Counseling Special Operations Forces

*What Clinicians Need to Know
About SOF Operators, Veterans,
and Their Families*

WES EASLEY
MFT, DAAETS, CWT

Ballast Books, LLC
www.ballastbooks.com

Copyright © 2026 by Wes Easley

ISBN: 978-1-966786-64-1

Printed in the United States of America

Published by Ballast Books
www.ballastbooks.com

For more information, bulk orders, appearances, or speaking requests,
please email: info@ballastbooks.com

TABLE OF CONTENTS

FOREWORD

by Jeffrey J. Denning

N o one suspected our backgrounds as we sat and ordered a meal in a small restaurant. A half dozen men gathered around the table. The group looked like any other—until you scratched the surface. In truth, it was made up of men with backgrounds most people only see in movies or on TV: a covert CIA operator, a Navy SEAL, Marines in Recon and Force Recon, an Army Green Beret, me, and a Tier One operator from "the Unit," or Delta Force.

To the latter, I casually mentioned Eric Haney's book *Inside Delta Force*. Immediately, a tirade erupted, laced with expletives and accusations. The usually laid-back operator didn't hold back. I could tell I had hit a nerve.

The one thing you don't do—you never do—is talk. You don't talk about the secret stuff. You don't write about it. You don't publish it. You don't say anything.

Opening your mouth is like breaking an oath. Secrecy is a weapon.

That's why when my friend from the Unit went public with his book, I had some insight into the struggle he went through to write and publish it. As a former Delta Force troop commander, he wrote *Kill Bin Laden* under the pseudonym Dalton Fury. His real name was Tom Greer.

Before Tom passed away a few years later from cancer, we worked together on different projects, both tactical as well as things unrelated to guns and firepower. I occasionally interviewed him for online newspapers and magazines. He wrote the foreword for my book *Warrior SOS: Military Veterans' Stories of Faith, Emotional Survival, and Living with PTSD*—the first book I'm aware of where not only one but multiple guys from the Unit specifically wrote about their trauma publicly.

At the time, Tom traveled more than I did. Still, we met up occasionally. One time at dinner with another regular Special Forces operator, I watched as Tom quietly let the guy chat and brag. He was truly a leader of leaders—both humble and brilliant.

Over the years, he introduced me to several other people and would often send me pictures just for fun. Once, he showed me a photo of himself in a tight spandex-like suit with a bunch of circle markers on it to track his tactical movements as the main character of a popular first-person shooter video game. We chatted about his *60 Minutes* interview and the giant fake beard they gave him to help conceal his real identity, as well as other supposed photos of him that filled the internet. He once sent me a photo of him with two other former Delta operators who went public after he did, along with another person everyone would recognize. He sent me a photo of his camouflaged kid hunting in a tree stand. Another time, he sent me the early manuscript of a fictional book he published, which he simply titled *BS*. Admittedly, I didn't read it.

He made a couple of custom 1911s. I helped him spread the word so he could auction them off in support of veterans and mental health. After the so-called Global War on Terror following 9/11, too many veterans were taking their lives by suicide. He was raising money to help stop veteran suicide.

Tom Greer was a friend to many, but not to enemies of the United States. He loved freedom. He loved liberty. He loved America.

I miss my friend.

This wasn't meant to be a eulogy. Thinking about my friends in special ops—including buddies who've died in war zones—brings up a lot of memories.

When you spend enough time with those in this line of work, you tend to believe they're invincible. Except for when they're not.

Wes Easley gets that. He understands the complexity of this community and its members' struggle to open up about the things that are not easily discussed. His research and insights span decades of real-world experience with unique and brilliant perspectives. Easley provides every counselor—regardless of their experience level—with the tools needed to work effectively with this population. Even with my own background and a solid foundation in working with and alongside SOF veterans, this book has already helped me in recent sessions with a client.

Trust is the most valuable currency in the SOF world—not credentials, not degrees. And when it comes to therapy for SOF operators, you must earn that trust. You won't get a second chance.

Easley unlocks the secrets of the SOF world—things that rarely, if ever, get talked about—without compromising what must remain guarded. What a privilege and blessing to have this information.

This book will prove to be a fantastic reference for SOF support personnel and operators themselves as they try to understand their own reactions and struggles while seeking a competent clinician. From PJs to frogmen, from Night Stalkers to Raiders, and quiet professionals anywhere, this book is essential reading for anyone working with or associating directly or indirectly with this population. Not only is this a great resource for therapists, but also for those who have ever been married to someone in special ops. It also includes those who've engaged in private military contracting or served on law enforcement SWAT teams.

This book reminds me of the courage my buddy had when he wrote *Kill Bin Laden*. He wanted the mission preserved, the story told. He wanted to help. And every dime he made from it went to the Special Operations Warrior Foundation. He told me his first check to them was for $26,000.

There's a parallel here. The information in this book is worth at least that much. Seriously, how much is it worth to save a life or change a life for good?

If writing were a contest, Wes Easley would win the Best Ranger Competition for this masterpiece. As far as mental health and special operations go, *Counseling Special Operations Forces* is, indeed, the tip of the spear—the crème de la crème—a Tier One hit.

This book belongs in the hands of every military leader, veteran, family member, and SOF operator. It should be purchased and studied in colleges, ROTC programs, and at West Point, Annapolis, and the Air Force Academy. It should be required reading for every clinician or intern working at the VA, Vet Centers, and Walter Reed Hospital, as well as for those working behind the fence or within other government agencies. It should be discussed in supervision and consultation meetings, referenced in continuing education courses, and used as a core training text. Therapists who work with law enforcement would benefit from reading it as well.

In short, *Counseling Special Operations Forces* is a field manual for understanding and serving our nation's most elite warriors. *Devour it. Study it. Reference it. Then put it into action.*

—Jeffrey J. Denning
First Responders First
FRFirst.com

Introduction

FROM THE BATTLEFIELD TO THE COUCH

Back when I started my career, guys in the military and in law enforcement didn't go to therapy. If you did, you were considered "weak" or "broken."

Since I had been both a soldier and a police officer, when I finally saw a therapist, I was skeptical.

I was also desperate for help.

A few years prior, I had responded to a domestic dispute call, where I suddenly had to wrestle a knife out of the hands of a parole violator who was high on crack cocaine. The scuffle ended when we both fell off a two-story-high balcony. I landed on my back, still holding the perpetrator, who had landed on top of me. The double handcuff case I had attached to my duty belt in the small of my back broke my fall—and my spine. The doctors eventually gave me the news that I would never fully recover due to spinal nerve damage, and I was forced out on disability retirement.

Not only did that end my law enforcement career—it also ended my fourteen-year military career. I had been in the US Army Reserve and, combined with my prior active-duty service, was only six years away from military retirement.

Right after my two careers ended, my wife at the time filed for divorce. For the next four years, I fought divorce and custody battles while half of my police disability retirement went to my soon-to-be ex-wife.

The disability, lawyer arguments and courtroom battles, loss of income, loss of my marriage, loss of seeing my children every day, loss of my two careers, and the loss of my identity attached to those careers was like living in a minefield. Every day, it seemed like I'd get hit with another explosion of stress, bad news, or depression.

Mental health care was (thankfully) covered by my insurance plan, so I decided I had nothing to lose. Maybe a professional clinician could help me make sense of it all and put me back on the right track.

In my first-ever session with a therapist, he did nothing but ask me questions about my past, my history as a cop, all the dead people I'd discovered and shootings I'd experienced and how many people I'd seen killed and how it made me feel. For fifty minutes, it was story time for the therapist. I got nothing out of it. In fact, I felt more exhausted leaving his office than when I had arrived.

After that appointment, I drove around realizing I had just rehashed and poured out all the crap I'd been dealing with and didn't receive anything in return. There was no mention of the next steps or how to move forward. I thought, *That was shit. I didn't like that at all.* There's got to be something better than this for people with my background!

That's when the lightbulb went off. I decided I would become the clinician I was looking for.

I didn't know what I was doing with my life or what direction I should go in. I didn't even know what the options were. But I realized that maybe as a therapist I could help others who served, so instead of having one crappy therapy session and never again seeking help, they could receive the care they needed and get their life back.

From Combat to Cop to Clinician

This introduction is to let you, the reader, know who is writing this book and how I have the experience to talk about this subject.

Everything I accomplished was done with the help and support of many others.

I joined the US Army out of high school, was stationed in Germany, then shipped out to the Port of Dammam in Saudi Arabia in preparation for Operation Desert Storm and Operation Desert Shield. While in-country, I made friends with some of the guys in 7th Special Forces Group (Airborne) who were staging in the tunnels under the airport.

As you'll learn from reading this book, to become Special Operations in any branch of service, you have to apply and be accepted administratively, pass a physical assessment and selection course, then pass a number of other specialty schools and training programs. However, there was a caveat during wartime that allowed the United States Special Operations Command (USSOCOM) to accept/acquire military personnel as needed for whatever reason through a shortened process. If accepted, you would join the unit in a support role, then complete the required assessment/selection upon redeployment to Fort Bragg.

The command at 7th Group was open to accepting me, but I still needed a medical exam. During what I thought would be a routine physical, the Special Forces medic examining me suddenly stepped back and said, "Whoa!" That scared the crap out of me. "You are red zone critical," he explained. "You need medical care immediately. Your blood pressure is way too high. We can't touch you until your hypertension is under control."

In Saudi Arabia, there were no amenities. It was summer, and the daytime temperatures reached 126 degrees Fahrenheit. Our food was bottled water and MREs (meals, ready-to-eat). MREs contain a lot of calories and a lot of salt, and the water was always hot because there was no refrigeration. I wasn't drinking enough water or taking care of myself. I had no idea my blood pressure was high, much less that I could've had a heart attack at any moment.

That Special Forces medic saved my life.

I was flown to "Tent City," which was a US Air Force compound that had complete medical care, from dentists to battlefield surgeons.

There I was prescribed hypertension medication and returned to my unit. I was hoping to get my blood pressure under control and continue the process into 7th Group when the Gulf War kicked off and the Army sent my unit into Iraq, where I worked as a crew chief on Black Hawk helicopters.

Later on during that deployment, I was able to succeed in my dream of working with Special Operations Forces, at least for a short while, and was temporarily assigned to Task Force 160th Special Operations Aviation Regiment (Airborne) (SOAR), known as the "Night Stalkers." 160th SOAR is the aviation unit that supports the military's Special Forces. I like to call it the stealth air taxi service. During that year-long deployment, I was also fortunate to be selected for a small team tasked with providing training on US light/medium weapon systems to a French Foreign Legion detachment near Najaf.

After that deployment during the Gulf War, I returned to Germany and accepted a spot in a specialized training program in Virginia known as X-1. I was part of the first group of soldiers to work on the experimental rotary-wing aircraft. It was so secret that I wasn't allowed to talk about it with anyone—until years later when I saw the crashed aircraft on the news during the Osama bin Laden raid.

After the stint in Virginia, I received orders for Fort Bragg, North Carolina, as part of the 82nd Airborne Division, where I jumped (parachuted) out of C-130s and other aircraft in a variety of conditions dozens of times, and I loved it.

Fort Bragg is home to many special operations units, and I was able to reunite with some of my buddies in 7th Group whom I'd met in Saudi Arabia. While I never became a Special Forces operator, I spent most of my off-duty time in their company area, where everything was a lot better—especially the food at their dining hall. I got to jump with those guys sometimes on the weekends during "Hollywood" jumps. I also volunteered to participate in Special Forces training exercises (like Robin Sage) when they needed extra "enemy forces" or "local civilians," which only made me more eager to join them. Five times I applied to Ranger School, and five times I was told "no" because I was in a shortage MOS (military occupational specialty) and my unit could not afford to lose anyone. The reality was that I did not have an infantry designation, and those who did were the ones who usually got accepted to try for Ranger School and other specialty schools. I realized it was a losing battle, so when I reached my ETS (expiration of term of service) date, I decided to try civilian life instead of reenlist.

Like many veterans still looking for the adrenaline rush, I became a law enforcement officer. I held many different positions over fourteen years, including hostage/crisis negotiator, explosive ordnance disposal (EOD) liaison, gang task force, emergency services unit, patrol officer, undercover, narcotics, bailiff, drug recognition expert (DRE) instructor, honor guard, and more.

In the meantime, I realized I missed the military, so I joined the US Army Reserve as an MP (military police) and later as an MPI (military police inspector) implementing installation security measures. One of my jobs was the NCOIC (non-commissioned officer in charge) of security for a SCIF (sensitive compartmented information facility) where special operations intelligence personnel held meetings, mission planning sessions, and monitored operations. I saw everyone in the "secret squirrel" community come and go out of that facility: CIA (Central Intelligence Agency), NSA (National Security Agency), DIA (Defense Intelligence Agency), Special Operations Forces, and special operations intelligence officers from all branches of the military. Some dudes that came through had no identification at all. They had no name tags, no IDs, and no uniforms, and most of them were bearded up. They didn't even have to sign in; they were escorted by a one-star general. I assumed they were ex-Special Forces guys working for the CIA. This only added to my admiration and respect for the special operations community.

When that all ended due to my disability after falling off the balcony, I was able to work as a contractor with the Department of Homeland Security (DHS) as part of the Secure Border Initiative Network

(SBInet). I served alongside many active-duty and former Special Forces personnel, which was great . . . until one day we realized we had driven too far. Without realizing it, we'd entered an Air Force bombing range and were surrounded by unexploded five-hundred-pound bombs. (They really should have posted some signs—there wasn't even a fence!) That's when I decided I needed to focus on my kids and get through my divorce—and maybe do something a bit safer.

At the Dominican University of California in San Rafael, I finished my undergrad studies in clinical psychology and got my master's in counseling psychology. During graduate school, I was connected with the West Coast Post-Trauma Retreat (WCPR) through Dr. Joel Fay, who became an amazing mentor to me. He co-wrote the book *Counseling Cops: What Clinicians Need to Know*, which inspired me to write this book. I went on to volunteer as an EMDR therapist at WCPR, where I was able to help many first responders, military veterans, and former special operations members.

During this time I remarried, and with the help and support of my wife and many others, I co-founded Brief and Strategic Integrated Counseling, LLC (BASICS) and the Men's Therapy Institute, LLC; taught critical thinking at Dominican University; and taught crisis intervention and mental health resources to first responders at Santa Rosa Junior College. While teaching, I developed the buoyancy-assisted psychotherapy treatment (BAPT) for physically disabled patients who would otherwise not be able to sit comfortably for fifty-minute sessions without extreme pain.

Why I Wrote This Book

The War on Terror (officially the Global War on Terrorism, or GWOT) raged for almost twenty years, starting right after September 11, 2001, and ending with the withdrawal of forces from Afghanistan in August 2021. During that time, Special Operations Forces were constantly deploying and conducting counterterrorism operations around the world. Even though the War on Terror is "officially" over, SOF operators are still fighting terrorism and assisting other nations against bad actors in every corner of the globe every day of the week.

This constant toll of continuous deployments, along with the constant and extreme training and preparation for those missions, has taken its toll on our nation's most highly trained and experienced warriors. Many come home suffering from post-traumatic stress disorder (PTSD), traumatic brain injuries (TBI), family problems, substance abuse, and other maladaptive coping mechanisms. Not all, mind you—many become extremely successful in civilian life. And all of them have the capability to do so. But sometimes, like many of us, they need a professional to guide them out of the darkness and get them back on track.

Through my personal experiences in the Army and law enforcement, the mentorship of Dr. Fay and others, and counseling many Special Forces members as a therapist, I learned what practices, techniques, and methods have worked best with SOF operators, veterans, and their family members—and a lot of what not to do.

I also know that many civilian therapists who lack this cultural understanding may inadvertently give a SOF member a first bad session, which may only serve to reinforce the stigmas and barriers to treatment that still persist in the military and first responder communities, and in society as a whole. At the same time, there are often stigmas and barriers in the behavioral health community against "tough" military operators, which only increases cultural misunderstanding. My aim is to lessen this gap in cultural competency, so you as a clinician can better help SOF members when they need it the most, and in doing so, help erase the remaining stigmas and barriers toward mental health care.

PART I:

THE ROAD TO CULTURAL COMPETENCY

1: UNDERSTANDING SOF: THE BASICS

But I fear they do not know us. I fear they do not compre-
hend the full weight of the burden we carry or the price we
pay when we return from battle. This is important, because
a people uninformed about what they are asking the military to endure is a people inevitably unable to fully grasp
the scope of the responsibilities our Constitution levies upon
them. We must help them understand, our fellow citizens
who so desperately want to help us.

—Admiral Michael Mullen,
former chairman of the Joint Chiefs of Staff

If you pay attention to the news, especially concerning our nation's
veterans, you probably know the statistics aren't good.

According to the US Department of Veterans Affairs' *2023 National
Veteran Suicide Prevention Annual Report*, veteran suicide rates have
generally increased since 2001. In 2021 alone (the most recent data in
the report), 6,392 veterans died by suicide that year. *That's over seven-
teen veteran suicide deaths every day.* This is "an increase of 114 suicides
from 2020" (5). The age- and sex-adjusted suicide rate increased by 11.6
percent in 2021, compared to a 4.5 percent increase rate among non-
veteran US adults. In summary, in 2021, "suicide was the 13th-leading

cause of death for Veterans overall, and the second-leading cause of death among Veterans under age 45-years-old," even as the COVID-19 pandemic was still getting under control (8).

It's important to note these are only the suicides the VA knows about. Not all veterans register for medical services with the Veterans Health Administration (VHA), so there are unknown numbers of suicides not accounted for in these statistics.

Garner (2018, 2) reports that from 2012 to 2015, "the USSOCOM [United States Special Operations Command] experienced an alarming increase in the rate of suicide within SOF personnel. Data indicates that 49 special operators committed suicide from 2011 to 2014, which exceeded numbers from the previous five years."

The Special Operations Forces (SOF) veteran community is sounding the alarm. SOF member suicides, as well as mental health and substance abuse issues, are becoming less taboo topics as more SOF veterans speak publicly about their struggles. I believe these statistics are only going to increase.

The War on Terror only ended in 2021 after almost twenty years of conflict, though in many ways it's not really over. Special Forces units are still operating around the clock and around the globe.

Suffice it to say, we as a country need to do more to help our veterans and SOF members. Lessening the lack of cultural competency is the first step.

Who Are SOF?

While terms like "Special Forces," "SF," and "special ops" are used by the general public, SOF operators will more often refer to themselves by their specific unit or job designation, or by specific names or nicknames such as "SEALs" and "Green Berets." The broadest term I use in this book is Special Operations Forces, often referred to as "SOF" (pronounced like "soft" without the "t").

Within the broader US Armed Forces Special Operations Commands, there are only a few units that are combat units, or "boots on the ground." For every one of those combat units, there are many more service members in special operations who are not on the front-lines, such as intelligence analysts, administrative and logistics personnel, and more.

Those who work in special ops *support* units are often stellar service members in their own right and are often specially selected for those assignments. The operational tempo ("op tempo;" i.e., workload) can be almost nonstop for all. However, this book primarily concerns itself with those who are, and were, in Special Operations *combat* units, or rather, combat teams.

SOF combat teams are the elite teams of the military, specially trained with various unique skills to fight foreign enemy forces, usually under the cover of secrecy. As such, they are understandably revered yet misunderstood by the general public. In the United States, less than one percent of the country's working-age population serves in the military at any given time, much less in SOF combat teams.

SOF personnel train constantly and are very mentally, physically, and emotionally fit. They live in a military subculture of close-knit camaraderie, operational secrecy, and a constant need to meet extraordinary requirements. As creative problem-solvers, they're adept at performing well in high-stress environments while conducting dangerous missions around the world. They are competitive, driven to be the best, and are constantly striving for perfection. Part of this is because any mistake could lead to mission failure and even a team member's death. Any injury, sickness, mental illness, or personal issue could interfere with an operator's ability to complete their mission, which, in turn, could let the whole team down.

Yet SOF team members are human, and they are certainly not perfect. Sometimes, SOF members recover after an injury or issue and get back in the fight. Sometimes they choose—or are forced—to end their SOF career or military career altogether. Either way, when they do call it quits, the transition to civilian life is often extremely difficult and can aggravate any issues they already have.

Regardless of the problems or situations SOF members are dealing with, they are not always likely to admit weakness or seek help, especially outside of their unit's medical facilities. For them, trusting a stranger with their personal problems is no small task.

A SOF member is likely to only seek care for mental health problems when they're in deep trouble. Any perceived misstep or misunderstanding with a mental health provider can send them away from therapy for good.

This book aims to bridge the gap in misunderstanding between the behavioral health community and those who served in our nation's most elite units. Whether you hope to work with this community or unexpectedly find yourself with a SOF veteran client, I hope that by reading this book, more clinicians like you are able to help them. If you decide helping SOF veterans is not for you, this book should also help you refer them to the appropriate clinicians and resources, so our nation's elite feel heard and get the help they deserve.

The Healer vs. The Killer

It might seem that those who serve in the military's Special Operations Forces are very different types of people from behavioral health specialists. When Richard Strozzi-Heckler, a doctor of psychology and creator of the Strozzi Somatics methodology, agreed to teach aikido—a martial art known as "the way of peace" and "the discipline of harmony"—to a group of US Army Special Forces (Green Berets), he encountered disbelief and hostility from his psychology peers. He writes in his book *In Search of the Warrior Spirit* that there was a clear us-versus-them mentality he hadn't expected:

> I was shocked. What did they mean *Them*? Are these men different in kind from myself? Won't they be the same men that I played basketball with, marched with in the Marines, knew in martial arts dojos, double-dated with? Was it only because I was raised in a military family and wore the uniform myself

that I think this? Was it because I have known many men in many different situations, some good, some bad, some I liked, some I would never want to see again, that I understood that these men would be different in degree, but never in kind? (Strozzi-Heckler 2007, 5)

This separation between clinician and warrior, "healer" and "killer," is one that must be addressed first, because in reality, we are more alike than different. People who serve in the armed forces come from all backgrounds and join for a variety of reasons. Similar to those of us who work in behavioral health, a main reason people join the military is to make a positive difference. They may also have a deep sense of patriotism, a yearning for adventure and excitement, a family history of military service, and other reasons. But ultimately, there is an altruistic motive to serve the greater good and be part of something bigger than the self. Those who go on to serve in Special Operations are no different.

When I served in the US Army, I never thought I would later become a cop, and when I was in law enforcement, I never imagined I would later become a therapist. Yet my past experiences made me a better clinician and helped me serve clients who had military and/or law enforcement backgrounds. From those encounters, I received many referrals over the years to treat former SOF members.

I believe my cultural competency has been a large part of my success as a therapist. But I know there are plenty of clinicians who don't have military or first responder experience and still may end up—either on purpose or happenstance—with a SOF veteran or family member in their office.

Because these elite warriors are part of a select and rare group, often undistinguishable from other civilians after they get out of the military, and because of the understandable biases that some clinicians have against "trained killers," I felt it important to educate my fellow behavioral health specialists on who Special Operations Forces personnel are, what problems they face—especially when entering the civilian world after service—and how best to treat them. The reality is that they are human, first and foremost. They are sons and fathers, sisters and citizens, neighbors and coworkers. And sometimes, they are our clients.

> There is certainly a legacy that distinguishes the warrior from war . . . It includes . . . Homer's hero Odysseus who outwitted his opponents rather than slaying them . . . the American Indians who lived in harmony with the land and whose ritual wars were exercises in bravery rather than slaughter . . . These historical and mythical warriors found their strength and integrity by defeating their own inner demons, living in harmony with nature, and serving their fellow man . . . instead of constantly fighting external enemies for petty ends. (Strozzi-Heckler 2007, 6–8)

I applaud you for reading this book and being curious about our nation's top forces. If you encounter one of these amazing people in your office, I hope what you learn here will help you to treat them with the compassion, knowledge, and cultural competency necessary to be the guiding light they're searching for.

The SOF Member in Therapy

> You are sitting across from the shell of a man—me. I am proud, I am fearless, I am a legend in my own mind. I am a broken man, I am an addict, and I am an alcoholic. I am a wounded animal. I am dangerous. Where to start? Do you address the addiction? Do you address the depression? Or the anxiety? Do you start by thanking me for my service? I have now worked with many operators and have worked extensively with first responders. In many ways there are similarities. With both, I start in the same fashion. I do it by

saying: "Don't trust me. I don't want you to trust me. What I am asking for is the opportunity to earn your trust."

—Thomas J. LaGrave Jr.,
LCSW and former US Navy SEAL

What I call special operations therapy is commonly used to treat veterans, first responders, and others who have experienced significant trauma. It is designed to help individuals understand their reactions to the trauma and develop ways to cope with the emotional, physical, psychological, and even spiritual effects of the experience. It typically includes modalities such as cognitive behavioral therapy, EMDR, SOF member peer support (if available), brainspotting, and other treatment modalities as needed. It may also include unconventional and non-psychological treatments, such as psychosomatic methods, hyperbaric oxygen therapy (HBOT), or a referral to use psychedelic-assisted therapy, especially for traumatic brain injuries.

A special operator's mental health is extremely important for their ability to function at such a high level and keep everyone else on their team safe. Today, there are more and more mental health positions available within the military than ever before, including in SOF combat units if you desire to work directly with Special Forces operators.

Even if you don't plan on serving the military directly, what the general public doesn't know—including most behavioral health clinicians—is that military veterans who served in a SOF unit at some point in their careers are often hiding in plain sight.

After the military, some seek other high-paced civilian employment as police officers, firefighters, or private military contractors. Some go on to be successful business executives or start their own businesses. Others retire and enjoy a quieter life.

Most importantly, there are many SOF veterans in jobs one wouldn't normally expect, which can be anything from tow truck drivers to construction workers to cashiers at the local grocery store. For instance, when I left active duty in the military, a SOF veteran and I worked as roofers in Ashland, Kentucky, until I decided to go into law enforcement.

> As the majority of military personnel enter soon after high school, they leave the military with a high school level education and often many acquired military skills that cannot be directly transferred into the civilian world. While many capitalize on government-funded educational opportunities such as the GI bill and live off of those funds while pursuing their undergraduate degree, many try and enter the workforce making minimum or entry-level wages. (Garner 2018, 83)

While the military in general, and especially SOF units, is becoming better at supporting service members' mental health, some SOF members may have issues they don't want their command to know about and therefore seek help from civilian providers. Others often develop issues over time and are unable to admit those issues to their command—or to themselves—for fear of jeopardizing their careers. But when their careers do end, those issues often hit them like a ton of bricks, forcing them to seek help.

Many veterans either don't have access to a Department of Veterans Affairs (VA) health facility near where they live, or they don't trust the VA to help them. When all else fails, they will search online to find a therapist with special operations experience in their area. If they can't find one (which is more than likely), they may settle for a therapist who served in the military or in law enforcement. Still, they may not be able to find what they're looking for. They may also visit a clinician *who was chosen for them* by a family member or their employer.

Therefore, whether you aim to work with SOF members or not, you may end up with a SOF member, veteran, or family member in your office. When that happens, it is probably the first time that person has opened up to a mental health clinician. They've probably waited until things got bad enough to force them to seek outside care. And they probably don't trust you.

You may only have that one session to show you are capable of helping them.

Special Operations Forces team members give their lives to near-constant training and dangerous operations. They have gone above and beyond the call of duty, and they are willing to sacrifice their own lives to save their teammates.

So when they're suffering from trauma, PTSD, substance abuse, family troubles, or even suicidal ideation, they expect a therapist to put everything on the line for them. They expect other professionals to be experts in their field and do whatever is necessary to provide them with the best care possible. As veterans who never flinched at danger or difficulty, they don't want a therapist who is easily offended or confused by their real-world experiences.

It's worth mentioning again: It's not usually easy for a person from the Special Forces community to seek mental health care, especially outside of their unit. If a session is interrupted frequently with questions, or it's clear the clinician is lost or can't relate to what's being said, the client may decide, unfortunately, that seeking a therapist is a waste of their time. Therefore, it is contingent upon the therapist to do their homework.

Another reason SOF veterans are reluctant to seek civilian mental health care is because so much of what they experienced is classified. They are not allowed to talk about the specifics of their training and missions. Luckily, you don't need those details to help them.

In order to adequately provide special operations therapy, it's important to have a basic understanding of military culture and the special operations subculture. The aim of this book is to provide that foundation of cultural competency, though it is just that: a foundation. Every special operations unit and occupational specialty has its own subculture, terms and acronyms, standard operating procedures, histories, traditions, and so on.

That being said, you don't have to be an expert in SOF counter-terrorism operations to help SOF clients. But you do need to know enough that you don't interrupt a session with too many questions or become distracted, bothered, confused, overwhelmed, or excited by details that don't really matter. What matters is helping SOF members with their issues so they can overcome their demons and move on with their lives. Doing your own homework on your own time to satisfy your personal knowledge and curiosity will greatly help you guide sessions with SOF members competently and efficiently. A SOF member will accept nothing less.

If you and the SOF client are not a good fit, your homework should also include knowledge of other clinicians in your area with military or first responder backgrounds who may be better able to connect with this population. Hopefully then, the client will understand that just one bad experience does not mean the end of seeking help. As my colleague Dr. William Ahern explained to me:

> Today, the first responders and veterans I work with will often tell me, "You know Doc, I've been to therapists before, and it usually takes about four to six weeks before they get what I'm talking about. But with you . . . you get it." It is important to my clients that I can relate to their experiences and am not shocked when they might reveal a disturbing or nightmarish incident. This is even more to the point when dealing with members of the "the warrior elite," to coin a phrase by former Navy SEAL Dick Couch, author of *The Warrior Elite: The Forging of SEAL Class 228*.

US Military & SOF Terms & Acronyms

I once had a client open a session with, "My HALO rig was trash." Because I had airborne experience, he didn't have to explain what he meant before we could do any therapy.

He was talking about parachuting from an extremely high altitude and opening his parachute at the last minute to avoid detection, also called "freefalling"—only his parachuting equipment (his "rig") was "trash." It didn't work properly or had a mechanical failure, and he had to quickly deploy the reserve parachute, which is much smaller. He didn't have a very soft landing, and he could have died.

Understanding these basics will help you communicate and understand your client and their experiences. I invite you to turn to Appendix I and familiarize yourself with the short list of terms and acronyms there. Many of the terms listed in Appendix I are further explained in this chapter. I also highly recommend the resources for clinicians listed in Appendix III.

Consider this part of your basic training, if you will.

A Profile of a SOF Member

There are Special Forces in virtually every military in every country in the world. Allied Special Forces often assist each other in both training and in operations. While this book focuses mainly on the United States Special Operations Forces, these concepts can be applied to elite warriors in almost any nation—many of whom are dealing with terrorists, drug gangs, and other bad actors around the clock, just as US operators are.

Someone who goes on the SOF path generally starts out like anyone else who joins the military: with basic training in their respective branch of service for enlisted personnel; and for officers, training during college or a military academy (or officer candidate school for prior enlisted service members) and becoming a commissioned officer upon graduation. From there, any military member must serve honorably and pass other requirements in order to qualify for and attend Special Forces training.

The training to become a Special Operations combat team member is different depending on the branch of service and the type of job specialty they aim to have. Regardless of those differences, Special Operations Forces training overall is called the "pipeline." If they successfully go through the pipeline, they will then be assigned to a SOF unit, depending on their job specialty and the military's needs at the time.

Only those who serve (or served) on a SOF combat team are truly considered Special Operations Forces.

The Army, Navy, Air Force, Marine Corps, and even the CIA each have their own special operations commands, and therefore their own training requirements, specialties, and units.

In real-world operations, SOF members can work individually, in small teams, in a bigger unit, or together with other units and even branches, depending on the mission.

Special Operations Forces missions primarily involve counter-terrorism, hostage rescue, direct action, special reconnaissance (often against high-value targets), unconventional warfare, foreign internal defense, and counternarcotics operations.

Tiers

US special operations units fall broadly into three tiers.

Tier 1 units are used for the most complex, dangerous, high-profile, and secretive missions, such as the killing of Osama bin Laden. As such, Tier 1 units are in high demand and can be commanded directly by the US president, secretary of defense, and the Joint Special Operations Command (JSOC). A Tier 1 unit is also called a special mission unit (SMU). The current SMUs are listed below.

- US Navy: the Naval Special Warfare Development Group (NSWDG), abbreviated as DEVGRU (Development Group), commonly known as SEAL Team Six
- US Army: the 1st Special Forces Operational Detachment–Delta (1st SFOD-D), commonly known as Delta Force, Combat Applications Group (CAG), or just the Unit
- US Air Force: 24th Special Tactics Squadron

- US Army: Regimental Reconnaissance Company (RRC) of the 75th Ranger Regiment (formerly known as the Regimental Reconnaissance Detachment, or RRD)
- US Army: the US Army Intelligence Support Activity (USAISA), or Intelligence Support Activity (ISA), also known as the Activity (not really a combat unit, but directly serves Tier 1 assets)

Tier 2 is considered all other Special Operations Forces units, such as the other SEAL teams, direct-action units in the Army's Special Forces groups (Green Berets), the rest of the 75th Ranger Regiment, the other US Air Force Special Tactics Squadrons, the US Marine Corps's Marine Raider Regiment (MRR), and the US Marine Corps Reconnaissance Battalions (Marine Force Recon).

Also considered Tier 2 is the Army's 160th Special Operations Aviation Regiment (Airborne) (SOAR), known as Night Stalkers. 160th SOAR provides aviation fire support (weapons and bombs), transportation, and in-flight refueling support to SOF units around the clock and around the globe, and therefore remains busy.

Tier 2 units conduct similar missions as Tier 1 units and may be tasked along with Tier 1 units, depending on mission requirements. They are generally based in certain geographical regions around the world, train other countries' militaries and Special Operations Forces, specialize in foreign languages, and conduct reconnaissance missions, among other specialized duties.

Tier 3 units are regular military combat units that have specialized training, such as the Army's 101st and 82nd Airborne Divisions, and the US Army's Psychological Operations (PSYOPS) and Civil Affairs (CA) units that are part of the United States Army Special Operations Command (USASOC).

The SOF members I refer to in this book are Tier 1 and Tier 2 operators and veterans, sometimes simply called "team members" or "operators."

This is just a basic overview. The United States Armed Forces is constantly updating and reorganizing to best meet current threats and geopolitical realities. Therefore, the details as stated here are subject to change. Also, most units would never refer to themselves as "Tier 2" or "Tier 3," but these terms give a basic description of how US SOF units are categorized and what they do.

For many who desire to be a Special Forces operator, earning a spot in a Tier 1 special mission unit is the ultimate dream. However, there are many other opportunities to serve in special operations units without being Tier 1. It's important to keep in mind that SOF units are all supported by various intelligence, logistical, administrative, training, and other support units and personnel. For those wanting to be a part of a SOF unit, there are many opportunities to do so without going through the pipeline and being an actual operator, though SOF support units are still very selective.

SOF Commands Throughout the US Government

The "special ops" section of the United States Central Intelligence Agency (CIA) is the Special Activities Center (SAC), which is responsible for covert and paramilitary operations worldwide. Two subgroups of the SAC are the Political Action Group (PAG), which is responsible for covert activities related to political influence, psychological operations, cyber warfare, and economic warfare; and the Special Operations Group (SOG), which is responsible for high-threat clandestine or covert operations with which the US government cannot be overtly associated.

SOF units "often work closely with US civilian intelligence agencies, particularly the CIA's shadowy Special Activities Division, which draws many of its personnel from the Special Ops community" (Mizokami 2021).

In the military, the United States Special Operations Command (USSOCOM or SOCOM) is the headquarters that commands all special operations units in the US Armed Forces. It oversees the development and deployment of SOF units and personnel for global special operations with government agencies and foreign allies to support activities against enemy state and non-state actors and to protect and advance US policies and objectives (USSOCOM 2022a).

The Joint Special Operations Command (JSOC) is a joint component command of SOCOM responsible for studying special operations requirements and techniques, ensuring interoperability and equipment standardization, planning and conducting special operations exercises and training, developing joint special operations tactics, and executing special operations missions worldwide (Wikimedia Foundation 2025). JSOC also commands and allocates special mission units for joint missions when necessary.

US Navy

The United States Naval Special Warfare Command (USNSWC/ WARCOM/NSW) is the United States Navy's arm of USSOCOM. This command oversees the training, sustainment, and deployment of the Navy's special ops units and personnel.

The Navy's most famous Special Operations Forces are the Navy SEALs. SEAL stands for sea, air, and land, meaning they can maneuver and fight in any environment. Today's "SEALs embody in a single force the heritage, missions, capabilities, and combat lessons-learned of five daring groups that . . . were crucial to Allied Victory in World War II and the conflict in Korea. These were (Army) Scouts and (Marine) Raiders; Naval Combat Demolition Units (NCDUs), Office of Strategic Services Operational Swimmers, Navy Underwater Demolition Teams (UDTs), and Motor Torpedo Boat Squadrons" (Navy SEALs 2025a).

Though these units were disbanded after World War II, many of them returned in various forms later during the Korean War and other conflicts due to the continued need for unconventional warfare units that could "carry out the types of clandestine, small-unit, high-impact missions that large forces with high-profile platforms (such as ships, tanks, jets and submarines) cannot . . . [and] essential on-the-ground Special Reconnaissance of critical targets for imminent strikes by larger conventional forces" such as covert reconnaissance of landing beaches and coastal defenses (Navy SEALs 2025a). In 1962, the US Navy SEALs were officially established by President John F. Kennedy.

As with any SOF pipeline, a SEAL candidate must have completed basic training and generally hold the rank of E-5 or above, hold an MOS that the SOF units need, be eligible for a secret security clearance, meet the height and weight requirements, and pass a specially-designed physical fitness test that is more difficult than the standard PT test. If those criteria are met, the candidate can request to enter the pipeline.

The US Navy SEAL pipeline officially starts with Special Warfare Combat Crewman (SWCC) training, which is divided into three phases: Alpha, Bravo, and Charlie. Each phase is seven weeks long. If a candidate successfully graduates those phases, they enter the most famous step in the pipeline: Basic Underwater Demolition/SEAL training, known as "BUD/S," which is also divided into three seven-week phases (First, Second, and Third). The most infamous part of BUD/S is Hell Week:

> Hell Week is the defining event of BUD/S training. It is held early on—in the 3rd week of First Phase—before the Navy makes an expensive investment in SEAL operational training. Hell Week consists of 5 1/2 days of cold, wet, brutally difficult operational training on fewer than four hours of sleep [total the whole week]. Hell Week tests physical endurance, mental toughness, pain and cold tolerance, teamwork, attitude, and your ability to perform work under high physical and mental stress, and sleep deprivation. Above all, it tests determination and desire. On average, only 25% of SEAL candidates make it through Hell Week, [considered] the toughest training in the U.S. Military. (Navy SEALs 2025b)

Special Operations Forces training in other branches of the military have similar "hell weeks" that test extreme hardship and sleep deprivation.

If a candidate successfully makes it through BUD/S, they move on to the final step in the pipeline: SEAL Qualification Training (SQT), which lasts for twenty-six weeks. This last phase teaches students the core, intermediate, and advanced tactical skills they will need on a SEAL team, including weapons training, small unit tactics, land navigation, demolitions, cold weather training, medical skills, and maritime operations. These candidates must also attend Survival, Evasion, Resistance and Escape (SERE) training and qualify in both static-line and freefall parachute operations (Navy Recruiting Command 2024).

The total pipeline to become a SEAL takes well *over two years* before a candidate is considered ready to serve on a SEAL team. Upon completing the pipeline, trainees receive their SEAL Trident, the emblem they wear on their uniform designating them as a US Navy SEAL.

Today, US Navy SEALs conduct small-unit unconventional special operation missions in maritime, jungle, urban, arctic, mountainous, and desert environments. Examples include rescuing hostages held by Somali pirates and raiding compounds to capture high-value targets in Iraq and Afghanistan.

SEALs are not the only special operators in the Navy. There are also Navy Divers who conduct underwater maintenance on ships, salvage military wrecks underwater, and lay or disable underwater mines; Explosive Ordnance Disposal (EOD) Technicians who spot and disable various IEDs in the water and on land; and Special Warfare Combat Crewmen (SWCC) who operate and maintain the watercraft that small special ops teams, such as SEALs, use for training and live missions (Navy Recruiting Command 2024). The pipeline for each involves many different specialty schools and over a year of training at least.

US Army

The United States Army Special Operations Command (USASOC) is charged with overseeing the various Special Operations Forces of the US Army. These units are the: 75th Ranger Regiment, several Special Forces units (Green Berets), the 160th Special Operations Aviation Regiment (SOAR Night Stalkers), Psychological Operations units (PSYOPS), and Civil Affairs (CA) units.

The US Army Rangers trace their history to the French and Indian War, largely based on Native American techniques of small unit guerrilla warfare. The Rangers' motto, "Rangers lead the way!" was coined during the D-Day landings in Normandy. Today's 75th Ranger Regiment officially formed in 1974. US Army Rangers specialize in raids, forcible entry, and reconnaissance operations within enemy territory (US Army 2024a).

To be eligible for the 75th Ranger Regiment, candidates must complete the US Army Airborne School. Airborne School trains service members on how to safely parachute out of aircraft. It is a requirement for many SOF specialties, whether they're in the Army or another branch of service. Then, Ranger candidates must pass the eight-week Ranger Assessment and Selection (RASP) process. If they are successful, they then attend and graduate from Ranger School. Ranger School lasts for sixty-two days and trains candidates to exhaustion in infantry, guerrilla warfare, and small-unit leadership tactics in a variety of terrain, including mountains and jungle. The total pipeline takes around five months, not including any specialized MOS training or optional schools.

Once a service member graduates from Ranger School, they are authorized to wear the Ranger Tab insignia on their uniform for the rest of their time in service, whether they are selected for the 75th Ranger Regiment or not. However, they are not a true SOF operator unless they are selected to serve in the 75th Ranger Regiment.

As the US Army website explains, "The distinctive headgear of the 75th Ranger Regiment is the tan beret. The beret is a mark of distinction . . . reminiscent of the leather caps worn by the original rangers of American heritage and lore" (US Army 2024b).

For soldiers opting to go further and be a Special Forces Green Beret, they must also complete Airborne School (Ranger School is recommended but not mandatory). Then, candidates attend the six-week Special Forces Preparation Course (SFPC), followed by the three-week Special Forces Assessment and Selection (SFAS) course. If successful, candidates enter the Special Forces Qualification Course, known as the Q Course, which includes specific MOS, language, and culture training along with small unit tactical leadership battle simulations. The Q Course lasts for over a year.

The pipeline to become a Green Beret, similar to becoming a SEAL, lasts for over two years in total. If successful, soldiers earn the right to wear the coveted green beret and Special Forces Tab.

Green Berets are guerrilla warfare experts who use unconventional tactics to fight terrorists abroad. They are required to be fluent in a foreign language and often hold other qualifications depending on their MOS, including the Military Freefall Parachutist Badge (high-altitude parachute training), Combat Diver Qualification Course (CDQC), and many more.

Klein (2023) explains the origin of the green beret:

> The U.S. Army Special Forces originated in 1952 . . . to operate as a stay-behind guerrilla force . . . in the event of a Soviet takeover of Western Europe. Initial recruits included OSS Special Forces veterans and Eastern European immigrants who spoke multiple languages and possessed skills ranging from parachuting to skiing to hand-to-hand combat . . . To distinguish themselves from conventional forces, the U.S. Army Special Forces unofficially adopted green berets, which had been worn by elite U.S. Army Rangers upon their graduation from an intensive commando school in Scotland during World War II . . . [T]hey became part of the official uniform

in 1961, when President John F. Kennedy requested they be worn when he visited the U.S. Army Special Warfare Center and School.

The final Army Special Operations Forces unit is the 160th Special Operations Aviation Regiment (SOAR). The SOAR Night Stalkers maintain and operate advanced, stealth military aircraft that SOF of all branches use during operations. These soldiers are expert helicopter pilots, mechanics, and fuelers who operate at night using night vision goggles (NVGs) and other means to avoid detection. The main course in this pipeline is the Basic Mission Qualification (BMQ) course, a six-week training program known as the Green Platoon.

Both SOAR and USSOCOM were developed after the failed mission to rescue hostages in Iran in 1980, known as Operation Eagle Claw. This failure resulted in part because of the lack of coordination between branches and because there were no helicopter units trained for special operations missions.

There are many other specialty schools that a special ops service member may volunteer for or be required to attend, such as the Reconnaissance and Surveillance Leaders Course (RSLC), Jungle Warfare School, and many more. For special operators, the training never stops.

US Air Force

The United States Air Force Special Operations Command (USAF-SOC/AFSOC) provides SOF mobility, strike capability, ISR (intelligence, surveillance, and reconnaissance), and air-to-ground capabilities in partnership with and in support of Special Operations Forces around the world. AFSOC is comprised of Special Operations Wings (SOW) and Special Tactics Squadrons.

According to the official United States Air Force website (2024):

[The] Air Force Special Operations Command ... activated 22 May 1990 at Hurlburt Field, Florida, but it inherited a legacy from the World War II theaters in Europe and China-Burma-India; secret missions during the Korean War; and major expansion in Vietnam. The distinctly-AFSOC communities . . . continue to execute the same mission sets of specialized air mobility, precision strike, battlefield air operations, intelligence, surveillance and reconnaissance, aviation foreign internal defense, and command and control.

The pipeline for airmen starts with the seven-week-long Special Warfare Candidate Course (SWCC) and continues with the Special Warfare Assessment and Selection Course, which lasts four weeks. If successful, candidates then move on to many other schools depending on their desired SOF MOS, including the Special Warfare Pre-Dive Course, Airborne School, the Military Freefall School, SERE training, and more. The pipeline lasts for over a year up to two years, depending on the airman's specialty and required training.

The SOF Air Force specialties are Combat Control (CCT), Pararescue (PJ), Special Reconnaissance (SR), Tactical Air Control Party (TACP), Special Operations Weather Technicians (SOWT), and Combat Rescue Officers (CROs). These forces conduct global special operations missions ranging from precision application of firepower to infiltration, aviation foreign internal defense, rescue and exfiltration missions, and the resupply and aerial refueling of SOF elements (U.S. Air Force 2024).

US Marine Corps

The US Marine Corps has two elite forces. One is Force Reconnaissance (FORECON), known as Force Recon. The other is the Marine Raider Regiment. Force Recon units fall directly under the Marine Corps but may work with SOCOM units if tasked to do so. They operate as part of the Marine Air-Ground Task Force (MAGTF) and report to the Marine Expeditionary Force (MEF). They specialize in direct action, deep reconnaissance and intelligence gathering, and other roles similar to the other SOF units mentioned.

The pipeline to become a Force Recon Marine starts with the Recon Training and Assessment Program (RTAP), previously known as the Basic Reconnaissance Primer Course (BRPC). This "is the first gut check of the Marine Reconnaissance pipeline . . . RTAP is a 5 week course that screens Recon candidates to see if they are physically and mentally prepared to attend the renowned Basic Reconnaissance Course" (General Discharge 2023). If successful, Marines then go on to the Basic Reconnaissance Course (BRC), which lasts for twelve weeks. The BRC is "designed to train Marines in the tactics, techniques, and procedures of land and amphibious reconnaissance operations" (General Discharge). The pipeline to become a Force Recon Marine is a minimum of over four months.

Zabalo (n.d.) writes:

> Marine Force Recon traces its lineage to the World War II era when the need for amphibious raids and reconnaissance missions was at an all-time high. They were not formally organized until 1957 . . . Today, Marine Force Recon personnel combine their amphibious nature with advanced capabilities, working alongside other elite units and providing a "first in" force, ready to assess and act in the most hazardous environments.

Because Recon Marine elements were not tasked directly by SOCOM, the Marine Forces Special Operations Command (MARSOC) was formed in 2006, along with the Marine Raider Regiment. "Raiders" was one of the names for the original Force Recon Marines in World War II. While very similar to Recon Marines in their specialties and missions, Raiders fall under SOCOM in terms of taskings, funding, and training.

The first step in the Marine Raider pipeline is the Assessment and Selection (A&S) process, which consists of two phases. Phase I is a grueling, three-week course that tests each candidate's physical and mental capability. Phase II continues to screen candidates on their physical ability, confidence, situational awareness, and acclimatization. As another psychological test, it lasts for a mysteriously undisclosed amount of time. If successful, candidates proceed to the Individual Training Course (ITC), a nine-month program that turns Marines into Critical Skills Operators (CSOs) or Special Operations Officers (SOOs). Then, depending on the Marine's MOS, the Raider then completes more MOS training and specialty schools (Marine Forces Special Operations Command 2024).

MARSOC specializes in direct action, special reconnaissance, unconventional warfare, foreign internal defense, counterterrorism, and information operations. All MARSOC operators receive advanced Special Operations Forces training in intelligence, communications, explosive ordnance disposal, and so on, according to their specific MOS.

Women in SOF

Over time, the US Armed Forces have continued to increase job and unit opportunities for females. There are many women serving in USSOCOM in support roles and in Tier 3 units, and their number continues to grow.

In 2016, the Pentagon effectively removed all gender barriers, opening all combat and special operations units to women. Since then, according to *Your Military*, two women are serving on Combatant Craft Crewman boat teams in the Navy; three females "graduated from the Q Course, earning the coveted Green Beret, and received assignments in Special Forces groups;" and the Air Force currently "has one female special tactics officer, and one officer and two female enlisted tactical air control party airmen . . . [and a] female enlisted special reconnaissance airman" (Seck 2024). According to that same article published in March 2024, no females have become US Navy SEALs or Marine Raiders . . . yet.

According to *Task & Purpose*, as of March 2022, one hundred females have graduated from Army Ranger School since 2015. "Capt.

Kristen Griest, one of the very first women to earn the Ranger tab, became the first female infantry officer in the Army. . . . Capt. Shaina Coss became the first woman to lead Rangers in combat" and is currently serving in the 75th Ranger Regiment (Britzky 2022).

Only a decade ago, females graduating from a specialty school, much less serving in and/or leading SOF teams in combat, would be unthinkable, even for many females in the military. It's true that we often don't know what we can achieve until we see it happen.

The Pipeline

> There is an ease and knowing in the way they shift the weight of their packs and hold their rifles. This is home. This is what the animal is trained for. All the conditioning is . . . to hump this unforgiving load over long distances at the highest speed possible.
>
> —Richard Strozzi-Heckler (2007, 26–27)

No matter the branch of service or occupational specialty, the SOF pipeline is designed to see who will keep going and who will quit. In fact, instructors of these courses often tell candidates to quit, give up, and go home to their comfortable beds. The combination of sleep and/or food deprivation, living out in the elements, continually completing arduous physical tasks while being forced to make leadership and battle decisions, all while being told to "Go home. You're not going to make it!" is a psychological test. Attrition rates for all SOF schools are very high.

A former instructor at the US Marine Corps BRC told *Task & Purpose* what it's like to go through the pipeline:

> Mentally and physically, it'll probably be the hardest time of [the service members'] lives. That's what the course is for. To

find mentally and physically strong, capable Marines who are willing to put their entire heart and soul into the training to obtain the [SOF military occupation specialty]. To find those types of Marines who won't quit and always put mission and team above anything else that may come up, personal or selfish. (Skovlund 2024)

It's not always the biggest, strongest, "baddest" types who succeed. Generally, those who succeed are driven to overcome the physical, mental, emotional, and spiritual obstacles they face.

The Marine who was interviewed also described, through his personal experience, how someone makes it through the pipeline:

By the six- to eight-week timeframe, I remember something clicked in my head. I was like, "Okay, if they told me we're running to Phoenix, Arizona, today, I'm doing it." Like, there's no hesitation. No internal dialogue at that point . . . It's amazing. No matter what they tell me to do, I'm gonna do it. So once you hit that point, it's pretty cool. Feeling that, and just knowing that I can do and overcome anything right now. Just because you're so physically and mentally strong. (Skovlund 2024)

As they say, "Quitters never win and winners never quit." Those who keep going through injury, illness, and setbacks, even if they have to be "recycled" and start over in a different class, are usually the ones who succeed. They want the emblem on their uniform, the lifestyle, and to be a SOF operator more than anything else in life, and they are willing to die for it. And in fact, because SOF training is so intense, some candidates do die, unfortunately. Of course, there are measures in place to prevent this, but it happens.

A colleague of mine, Thomas J. LaGrave Jr., LCSW, is a former US Navy SEAL. He describes his experience going through the pipeline below:

> After boot camp, I went to my rating school [MOS school], becoming a Hospital Corpsmen [Navy medic]. Ten weeks later, upon completion, I checked in on the quarter deck of Basic Underwater Demolition/SEAL (BUD/S) training. Here I would spend the next six months in the ultimate rite of passage, including Hell Week. Hell Week was five days that I went without sleep, being physically, mentally, emotionally, and spiritually abused in an attempt to break me.
>
> The rite of passage is a key marker for understanding a Special Forces operator. No matter the military branch or type of special operations career, each are the same in one crucial respect—you have to volunteer. Whether it's for a Tab, Beret, Trident, or Freefall Wings, an individual must willingly volunteer.
>
> These schools are extremely difficult. They are designed to push each volunteer physically, emotionally, mentally, and spiritually beyond what each individual thinks is possible. As a clinician, when you sit across from your operator, understand this: "Possible" is different from what you think and what they think is possible.
>
> Few human beings are tested to find their personal breaking points. It is not possible for a human to find this breaking point without being pushed there by another or others. One of the most important requirements of the various Special Forces training commands is to do this very thing. An individual must be pushed to the breaking point to find where it is. What differentiates an individual who succeeds and graduates from one who quits is their breaking point. The man

(or woman) operator sitting across from you did not quit. They did not give in. They did not give up.

As you can imagine, those who succeed end up feeling, in a way, invincible. Nothing can stop them—not even their own minds.

But no one is invincible. And when SOF members are no longer in control of their minds, their lives, or their situations, they will need you to guide them through it.

Not Always Invincible

SOF members are typically chosen and trained for a high state of mental and physical health. Unfortunately, the Global War on Terrorism has kept SOF members active at an extremely high level for over twenty years, and this can take its toll on both the SOF members and their families.

Furthermore, SOF members can find the transition back to civilian life extremely difficult, as their skill sets and experiences don't always relate to a non-military environment, especially if they're dealing with mental or physical injuries that make daily life difficult. Many SOF veterans (as well as other combat veterans) may find themselves unable to find or keep steady employment. They may also opt for jobs that require as little interaction with other people as possible.

As a therapist, I have worked with many SOF members over the years. SOF members are typically Type A alpha males (though not always) who are used to being self-sufficient, working in highly complex operations in small teams under high stress with surgical precision. In other words, they don't generally like to admit their weaknesses or ask for help.

So when an SOF member does sit down with a therapist, it's often because they're at their breaking point. Due to these factors, that also means one bad therapy experience might convince them there's no hope.

I've seen this too many times, and that's why I wrote this book. Whether you hope to work specifically with SOF members or not, it's important to be prepared. If you know you aren't a good fit for them, you can at least point them in the right direction so they don't give up.

I hope the information here prepares and educates more clinicians to better serve our military's most elite forces. Being elite can often mean feeling alone, but we should all be determined to leave no operator behind.

2. SOF CULTURE

The cultural competency of most clinicians is limited to race, ethnicity, gender, and sexual orientation. Far fewer of us have been required to study the world of work. If you want to be successful with law enforcement, the first thing you need to do is immerse yourself in the culture.

—Ellen Kirschman, Mark Kamena, and Joel Fay
in *Counseling Cops: What Clinicians Need
to Know* (2014, 241)

Cultural competence is vitally important, especially when dealing with military and SOF personnel. Those who live or have lived in a military culture, and especially within a SOF subculture, will often have different expectations and reactions to mental health care when compared to the civilian population. Meyer, Writer, and Brim (2016) researched the importance of military cultural competence in the fields of behavioral health. One study they found stated that it is unethical for a "culturally incompetent individual to provide care for culturally diverse patients." Another declared that culture was a central component in "nearly all aspects" of mental disorders. A third study posited that providers need to be "more aware of themselves, understand the worldview of their culturally different clients without negative judgments, and finally develop strategies and skills when working with diverse clients." The authors concluded that mental health professionals not fluent with military culture and language could struggle to provide effective treatment (Meyer et. al. 2016).

> Military cultural competence has recently gained national attention. Experts have posited that limited outcomes in the treatment of posttraumatic stress disorder and depression in the military may be related to limited familiarity with the military. National surveys have indicated low military cultural competence among providers and limited educational efforts on military culture or pertinent military pathology in medical schools and residency training programs. Military families, with their own unique military cultural identity, have been identified as a population with increased risks associated with deployment . . . The clinical impact of enhanced cultural competence in general has thus far been limited. The military, however, with its highly prescribed cultural identity, may be a model culture for further study. (Meyer et al. 2016)

Military cultural competency in behavioral health is especially vital today due to the fact that 70 percent of service members who deployed to Operation Iraqi Freedom (OIF) and/or Operation Enduring Freedom (OEF) are now seeking care. This chapter aims to lessen the cultural gap between Special Operations Forces and clinicians, so that us clinicians can serve our most elite veterans in the best ways possible. Here I describe the SOF lifestyle so you have an idea of what your SOF clients have gone through, how they think and behave, and why.

The Special Forces Lifestyle

> Somewhere, a true believer is training to kill you. He is training with minimum food and water, in austere conditions,

day and night. The only thing clean on him is his weapon. He doesn't worry about what workout to do—his rucksack weighs whatever it weighs, and he runs until his enemy stops chasing him. The true believer doesn't care how hard it is; he knows that he either wins or he dies. He doesn't go home at 17:00. He is home. He only knows the cause.

—Jack Carr

Special operators come from every walk of life, spanning middle to lower socio-economic classes to upper classes. Amongst this cadre are two distinct classes. The first class is an officer corps made up of individuals who are expected to lead and are college-educated. The other class is the enlisted rank, which has varying levels of education and is considered the workhorse of the military.

Special operations culture is characterized by a deep respect for the chain of command, a commitment to strict operational security and secrecy, a strong sense of mission, high standards of performance, and a commitment to the team with a focus on results rather than accolades. Due to the nature of SOF missions, special operators often have a deep degree of camaraderie and loyalty.

SOF members are very smart. Because they often work in small teams, they must be innovative, creative, adaptable, and able to instantly adjust to the enemy and changing circumstances within the fog of war.

Because team members must complete top-secret missions with little room for error, they train and plan as much as possible. For instance, they don't just get told they're going to parachute into an area and grab a target. They are given as much detailed intelligence as possible, do research, train as realistically as they can, and go through every conceivable scenario. If they need to break into a compound, for example, they create a mock-up of that same compound and terrain, scalable to the real thing, built with the same materials at the level of architects. Then they must use the right type and number of explosives to breach the compound successfully. Not enough breaching charge, and they don't get through and also compromise their position. Too much, and they can kill their entire team and other civilians inside the compound— along with the target they were supposed to capture for intelligence purposes. They use mathematical and scientific skills to ensure everything goes according to plan, so they succeed even when the unexpected happens.

Despite any first impressions, there are similarities between clinicians and SOF operators. In large part, they each have a desire to make a positive difference in the world. Of course, everyone is different, but the majority of individuals I've worked with got into special operations because they wanted to help people. A lot of that is because they felt helpless as a child. As a matter of fact, a lot of cops I've worked with saw domestic violence as a child, and that was a driving motivator for them to go into law enforcement and assist other people who are in similar situations and stop those bad situations from happening. It is often the same with SOF members.

Yes, many young people who join combat units are "itching for a fight" and enjoy the adrenaline rush of high-intensity training and even combat. It's usually when things go wrong on the battlefield, often combined with some experience and age (and in retrospect, sometimes in the form of PTSD), that the realities of war leave their scars. All the same, most of these young men are trying to do good. They want to fight the "bad guys" and protect the innocent.

For example, Rudy Reyes, a former Recon Marine, grew up as an orphan protecting his younger brothers. He said this in a podcast interview:

> I never thought I was going to join the military, probably because I'd been around so much gun violence being in the hood . . . I wanted to be the antithesis of that . . . I never really wanted to hurt people . . . But when Kosovo happened [and I saw the orphans in the news] . . . I said, "Wait a second . . . other

men are going to go fight. It is responsible for me to do my part." So I joined the Marine Corps. (Ritland 2023)

It's important to remember that both SOF members and clinicians ultimately want to help others and make the world a better place.

Then, of course, there are the differences between special operators and clinicians that, when observed from a distance, can be vast. SOF members are action-oriented and trained to make split-second decisions. Clinicians are contemplative and introspective, and they may take time to declare a diagnosis or treatment plan.

Through an initial observation, possibly considering posture and early conversations, a jump to the conclusion that you're looking at an antisocial personality or a narcissist would be a mistake. As a therapist, you must be very careful when evaluating a SOF member or veteran. You must distinguish between arrogance and confidence, as special operators gain incredible confidence—and must exude that confidence to their team—after years of overcoming incredible obstacles, training, and dangerous missions.

Many clinicians may not understand the idea of training to kill others, which is essentially what the military is about. Lt. Col. Dave Grossman, psychologist, researcher, and author of *On Killing: The Psychological Cost of Learning to Kill in War and Society*, explains it this way in an article he wrote:

> If you have no capacity for violence then you are a healthy productive citizen: a sheep. If you have a capacity for violence and no empathy for your fellow citizens, then you have defined an aggressive sociopath: a wolf. But if you have a capacity for violence and a deep love for your fellow citizens, then you are a sheepdog, a warrior, someone who can walk into the heart of darkness, into the universal human phobia, and walk out unscathed. (Grossman n.d.)

SOF individuals operate at the "tip of the spear," meaning they are often the first—and sometimes the only—troops in harm's way. Many special operations forces conduct reconnaissance missions, meaning they're ahead of the main fighting force, usually in a small team with, at times, limited artillery or air support. That means it's just them and whatever enemy forces are waiting for them. Many operators have dealt with the realities of military conflict around the globe. They have had to take human life on missions because if they didn't react with deadly force, they or their team member would be dead. In many other settings, this would be considered aberrant behavior in what it is to be human. This is where the clinician must think outside of their experiences and attempt to imagine what it would be like if they were required to kill and deal with life's extremes on a regular basis.

A simple way of embracing this mindset would be to imagine your family, your children, your spouse, your parents, or anyone else you love dearly. If they were in harm's way and their well-being was threatened, what would you be willing to do to keep them safe?

Most SOF members don't have a problem killing the bad guys, especially since they're not fighting large, conventional forces. Rather than Private Snuffy sometimes wondering why he has to kill an enemy soldier who is simply defending his home just as Snuffy would in America, special operators are usually targeting specific terrorist leaders or known combatants who are holding people hostage, for example. To them, it's their job to get rid of the bad guys and save lives. It's just business.

Furthermore, as Lt. Col. Dave Grossman says in his book *On Killing*, Special Ops Forces are not always sent to kill. As a former infantry company commander and Army Ranger, he explains how the small-unit, secret SOF patrols often work:

> On a recon patrol a small, lightly armed body of men is sent into enemy territory with specific orders *not* to engage the enemy. Their mission is to spy on the enemy, and if

a recon patrol runs into an enemy force it will *immedi-ately* break contact with the enemy. The essence of a recon patrol is *not* to be found or seen, and there is not enough firepower with such a patrol to support any kind of offensive operation. [. . .]

If a patrol is not a recon patrol, it is usually on an ambush or a raid, in which a select group of men will attack the enemy at a planned point. Just as in a recon patrol, a combat patrol will *immediately* break contact with the enemy if it is spotted while moving to or from its objective. The killing actions of a raid or ambush are focused on one particular spot for one brief period of time; at all other times the patrol, which depends on surprise for its success, will run from the enemy.

A raid or ambush patrol is carefully and thoroughly planned and rehearsed prior to leaving friendly lines, and the time in which killing takes place will be extremely brief, and very much like that practiced in rehearsal. And, if conducted properly, the enemy will be caught by surprise and will have very little chance to fight back. The psychologically protective power of (1) hitting a precise, known objective, (2) conducting such exact rehearsals and visualizations prior to combat (a form of conditioning), and (3) attacking an enemy who is caught by surprise and will hopefully have little chance to fight back is tremendous. Thus, by their very nature, such combat patrols involve far less random killing and are therefore less conducive to psychiatric casualties. (Grossman 2009, 59–60)

Grossman further explains that many service members in war don't usually feel a huge amount of guilt or remorse when killing from a distance because it's impersonal. It's when they must kill up close—when they see or hear the suffering of the other individual or see the dead body—that they endure a serious psychological toll.

What often bothers SOF members greatly is when a mission didn't go according to plan, such as when there was an unexpected civilian casualty, or when a team member was wounded or killed. Usually, there is at least one member on every SOF team trained and designated as a medic, and all SOF members are trained in Tactical Combat Casualty Care (TCCC). SOF members who encounter wounded civilians will, if the mission allows, try to help as much as they can, or they will take the civilians to a military or local medical facility when possible. Many SOF clients I've worked with had troubling memories about those types of issues.

Special Forces vs. Regular Military

There are many similarities between the men and women who serve in our nation's Armed Forces and those who go on to serve in SOF. Most notably, they share an understanding of basic military culture comprised of a hierarchy/chain of command, a responsibility to obey commands, a willingness to endure hardship in training and occasional deployments, and a desire to serve their country. Service members and their families sacrifice much over time, as their lives are generally dictated by the military's needs. (If you haven't already worked with members of the military, veterans, or their families, then understanding general military culture will be tremendously helpful when working with SOF individuals and their families.)

The main difference between SOF folks and regular service members is that special operators and their families deal with a much higher level of training and deployments, which requires even more sacrifice. On top of that, SOF operators are not allowed to tell anyone outside of their unit much about what they do. This includes their spouse and children. This secrecy can add stress and conflict to personal relationships. Many SOF units now have a good spousal support system that can be of great assistance when used, though not every spouse is engaged or willing to participate. Additionally, there can always be miscommunications and personality clashes as well as unit support shortcomings, just as in any organization.

Special Operations Forces have always trained and deployed more intensely and frequently than regular military service members, and since the declaration of the War on Terror after 9/11, the pace has only increased. Depending on what their mission or tasking is, this may be a high operational tempo (op tempo) with Tier 1 units, or a variable to high op tempo with Tier 2 and SOF support units.

This can't be stressed enough: SOF members are constantly deploying, and when they're not deployed, they're training for the next deployment. They train as hard as they fight—as realistically as possible. In fact, more injuries happen during training than on real missions, which is the point of training. SOF teams don't want anything to go wrong when combating the enemy or operating in enemy territory.

Many SOF units have basically been operating on an around-the-clock basis ever since September 11, 2001. The War on Terror is operating twenty-four hours a day, seven days a week, around the globe. As they say, the enemy doesn't take time off, so neither can the good guys. There are always operations going on, whether it's to snatch and grab high-level al-Qaeda or ISIS targets, rescue hostages, gather intelligence, disrupt enemy capabilities, or support indigenous forces in foreign countries.

SOF members do not usually operate as lone warriors like they do in the movies. They do, however, operate in small teams of about a dozen personnel or more, depending on the mission, and they may work with other SOF teams. Because they often operate behind enemy lines, the goal is to be secret, surgical, and fast. The majority of these operations are not meant to be long, drawn-out combat situations like what the regular military is trained to do. Therefore, each special operator is expected to act with the utmost professionalism and competency. There is no room for error.

Additionally, there's a whole cast of individuals who support all of these operations—individuals behind the scenes that no one even thinks about. There are supply and logistics personnel who inventory, order, maintain, and prepare all the equipment for each mission and training, from weapons to uniforms all the way to the oils needed for weapon maintenance (and there are different oils for cold, arctic environments versus dry, desert environments). The team members themselves also inventory and train on the equipment for each environment they'll be working in.

Then there are intelligence and communications personnel, such as signals intelligence (SIGINT) and satellite communications (SATCOM) personnel, to name a few. There are people who fly drones, such as the Predator drone, who must be on duty and away from their families for the duration of the mission, even though they're in a cubicle on another base rather than on the frontlines. And there's the 160th Special Operations Aviation Regiment (the SOAR "Night Stalkers"), which is basically the air taxi service for all special operations around the globe. They fly teams in and out of operational areas using stealth aircraft and methods, usually at night. SOAR is comprised of not only the pilots for these aircraft but also the gunners, navigators, mechanics, fuelers, and logistics and supply personnel. It also comprises the ordinance experts who equip the aircraft and SOF teams with the necessary weaponry, such as Hellfire and Sidewinder missiles, and a Tactical Air Control Party (TACP) who communicates with Air Force assets, such as if a five-hundred-pound bomb or an AC-130 Spectre Gunship is needed at a location.

All these personnel support an incredible pace of deployments, which may last a few weeks to a few months at a time. Generally speaking, Tier 1 units may get about a month at home before they deploy again. And when they are home, they're training for that next deployment.

My SOF clients have often talked about how the op tempo and numerous deployments affected their family in negative ways. Sometimes they would be gone for three or four months, come home, have to switch gears to home life, then be back out for another three months.

That pace could go on for two, three, or four years straight. Imagine what that does to a marriage and to raising children, or the lack thereof.

Special Ops Forces are training and deploying constantly, almost always at 110 percent of their physical and mental capacity. As much as we would love to think these people are superheroes (and they certainly feel like superheroes at times), they are human beings, and the human body and mind can only take so much before they break down. The knees can only take so many times of hitting the ground. The brain can only take so many explosive blasts before it starts having traumatic brain injury (TBI) symptoms. Not to mention, these guys are usually operating at night in pitch black, constantly running, jumping, shooting, moving, and communicating, and accidents do happen. Always operating at 110 percent with little downtime causes what I call special operations exhaustion syndrome, among other issues. It's the years of constant, high-level training and op tempo where a lot of my clients indicated they developed mental health issues and maladaptive coping skills.

Special Forces Psychology

Everyone must go through a mental health screening to get into special operations, which is not required for the regular military at the same level of detail. Once in a SOF unit, SOF members are routinely psychologically evaluated. SOF units today typically have mental health professionals on staff specifically assigned to them, whereas the regular military's psychologists, psychiatrists, and therapists are generally assigned to health clinics and hospitals, not as part of a unit.

The reason for this heightened mental and emotional screening is that SOF operators need to be calm under pressure and think on the go. They're not the "Billy badass" types you see in the movies. They are real-world, real-time problem solvers who must work in a team. This is why the biggest, most muscle-bound guys don't always make it through the pipeline. Those who do are not just physically capable but also mentally and emotionally skilled in the most difficult of circumstances. This is why mental health disorders (e.g., depression, anxiety, post-traumatic stress disorder) are actually less prevalent among special operators than in their counterparts in conventional forces (Cooper et al. 2020; Hanwella et al. 2014; Hanwella and de Silva 2012).

The SOF members I've interacted with, generally speaking, tend to see the benefit of keeping their mind, body, and spirit as healthy as possible. They work on all aspects of themselves and aren't as opposed to visiting their unit's mental health specialist as the typical infantry grunt might be. Acceptance of mental health continues to grow in society in general, so younger generations are continually more open to understanding and seeking mental health care. I was surprised when some Navy SEALs told me their command brought in a yoga instructor for PT one day. Most regular combat units, such as the 82nd Airborne Division I served in, would ridicule the idea of yoga for PT.

That being said, it is extremely difficult for a special operator to admit they have a problem and seek a therapist for regular visits. The counselors embedded with SOF units generally walk around and talk to guys at the gym, pop into offices in the unit area, and check in on people. They may be there for a team or team members after a particularly difficult mission. And operators may visit the counselor's office from time to time if there's something on their minds. But generally speaking, no operator wants to be the weak link. No SOF member wants to be the one who, in their mind, lets their team down. They must be at their best physically, mentally, emotionally, and tactically at all times. Once an operator is injured or otherwise incapable of performing the mission, they will no longer be able to serve at that level, if at all. Their entire career could be in jeopardy.

Even when I was serving in the 82nd Airborne Division, a Tier 3 unit, when someone went to the troop medical clinic (TMC), other soldiers thought they were suspect. Any airborne-qualified service member needs to be 100 percent well to remain on "jump status," or they could complicate their own injury and possibly hurt others when parachuting. So when someone had an illness or injury, they would be taken off jump status for a time. And when that happened, many people in the unit were very judgmental toward them. They would wonder out loud if those guys were trying to fake something to get out of jumping, a training exercise, or a deployment. Being nonoperational is not something most people want, especially at that high level.

While being tough at every level has advantages, it has downsides as well. Special Forces are accustomed to pushing through any physical or mental pain and ignoring personal or family problems until the problems become too serious to ignore. That's when you're most likely to see a SOF operator or veteran in your office.

Young Man's Game

The evolution of a SOF operator has several phases. The first is newbie status, when everything is new and exciting in the initial years. Then is the honeymoon phase or middle years, when operators have real-world operational experiences, feel more confident, and are respected and looked up to by their subordinates and peers. Plateauing in the end to late years is when they have become an extremely valuable asset because of their expertise, but one that has been, in many cases, completely worn out through multiple deployments and targeted specialized operations. Military retirement is possible for all branches after twenty years, though rarely will anyone work in a special operations combat unit for their entire twenty-year career. Many special operators get out before retirement due to exhaustion, injuries, or medical reasons. Others opt to get out and join the CIA or other government entity as a government contractor, doing the same things but making more money—and with less military "bullshit."

Whether a SOF member retires, becomes a government contractor, or gets out without any plans, the transition from the military to civilian life is often difficult. While many special operators have an impressive resume and will go on to other careers, some find the loss of the SOF identity and camaraderie very difficult, especially if they lost their spouse and kids along the way.

Because the SOF lifestyle is so demanding, an injury or mental illness can end a SOF member's career prematurely, and then also prevent them from doing what they would like to do in the civilian world. This can make the transition even harder, since the individual deals with the loss of their career, identity, and more—especially if these losses happen at a relatively young age when compared to regular military service members, and especially when compared to most civilians.

Bonding and Brotherhood

Bonding and brotherhood among members of Special Operations Forces is profound and distinctive. It is shaped by the intense experiences, shared challenges, and unique demands of their duties. This deep camaraderie is not only a fundamental aspect of life within these elite units but also a critical operational asset.

The roots of this brotherhood stretch back to the rigorous training and selection processes few candidates pass, designed not only to test physical stamina and skill but also to forge psychological resilience and team cohesion. The extreme nature of SOF training ensures that only those with the highest levels of perseverance, mutual trust, and dedication to the team succeed. These experiences lay the groundwork for strong bonds that extend into their operational duties.

In the field, special operators depend on one another for survival, success, and safety. This reliance under high stress and danger cements a sense of brotherhood that is difficult to replicate in civilian settings. The shared experiences of frequent deployments, secretive missions, and high-stakes operations contribute to a collective identity and a profound sense of loyalty to one another.

SOF operators are often unable to discuss the full extent of their work with outsiders, including their own families. Unit cohesion provides crucial emotional support, as members understand the mental and emotional tolls of their work without needing to articulate them. This unspoken understanding allows for a supportive environment where members can rely on each other not only for physical backup but also for psychological and emotional sustenance.

SOF culture emphasizes honor, courage, integrity, and self-sacrifice. The ethos of placing the mission and the team above oneself cultivates an environment where personal bonds are as crucial as tactical maneuvers. Ceremonies, memorials, and traditions that revere unit history and legacy and honor those who distinguished themselves in battle and those who died reinforce a sense of continuity, purpose, and connection.

The brotherhood formed in SOF often lasts a lifetime, enduring well beyond the end of active duty. Veterans of these units frequently maintain close contacts through reunions, social media, and professional networks. And, if they're willing and able, they often turn to one another for support in transitioning to civilian life or in facing post-service challenges.

That being said, operators are human, and personality conflicts do occur, which can make a SOF member's career and overall life satisfaction less than ideal. It may also tarnish that SOF member's ability or willingness to reach out to other SOF members once they have left the military, possibly causing more isolation and maladaptive coping behaviors. And when a SOF member leaves the military, they may no longer be geographically close to their brotherhood. It can take time before they are able to find a new civilian "brotherhood" or other veterans they can relate to.

This brotherhood can also have a negative impact on SOF family members, especially due to the secretive nature of SOF operations. Many SOF members may be closer in some ways to their SOF teammates than to their own spouses and children.

Perfectionism

In the special operations community, you are always striving for perfection. Everything is a competition—fastest shooter, fastest runner, fastest swimmer, strongest guy, most kills, most operations, longest in. It doesn't matter—everything you do in special operations is to prove your worthiness, to strive for perfection, and to earn your keep.

—Shawn Ryan,
former US Navy SEAL and CIA contractor (Ryan 2023)

Perfectionism is the tendency to set excessively high standards for oneself or others, and to engage in excessive critical self-evaluation. It is often driven by a desire to avoid mistakes or to achieve a sense of accomplishment or approval.

Operators have been extensively trained for one overriding reason—to avoid making mistakes. When an operator makes a mistake, someone could die. That's why perfectionism is a characteristic sought through continuous training and practice.

As mentioned, SOF members receive an incredible amount of intelligence and create a workup of their mission so they can train as realistically as possible before any operation. The in-and-out, very quick operation is the best they can hope for. It's when things go wrong that can cause issues, such as survivor's guilt, moral injury, organizational betrayal, and so on—though SOF members plan for things to go wrong as well. This could be where a team gets dragged down and they're not able to exfil (leave the area) in a quick manner, like in the movie *Black Hawk Down*, for example. While Hollywood tends to get a lot of things wrong, that movie is a perfect example of how a mission can go really bad, really fast if things don't go according to plan. This is why SOF members strive for perfection, train incessantly, and need to be able to think on their feet.

While perfectionism can be a positive quality when it helps individuals set and reach high goals, strive for excellence, and be highly competent, it can be problematic when it becomes all-consuming and interferes with an individual's home/family life, their ability to achieve a healthy work-life balance, their life satisfaction, and their ability to recognize their own accomplishments.

Discrimination in SOF

Despite the highly professional environments in which they work, SOF operators are not immune to the broader societal challenges and discriminatory practices based on race, gender, ethnicity, religion, or sexual orientation.

Historically, the SOF community has been predominantly male and often skewed toward certain demographic profiles. This has sometimes resulted in environments where institutional biases subtly influence everything from recruitment and promotions to unit cohesion and operational effectiveness. As SOF units have increasingly recognized the value of diversity for broadening their operational capabilities and perspectives, efforts have been made to address these biases.

Obviously, discrimination within SOF can severely impact morale and unit cohesion, as with any other organization. This can lead to feelings of isolation or resentment among members who feel they are not receiving equal treatment or opportunities. This erosion of trust and reliability can, in turn, negatively impact critical, high-stakes SOF operations where team members must implicitly depend on one another for their livelihoods.

So far, all my SOF clients, for whatever reason, have been Caucasian and male. However, when I was active duty at Fort Bragg hanging out with 7th Group, Special Forces, I had Black and Hispanic friends who were SOF members, and I could see that even at that level, racism and discrimination existed. It was much more subdued than what I saw in the regular Army because SOF is more selective and small, and therefore more disciplined and professional overall. But it was still there.

David Goggins is a famous former Navy SEAL who talks a lot about dealing with racism throughout his life—before, during, and after the military. Even at elite levels of society, there is always somebody higher up making decisions about who goes where and who does what. The reality is that everybody brings whatever upbringing they had and whatever political views they have to their situation, wherever they go. We all have to deal with our own and with others' preconceived notions and biases, whatever those are, especially as clinicians.

We are taught as clinicians about discrimination in regards to race, ethnicity, gender, sexual orientation, economic status, religion, and so on. But the discrimination I've seen most with SOF clients has been more about who's getting specialty assignments, especially in terms of specialty training. Because of the perfectionism and drive SOF members have, they all want to be the best, which means getting the most training and becoming the most decorated and tactically proficient warrior possible. Of course, not every SOF member can go to every school and be awarded every accolade. There are only so many student slots, only so much time in someone's career, and only so many opportunities. Everyone's path is different.

Even so, SOF members have described some environments as a good-old-boy network, where they felt certain people in the network were taken care of and favored over others. This discrimination seemed to be more group-based than anything else. I've had clients complain they were not recommended for a promotion, or weren't allowed to attend a special school, or were reprimanded for something minor and felt they were treated more harshly than they should have been. Because most of these folks are super high achievers, these grievances can stay with them even after their service.

Myth of Uniqueness

The myth of uniqueness refers to the belief that one is special or exceptional in some way, and that their experiences, challenges, and struggles are unique and cannot be understood or appreciated by others. The myth of uniqueness can be fueled by a range of factors, including cultural messages, social media, and personal experiences. It can lead to individuals feeling they are somehow different or better than others, or that they have a special purpose or destiny.

This is especially true of SOF members, as they go through experiences and conduct operations that few others go through or can even know about.

While it is important for individuals to recognize and value their own unique qualities and experiences, the myth of uniqueness can be harmful if it leads to feelings of isolation and disconnection from others. Many SOF members feel frustrated around civilians who aren't as highly proficient in their jobs as the SOF member was in theirs. This can come across as condescension and can result in arrogance and irritability. Additionally, the myth of uniqueness can prevent individuals from seeking support or help when they need it, because they may feel no one else can understand their experiences or that no one is competent enough to help them.

The myth of uniqueness can be a huge barrier for a SOF member reaching out to the behavioral health community. What I try to tell SOF clients is that it's impossible to be perfect. Even though they are extraordinary at what they do—there's no doubt about that—they still have the same human emotions that we all deal with.

Vigilance

Vigilance is the state of being alert and paying attention to any danger. It involves being watchful and ready to respond to any sign of threat or emergency at any time. Vigilance is an important quality for SOF individuals and teams to maintain, as it helps to ensure safety and security. SOF units and service members are trained to always be vigilant, as one moment of complacency can cost someone's life. You will find that special operators are constantly evaluating their environment. Often, they will not put their backs to an open door, nor will they sit randomly. Instead, they will sit in a corner where they're most comfortable, usually with a wall behind them.

It's one thing to be vigilant and another to be hypervigilant. Hypervigilance is when a person is unable to slow down or find balance in their environment and, most importantly, is unable to relax. This inability to shift gears causes them to stay in hypervigilance mode, which is detrimental to their mental health. It's important to distinguish between vigilance and hypervigilance.

Command Presence

Command presence refers to the ability of a leader to project confidence, competence, and decisiveness, and to command the respect and attention of those around them. In SOF culture, command presence is an important aspect of leadership.

Effective command presence involves being able to clearly communicate expectations and goals, make difficult decisions, and inspire and motivate others to achieve success. It also involves being able to adapt to changing circumstances and demonstrate flexibility and resilience.

Command presence often comes in the form of supreme confidence, competence, and experience. Remember that confidence should not be confused with arrogance. While a SOF operator may come across as arrogant, it's more often than not the result of years of training, real-world operations, and mastery of various skill sets.

A SOF member's command presence is their modus operandi; it's a part of their personality. Therefore, a clinician must not be offended by it, but instead recognize that it may mask a SOF member's feelings and problems. A SOF member would never allow their mask to slip during a mission. However, they would also not want to hide a serious issue if it could become a problem for the whole team. I tell clients it's better they fix what's wrong and become whole again rather than hiding and suffering forever.

Dark Humor

Dark humor is a type of humor that comments on or makes light of difficult or taboo subjects, such as death, suffering, or tragedy. It is often used as a way to defuse tension and cope with difficult or uncomfortable experiences. It can also be used to challenge societal norms, satirize controversial subjects, or expose the absurdity or injustice of a situation.

Many people, especially those working in certain professions such as SOF or law enforcement, appreciate dark humor's ability to provide a lighter perspective on painful or sensitive subjects. However, it's not for everyone and can be easily misconstrued or taken the wrong way. And not everyone who works in "extreme" professions appreciates dark humor, either. It's really up to the individual.

Because it can be seen as insensitive, inappropriate, and downright offensive to some people, it's important to know where it's coming from, and to know your audience when using it yourself. If you don't appreciate dark humor, it's important to understand the context so you aren't shocked or offended by it, as that could hinder a therapy session.

To put dark humor in context, when I was in law enforcement, it was incredibly painful to attend a funeral for a fallen teammate who had been killed in the line of duty. I always teared up when I heard the bagpipes; I just couldn't help it. So at one of those services, I leaned over to my buddy and said, "You see those flowers? They fucking suck. Where did they get those from, the grocery store? When I die, I don't want those cheap-ass-looking flowers. You better go to the top florist and get the best displays, man!"

Another time, also while in law enforcement, I responded to an active shooter situation as part of the Emergency Services Unit. The guy in front of me engaged and killed the active shooter, then our team split up to secure the scene and assess the situation. Another team member and I stood next to the dead shooter to ensure no evidence was tampered with until the coroner arrived. As it happened, the shooter who had been killed had fallen face-first into a planter box, and his face was buried in dirt. My team member, an Italian guy, looked at me and said, "Heeeey, that's what we call a 'dirt nap.'" I lost it right there. In that moment, that was the funniest thing I'd ever heard. Keep in mind, our adrenaline, our vigilance, and the reality of our situation were through the roof. When he said that, it released all that tension.

If someone had seen me standing there laughing like crazy over a dead body, they might have thought I was callous or even a sociopath. But you can't be stoic and absorb all the pain of the world, especially in those types of professions. There's got to be some type of deflection or release, and dark humor works for some people. It doesn't work for everyone—I've made jokes around other seasoned cops who didn't respond well to dark humor—but it can be a way to lighten the load of serious situations.

Dark humor is a coping mechanism. Personally, it has helped me and many of those I've served with deal with the difficulties that come with the professions we worked in. And in a way, some people end up being able to talk about death and other difficult subjects more easily by using dark humor. From my perspective as a therapist, when a client uses dark humor, I see it as a good sign. It's usually the stuff my clients don't joke about that needs to be addressed.

3. MANAGING THE THERAPEUTIC ALLIANCE

That's the thing . . . you don't get training for . . . how to cope. I think it's just how you personally deal with things. It differs with everybody. Like, they train you up to be able to do a job . . . but after the fact, you gotta figure it out on your own. You can go seek help. But during your entire time in the military, you're told not to seek help, or you're told to mark "No, I didn't see this, I didn't do that" so you can go home early. So you're kind of brought up in that mindset to not show any of that weakness until you get out.

—Nicholas Irving,
former Army Ranger (Prez 2024)

The difference between the working culture of the military and behavioral health professions can be wide. For the military, and especially for SOF folks (as well as law enforcement and other first responders), members are trained to communicate directly and concisely, quickly solve problems and reduce threats, be highly competent, and be willing to sacrifice themselves for the team.

In stark contrast, I've found that a majority of clinicians follow a behavioral pathway that focuses on cautious, indirect, and ambiguous interactions. Generally speaking, this soothing, get-in-touch-with-your-feelings, let-me-gently-guide-you-until-you-figure-it-out-on-your-own kind of therapy is not going to work with this group of people. Many of them are simply not comfortable in a traditional therapeutic environment because they need a more direct approach.

The clinician must understand that these types of clients—especially SOF clients—are momentarily ceding their competency and skill sets and entering a world they're unfamiliar with. They are looking at you to be a competent and knowledgeable guide in those moments. Instead of coddling them, they want you to take charge; to be direct and show your expertise without being condescending or arrogant; to be understanding and sympathetic without expressing too much emotion or being trite.

When someone enters my office, I know I need to find the underlying issue that's kicking their ass and causing them to seek help in the first place as quickly as possible, not simply get them to express their feelings in an unending talk session. I know they had to overcome a lot of barriers and an unwillingness on their part to seek help in the first place, so I take it very seriously when they make it over that hurdle. It doesn't happen very often—at least, not as often as I would like.

Not every clinician will want to deal with this population and want to hear about some of their combat experiences, which is understandable. For me, because of my background, I enjoy it, but not because it's entertaining. It's because I understand it. It's important that stories of combat and difficult situations like suicidal ideation don't distract you from helping the client.

When a client tells me that they bombed an enemy location but later found there had been children at the location who were killed, for instance, I'm not focused on the children who died, nor am I thinking about war or politics or anywhere else my mind might wander. My focus is on the fact that this person sitting in front of me had to deal with that situation, and the experience is now affecting their ability to live. I need to find the behavioral threads that are unraveled because of that incident and figure out how I can bring that person back to emotional health.

In my experience, too many therapists want to focus on the incident itself, either to try and understand it because they lack cultural competency, or because they want the client to walk themselves through it and process it. But that is not always the right approach with this group. I don't usually want that person to sit there and stew in the worst day of their life for an hour. Instead, I want to see how that incident is affecting them and if that's the main reason why they're not sleeping at night, abusing alcohol, lashing out at their own children because they're overprotective, or whatever the case may be. And then I walk the client through the healing processes to find ways to mitigate those negative behaviors and maybe help provide them with a new perspective on the past.

It's okay if you decide not to work with this population, but it's important to do your homework and have the appropriate referrals ready. That way, your due diligence and research can still put them on the right track.

Barriers to Seeking Mental Health Treatment

> We get good at putting a mask on . . . I can come to work and look like a Spartan all day . . . until I put my car in drive to go home. It takes a true leader and a true mentor to be able to look at somebody and understand that's not the normal person [they're] used to seeing . . . Sergeant Major Donaldson pulled me in his office, and he was like, "What's going on, Ranger buddy? Where you at? I can tell you ain't here." And we just talked. It was emotional, the stuff I was dealing with at the time . . . it was like an atomic bomb in my head . . . [And he] developed me and gave me the time I needed.
>
> —First Sergeant Jason Belford,
> Army Ranger, interviewed on *SOFCAST*
> (USSOCOM 2022)

When a SOF member comes into a therapist's office, it's usually because: (a) they realize they're about to go off a cliff; or (b) a family member (usually the spouse) realizes they're about to go off a cliff.

At this point, not only are they suffering internally with their mental and emotional health, but their external life is suffering, too, as a result. They've been fired from a job, or their spouse has threatened to leave them and take the kids, or they can't connect with their children. To put it in military terms, it's like they're pulling the ripcord for the parachute at the last minute because they finally saw the ground rapidly rising to meet them.

The reason for this is partly due to the barriers SOF members must overcome before seeking treatment. Therefore, it's important for clinicians to try and reduce the barriers that prevent many SOF members from getting the help they need. Understanding SOF members' reluctance to seeking treatment for psychological injuries was a main focus for writing this book. It's important to understand that for many SOF clients, you have only one chance to show them you can handle what they're going through and that you have the skill set to assist them. If you don't prove yourself in that first meeting, chances are they won't come back.

Stigma of Seeking Treatment

Stigma is one of the biggest barriers to seeking treatment, and it's why so many SOF members don't seek help. Many SOF folks feel that seeking psychological treatment will expose them as weak or broken, as unfit for duty or unreliable in high-stress situations. This is unacceptable to them, because when they're in a SOF unit or on a mission, if they're not 100 percent, it puts the whole team at risk.

Active-duty SOF members will also fear that their careers will be negatively impacted, such as loss of security clearance, loss of promotion opportunities, loss of the ability to carry a firearm, disdain from fellow SOF members, and even discharge from the service and loss of their job—and their identity. The same goes for SOF veterans seeking care through their employer's insurance or medical program.

Unfortunately, these are not baseless fears. They have all occurred to those seeking mental health treatment in the past. Based on my clients' input, the military branches have made improvements in taking care of their members' mental health, but treatment can still be seen as a scarlet letter or "shit stain" on members' careers.

The same can be true in the civilian world.

What clinicians need to understand is if a diagnosis of PTSD ends up on a client's employee medical record, it will follow that client back to their job and to every future job application they submit. So while there is a stigma that keeps people from seeking treatment, the truth is that there is still a stigma against those who have been treated.

A potential employer may decide that hiring someone diagnosed with PTSD or other mental illness is not worth the risk. I have seen a diagnosis hurt a lot of people over the years, and it's unfortunate. So while therapists often need to determine a diagnosis for insurance purposes, doing so without taking into context the whole picture of the client's life and current employment situation can sometimes do more harm than good.

I actually tell all my clients that if they're seeing me through their employee assistance program (EAP), it's not really confidential. I tell them that if they can, it's better for them to spend their own money and pay out of pocket. It's money well spent because they're investing in their mental health, and then it goes nowhere; it truly is confidential. When someone seeks health care on behalf of any employer insurance, whether it's EAP, worker's comp, or whatever, then the employer can get that record because the employer is paying for the service. And that's when it sticks; it stays on the client's record forever. So when someone pays out of pocket, preferably outside of their hometown or small-town area if needed, then those notes are protected, and no one will know about them.

Many therapists are too eager to place labels of disorders or illnesses without differentiating the fact that what their clients are experiencing is, in many cases, normal under their unique circumstances. Unfortunately, the current mental health model often requires a diagnosis in order for the therapist to get paid for services, which only adds to reasons why a SOF member will avoid seeking care. Therefore, it's important to be culturally competent and weed out as many diagnoses as you can so you're confident the diagnoses listed on the client's record are accurate and won't cause them undue harm outside of the clinician's office.

Erasing Stigma

To be a good leader, you have to be a good communicator. As a leader, you have to communicate your intent every chance you get, and if you fail to do that, you will pay the consequences.

—William H. McRaven, Admiral (Ret.),
former SOCOM commander

The younger generations have fortunately been raised with a more open attitude toward mental health. They're often a bit more accepting of seeing a therapist when compared to old-timers like myself, who were in the military or law enforcement in the 1980s and early '90s. Older generations like mine were taught not to show emotion. If it was something we couldn't shake off with a stiff drink and a couple of laughs with our buddies, we were considered suspect. And if we did ask for clinical help, others would often assume something must be seriously wrong.

While I'm glad our culture is becoming more aware of the importance of mental health, the military—especially SOF—trains its members to sacrifice themselves for others, for their team, for their country, and for the higher good. A SOF member's personal fears, reservations, views, or political opinions usually have no place.

Transitioning to civilian life often results in an awakening of sorts, where the service member is suddenly free to listen to their own desires and to express their own opinions, while they look back at who they were and wonder how that fits with who they are now and who they want to become. This can be a disorienting experience, especially when entrusting a stranger to help them with deep, complex, and personal struggles.

One way I combat the stigma of seeking help, especially when I have clients who are having difficulty accepting the fact they're not always 100 percent, is to educate them with analogies. Automotive analogies seem to work well, especially with men. I might ask them if they would buy an $80,000 truck and just drive it till it explodes. And they say, "Of course not." Then I ask, "So, what would you do to make sure your truck didn't explode?" They answer, "Get regular maintenance on it." I explain to them that it's the same with our mental health. It's like a tune-up; we don't want to ignore our problems until we explode. This is, unfortunately, what many SOF members end up doing.

In the military, whenever we have a vehicle fleet or other equipment assigned to the unit, we need to take care of it on a routine basis, usually called PMCS (preventive maintenance checks and services). For instance, you can't keep firing a rifle or pistol for three years without cleaning the damn thing; it would seize up and explode in your face. So I'll ask my clients, "What did you have to do with your weapons and vehicles in the military?" They answer, "Oh, we had to clean our weapons," or "We had to PMCS our vehicles." And I say, "Okay, so what does PMCS mean?" They go through all the maintenance and checks they had to do. And I say, "That's what you have to do with your mental state. You need to do ritualistic things to keep yourself and your relationships running smoothly so they don't seize up and explode in your face in the form of substance abuse, suicidal ideation, divorce, or infidelity."

It's the same with our bodies, and SOF members understand how to train, work out, eat right, and recover. I tell them that seeing a therapist doesn't have to be labeled with something; it's just to get under the hood and make sure everything's okay. Eventually, they'll be back out on the road and running smoothly again.

Because SOF members push their bodies and minds to the limit and deal with things most humans rarely deal with, much less on a regular basis, it only makes sense that they would need a checkup every once in a while.

When I use metaphors like that, I generally see the light bulb go on. They realize that if we need to take care of our equipment and our bodies, then we need to do that with our minds as well. I remind them that what they're going through doesn't mean they're crazy. It just means they're human and that they need to work through some stuff so they can be mentally fit again.

Efforts to change the negative perception of seeking help go beyond individual clinician-client relationships, such as peer-to-peer support programs, leadership advocacy, and education campaigns that emphasize mental resilience as a component of operational readiness and basic human health.

I once went to see a therapist myself for a checkup after I had gotten my clinical license and was working as a therapist. I went just to bounce ideas off someone else who was similarly trained. The therapist was very puzzled when I told her I didn't really have anything clinically significant going on and just wanted to make sure everything was good. Fortunately, now that some insurance plans pay for mental health services, I knew it was a benefit I had with my health plan, so I decided to use it. The therapist and I had a good chuckle about it, but even therapists should get their stuff checked every now and then. Everyone should, because we're only human.

If someone tells me they've never had any issues in their life, that just tells me they're good at hiding it. We all go through mental problems and life problems. People are so scared of getting labeled with a disorder, like there's something wrong with them, when a lot of the issues we have are just part of being human.

Unfortunately, because of our insurance model in the US, we clinicians can't really get paid unless we diagnose something that's listed in the *DSM* (the *Diagnostic and Statistical Manual of Mental Disorders*). I wish that would change. If people could see a professional and get help for whatever they're dealing with without worrying about the fact they may get labeled as mentally ill, we might be able to help more people and even prevent more serious mental illnesses from forming. People would know that hitting road bumps and taking detours is okay, and it doesn't necessarily mean there's anything wrong with them—and if there *is* something wrong, it can get fixed or they can learn how to cope with it.

Confidentiality

Concerns about the confidentiality of mental health treatment, for fear of reprisal or stigma and particularly regarding the impact on employability, can deter SOF personnel from seeking help. Losing one's security clearance, whether they are still serving or are working in a civilian job that requires one, is another important concern. SOF clients may also be reluctant to disclose sensitive information because of the secretive nature of their military experiences.

As a therapist, you must navigate the need to maintain confidentiality while fulfilling your duty as a mandated reporter, including any information that might affect national security. This is where cultural competency comes into play, so you don't need all the details and can assure your client as much. If details come up, your client can rest assured knowing you won't record them.

When suggesting a client does not use their employee insurance or medical program when possible, it's important to address these concerns using clear communication about confidentiality policies, what is reported and what is kept confidential, what is written in confidential notes, and how the client can access those notes for their own benefit and knowledge.

Of course, it is necessary, as it is with all clients, to explain your confidentiality rules, and to share the five issues that cannot be kept confidential: (1) severe/probable suicidal ideation; (2) severe/probable homicidal ideation; (3) domestic violence; (4) sexual abuse; and (5) child abuse. It's important your SOF client understands where these boundaries are. It's also important that you as the therapist not over-react to anything that may not yet cross those boundaries, which is part of the crucial process of gaining trust.

I would even encourage clinicians not to take notes when working with SOF members. It will help make them feel more comfortable, and it may protect both of you if subpoenaed in court. In those cases, there wouldn't be any notes on that client that could be used as evidence. You would verbally tell the court you had a session with the individual and that you talked about certain things, about post-traumatic stress disorder or depression or substance abuse or whatever, but then you would be able to downplay or keep out of judicial record anything that was specifically said. When you start taking notes, those notes can be sought by legal teams in litigation, and there are times when SOF members will actually seek therapists only when they're dealing with litigious situations, so taking notes can be an important boundary issue to consider.

Overall, it's important to keep what is said and done in session private and not report anything to the client's employers or command staff or the like, unless it's necessary to do so.

Other Barriers to Treatment

Operational Tempo and Deployment/Training Schedule

When a SOF operator is on active duty, the demanding nature of SOF missions often requires a never-ending cycle of training, deployment, and brief recovery periods, leaving little room for mental health care. You can mitigate this barrier by integrating mental health support directly into the operational cycle, offering flexible and accessible care options like telehealth, and ensuring mental health professionals are available before and immediately after deployments.

Civilian Job Schedule

In the military, troop readiness is vital to mission success. Every service member's medical, dental, and vision health is tracked at the command level. Therefore, when a service member needs to attend a medical appointment, the command is usually accommodating. The civilian world, however, is not always as understanding, especially when a SOF veteran is transitioning into a new civilian job.

Missing work for steady mental health appointments could put the client's future career in jeopardy. Therefore it's important to understand your client's schedule and be accommodating by being available after hours or on weekends if needed, providing telehealth appointments, and/or recommending other clinicians and resources that can help the client without putting that client's employment at risk.

Limited Access to Specialized Care

Sometimes SOF personnel require specialized care, such as tests or treatments for neurological issues or sleep disorders, or they want to try specialized treatments such as electroconvulsive therapy. Unfortunately, specialized testing and treatments can be quite costly and further limited based on the client's insurance situation and geographic location. It's important to work with your clients as much as possible and do the necessary homework to learn about other treatment options, insurance coverage, and veteran and low-income programs that can assist with funding and access.

Limited Access to Basic Care & Basic Information

A study by the RAND Corporation noted "only about half of all veterans who need mental health care ever receive it" due to "[a] perfect storm of provider shortcomings, access problems, and personal and social attitudes" (Farmer and Tanielian 2019). These barriers include "shortages in the mental health workforce [that] can make it difficult for veterans to schedule a timely appointment. And some providers aren't as extensively trained as they could be in evidence-based practices, which means fewer veterans are likely to receive the highest-quality care in the private sector" (RAND Corporation 2023).

Other barriers the study noted include the fact many potential clients are often skeptical about the effectiveness of treatment and whether they'll experience side effects from any medication. These are valid concerns and need to be discussed openly during therapy.

Limited Time Transportation & Finances

Other often overlooked barriers are the facts that many veterans struggle making it to care appointments due to scheduling conflicts, transportation difficulties, or financial issues. If they do have transportation, a long drive can also deter veterans from following through with appointments, as it takes time away from their job or home life and can add stress. Lack of information about things like provider eligibility and first-line treatments can further hinder them from receiving the best possible care. Additionally, "insurance and provider financial models bring more issues into play, such as coverage eligibility and care financing" (RAND Corporation 2023). It's important to keep these barriers in mind and do what you can to remove them.

Lack of Culturally Competent Providers

Another major barrier that prevents SOF members from seeking treatment is the perception that therapists will not understand what they have been through during their careers and will be unable to help. Unfortunately, I believe there is a lot of truth to that perception of the current field of therapists. As a combat veteran and career law enforcement officer, I've had a hard time finding therapists who were competent at dealing with either military or law enforcement personnel who I felt comfortable referring clients to.

One reason for this is the lack of cultural competency, as discussed in the previous chapters. And even though there is more mental health support now in the military for active duty personnel and in the Veterans Affairs medical system for veterans and retired personnel, the military and the VA still have a long way to go before the mental health care they provide is truly adequate to serve the number of combat veterans today. Most mental health clinicians at these government facilities are booked up months in advance, even more so if they have a specialty in high demand. This is why, in my experience, many SOF veterans may try and find a civilian therapist who is retired military before they go to the VA—say, a Vietnam-era veteran who specializes in PTSD. Or they may have tried the VA and weren't happy with the results.

Unfortunately, that doesn't mean mental health care in the civilian sector is always better. It may often be worse, because at least therapists in the military or VA have some cultural competency by virtue of working in a military environment.

As you can see, not all barriers to treatment are psychological. It's important to understand that when clients are under stress and dealing with mental health issues, what may seem like a slight inconvenience to us as clinicians can be a true impediment to getting care. Therefore, it's important you be flexible and do whatever you can to ease or remove the barriers your clients face.

Developing Clinician-Client Trust

SOF personnel are often selected and trained to be highly self-reliant and resilient, which can lead to a tendency to handle problems independently rather than seeking help. Continuous exposure to high-stress environments and traumatic events can lead to a normalization of these experiences, causing individuals to underestimate the impacts to their mental health and to dismiss their need for help.

I've frequently found that by the time a SOF member or veteran overcomes their personal, organizational, and societal barriers to seeking help and actually goes to therapy, they've been suppressing their mental health problems for a very long time. They're on the edge. Stuff has gone badly. They're at a breaking point.

It's rare that I run across anybody in Special Operations Forces that who self-identified when something was wrong and immediately went to a therapist. Usually, they've "muscled through it" for as long as they could, just as they muscled through their physical and psychological pain to get through years of strenuous training and dangerous missions. They never want to let their team down, their family down, or themselves down by "going to medical" and being forced to miss out on a training exercise or mission.

When working with SOF members in treatment, it's important to recognize that the barriers to treatment make it even harder to trust a potential care provider. Many members have experienced a high level of trauma or difficult situations during their time in the military, including multiple combat deployments, exposure to high explosive blasts, civilian death, and even child death. These experiences can lead to feelings of anxiety, depression, and PTSD, which may make it even more challenging for them to open up about their experiences to a stranger.

Overall, building trust in SOF treatment requires a direct and honest approach that takes into account the SOF member's unique experiences, training, and community lifestyle. This might involve creating a safe and confidential environment for discussing classified or sensitive issues, providing education and honest support around mental health concerns, and by addressing potential barriers to treatment, such as stigma or concerns about career consequences.

In my experience, the two most important components to building trust are transparency and honesty. You as the clinician must be willing to acknowledge when you don't know something or don't understand something.

When I was studying and training to be a therapist, I heard the term "Fake it till you make it" a lot, but this is the wrong approach when dealing with SOF folks. It's counterintuitive and counterproductive. SOF members are professionals at reading other human beings; they'll know when you're just going through the motions. Do not fake a thing.

The best thing any therapist could ever do is be 100 percent transparent. If you have no idea what your client is talking about, then say so. Ask them, "Are you willing to talk to me about that? Can you explain that to me?" I always give the individual an opportunity to say yes or no, because they may not be able or willing to give more information.

What you don't want is for the session to turn into story time, when the therapist is asking questions about their clients' experiences and the client is doing most of the talking to help fill the gap of cultural competency. Many SOF members I have worked with in clinical sessions were worried that the therapist would ask endless questions of past combat missions and what the operator saw and did. I know what they're worried about, because I've had those experiences myself. The first time I went to a therapy session I walked away realizing the clinician got more out of it than I did; I had spent the whole time giving them information and getting nothing in return.

In those situations, the client is teaching the therapist instead of the therapist giving the client assistance, guidance, and help with their problems—the reason the client is visiting the therapist in the first place. Story time will cause a SOF member to quit therapy.

Many therapists want to hear about their client's horror stories because they think by knowing all the details about what someone has experienced, they'll be able to formulate a better treatment plan, but that doesn't usually work at all. In fact, making a client relive all their trauma by asking questions about it without providing any relief or recommendations or treatment is, for the client, frustrating at the very least, and retraumatizing at the worst.

That's why cultural competency is so important, and this book is not the only way to do that. You should do your own research and due diligence if you want to work with this population —and they will expect that of you. You must also do your homework on your individual clients so you get an idea of what they have been through and what you're dealing with.

You have to be willing to be "butt naked." That's my own term, and it means that during a session, you're stripped down, rawdogging it with another human being, because that's how they feel coming into your office. They're dealing with hardship and pain, and they're not the badass SOF operator they're used to being. They feel incredibly vulnerable, so you have to meet them where they're at while showing you can lead them out of the darkness. You cannot show yourself to be broken or fragile, but you don't want to be aloof to their pain or talk down to them as a know-it-all clinician. You need to connect with them.

Personally, I use this style regardless of who I'm working with, while adjusting for each individual and listening to what my instincts tell me. I think when any of us show up in a therapist's office, we want our therapist to "lead the way" out of whatever issues we might have in a professional manner, without getting sidetracked by stories, clinical elitism, or emotionalism.

When you strip everything away, SOF members are still human beings. While their experiences are unique, they have the same emotions and deal with the same anxieties and stressors that we all deal with in life. So, when they're talking about whatever happened in Afghanistan or wherever in the world, they're really talking about how it's affecting them now in daily life. They're saying that they're having a hard time sleeping, or expressing how they feel to their spouse or their loved one and it's causing problems at home, or they're not able to connect with their children and be a part of their children's lives the way they want to. They want to be productive, good people, and they want what's best for them and their families, just like you and I do.

It's important not to sugarcoat anything, but to get to the root of the issue as soon as possible and start helping them address their issue and their negative behaviors. They need to see that there is a way out, that there is value in seeking treatment, and that they don't have to suffer forever.

Strip away all ego, education, training, background—everything. It all has to go out the door, because they'll sniff it out in a minute. Even if you're really nervous or excited to be working with a SOF member and you can't wait to tell your colleagues, a SOF client will read that in your session, whether it's through body language or your choice of words. Whatever it is, they'll read it. So be honest and transparent, do your homework, say when you don't know something, and be yourself.

In order to gain the client's trust, you should be as straight up and honest as possible. They are professionals of the highest caliber. They expect to be treated as such, and they expect you to be a professional in your field. If you are transparent with them and don't make the mistake of coddling them or treating them like a wounded animal, you will have a much better relationship.

On the flip side, if you feel the need to confront the client about possibly nonfactual or unrelated issues, then be direct and clear. You don't ever want to call them a liar, but you must stand your ground when you doubt the validity of their story or feel the information shared is irrelevant and deflecting from the root issue. They will respect you for it.

As clinicians, we're used to thinking about and trying to fix problems. No matter what a SOF member has gone through, they're human and are dealing with human problems. That's why you don't need their whole story or the nitty-gritty details; you want to focus on the human issue that the client is facing.

It's also easy for clinicians to have a cookie cutter approach and treat their clients as though they're just another problem that needs fixing. This is also the wrong approach. The problems may be the same, but the individual is different. You must get to know each of your clients as individuals and tailor your approaches and solutions to each person. If you don't, both you and the client will end up frustrated.

As my colleague Thomas J. LaGrave said:

> There is a statement that goes like this: "All Navy SEALs are alike, no two are the same." Let me explain. When we operate, we behave as Navy SEALs—we move, we shoot, and

we communicate the same, better than anyone in the world. When we go home to our families and our friends, we are just like everyone else—unique. We are the same as any other father, brother, husband, wife or mother.

It's important to remember that while human problems are the same, each client has different values, perspectives, beliefs, and thoughts. You must get to know what those are for each individual client before you can understand how to help them.

Quickly reading and helping your clients comes with experience. Of course, some clients may take longer to understand and help than others. No matter how difficult a client is, the more trust you develop in that first session, the more likely they are to come back and share more with you.

Guns in the Office

Many clinical and behavioral health settings, including the VA, have policies against firearms on the premises, for obvious reasons. However, SOF operators are used to having at least one weapon on them at all times. Similar to law enforcement, this is their protection, a part of their armor, which can save their life and the lives of their team members. For a lot of these folks, their firearm is one of the most critical pieces of lifesaving equipment they have.

Remember that they're not supposed to be vulnerable, so when they have to see a mental health specialist and don't feel like they're in total control, their firearm may be the one thing that keeps them feeling safe and secure. When a "civilian" tries to strip them of that and take away part of their armor that could keep them alive and safe, it can rub them the wrong way, to say the least.

You're not going to get much therapy done if certain things cause that person to shut down. They may just leave and not come back, or they may just go through the motions and not get anything out of the session. This is especially the case when the client is only there because their spouse, their chain of command, or a court order made them attend therapy, which means you have to work even harder to gain their trust.

I know therapists who are totally okay when a SOF client has a sidearm with them in session. They know that their client—especially a SOF client—is a professional who knows how to use that weapon better than anybody else in the world. But this all depends on your own personal comfort level.

Another colleague of mine was not as comfortable with guns in his office, but to ensure he didn't try to confiscate anything from them or disrespect their boundaries, he went out and bought a small gun lockbox that he keeps in his office. Whenever one of his clients comes in who legally carries a firearm, he asks them to lock it in the safe, and they—the gun owner—get to keep the key during the whole session. This way, the client has easy access to their weapon and doesn't feel powerless, but the gun is not so easily accessible that it makes the therapist feel unsafe.

Bullshit Detector

They are guarded and probing—psychic radar. I feel them take in every detail. They're sharp and accustomed to camouflaging themselves . . . Nothing will be swallowed at face value. These are practical men and everything we put before them will have to be backed by our own personal experience and relevance to their job. They're interested in results, not theory.

—Richard Strozzi-Heckler (2007, 12)

The shit detector can go both ways: when you as a therapist call out your client for evading or talking around the real issue that's bothering them, or when your client calls you out for not adequately addressing their concerns. I will talk about both in this section.

First, SOF members have extensive training in human psychological behavior and are adept at reading people and situations. This provides them with valuable skills when interacting with both friendly and enemy forces as well as unknown individuals, such as family members or other people in an area. Quickly and accurately reading body language, facial expressions, clothing, environment, details of the surroundings, and more can mean the difference between life and death.

You as the therapist should know that as you are evaluating your client, the SOF client is evaluating you. Right from the minute they arrive to their appointment, they're noticing the location of your building and office, how your office is set up, where the exits are, what you're wearing, how your hair is cut, what stationery you use, and anything else you can think of.

If your office is not clean and orderly, it may give them the impression you don't really know what you're doing or that you're too stressed to help anyone else. If it's old and needs an upgrade, it might give the impression you're barely making rent. If you have a lavish office and dress very formally, it could give the impression you're out of touch and that you charge high prices but don't actually know how to deal with serious issues. (These are just examples, of course.)

Even before their appointment, a lot of SOF clients will do a deep dive on you and your history, past clients, practices, education level, where you've lived, and so forth. Anything a military intelligence analyst would be able to pull up on somebody, they're doing that to the clinician, especially if they still have access to government security databases. And what they're looking for is anything in session that diverges from that narrative of information they've already gathered. That's why I suggest being "butt naked," because you won't be able to be anyone else than who you really are. So just go for it. Be open. Be willing to talk about anything that will help develop trust and lead your client out of their pain and suffering, while maintaining your professionalism at all times. Because, of course, when you cross those boundaries, they'll notice that too.

That's how I was when I was seeking help. Before I would ever sit with a therapist, I researched every damn bit of information I possibly could about them ahead of time. I wasn't trying to find dirt or anything bad; I just needed to know who they were, if they could be trusted, and if they had the skills to help me. But if anything they said or did in session countered what I had learned already, that trust was broken and I wouldn't bother going back.

While that may sound intimidating, the SOF individual basically just wants to know if you are worth their time, if you can handle what they might say, and if you can help them deal with their problems. That's all they want. They want a clinician who brings their knowledge and experience to the table right away so that they don't have to give their whole life story and then hear something like, "Okay. Well, it was nice to meet you. See you next week. Maybe then, the real therapy will begin."

If you are unable to show your competence in helping them, or keep trying when you know you're unable to help instead of referring them to the right clinician and/or resources, they may literally walk out of the session and never seek therapy again because they'll assume all clinicians are the same. Honesty and transparency are valuable assets to SOF operators, and they expect that from others. If something doesn't seem right, they notice it.

On the other hand, some SOF clients may actually use "story time" themselves to deflect from the true issues that are causing problems in their life. The truth they share may not be absolute. If I feel the client is not being forthcoming on the core issues, I call them on their bullshit. To be clear, I don't use that language, but I would not be doing them any service if I didn't cut through the haze and hit the issues directly.

This is where cultural competence is very useful. The more cultural competency you have, the less interruption there will be as the SOF client relays their experiences, and the conversation can move more fluidly. They don't want to take up the entire forty-five- or sixty-minute session explaining their years of military service. However, if they mention something you don't understand and it's causing confusion that could hinder your ability to help them, be honest and ask questions. The worst thing you can do is fake cultural competency. The SOF client will spot that right away, which will ruin any sense of trust.

As a clinician, this is where you must rely on your instincts. Filter your knowledge of what is right and wrong in civilian society through the lens of what is right and wrong in the SOF world of clandestine operations and counterterrorism. This ability to use your instincts can help you sense a lack of complete truth and determine when you need to stand your ground. If you do this in a professional manner, the SOF member should respect the fact that you're trying to get to the root of their problems and help them, and it shows your competency.

4. CAREER LOSS AND REINTEGRATION

I found retirement to be extremely difficult. Very difficult. Because I hadn't planned it. I hadn't planned to stay for twenty years, either. But . . . I had no job lined up. I didn't have a place to live. I had nothing. No savings. Nothing.

I spent five hundred days [on active duty] in recovery and treatment for my injuries. But those injuries also included the nightmares. And my inability to balance when I closed my eyes or when people turned off the lights. Or all this damage that had been done to the way that my brain put information together... So I spent a lot of time rewiring the way my brain works. Because we [SOF members] actually rewired [our brains] in all the training and conditioning and things we'd done. We wired it so we did crazy crap. Like we ran toward gunfire instead of away from it. [. . .]

I think I was blessed. [. . .] I had a very supportive family. I had something to live for other than myself—my daughters. My mom. [. . .] I had friends who were already retired who knew what I was going through . . . I had an amazing [medical] colonel through my recovery . . . [who would say,] "Oh, you need to go teach a low-visibility shooting course to feel better? Go do that." [. . .]

Because I needed purpose. I was literally drowning in absence of purpose.

—Medically retired Green Beret (S. Williams 2024)

Of all the mental health issues SOF personnel may face, transitioning into the civilian world is probably the biggest for most.

Many might think that someone who operated at the highest levels of the military would go on to excel in civilian life, and sometimes that is the case. But the loss of a SOF career and subsequent reintegration to civilian life is daunting for many SOF members, which can lead to and/or aggravate many of their psychological, social, and maladaptive coping problems.

As a clinician, unless you're working in a military or government environment, most of the SOF members you're likely to meet in a therapy setting are SOF veterans who are struggling to transition to civilian life. They're not likely to be the SOF members who became *Fortune* 500 CEOs (at least not yet). You're going to see SOF members who are enduring really hard life challenges. Hopefully, you can help ensure that whatever setback they're experiencing is only a temporary pause, and they'll be able to get back on their feet and find something that gives their life new purpose and meaning.

Many SOF members encounter both external and internal hardships when attempting to transition and integrate into civilian society. Some of those hardships include physical injuries sustained during military service, such as a loss of limbs, eyesight, and hearing; non-visible wounds such as traumatic brain injury (TBI) and substance addiction; and psychological injuries such as moral injury and PTSD.

Many SOF members are experiencing co-occurring symptoms or injuries both physical and psychological. This can add to the member's struggles with reintegration into civilian society. Not only do these injuries make it difficult for the member to gain a sustainable, living wage, but injuries can also restrict certain types of employment they might be most interested in, such as law enforcement. Therefore, it's important for you as the clinician to help them navigate these difficulties so they can find a new, meaningful path.

I've noticed many combat veterans seemed okay when they were deployed, even during and after traumatic events. It's after they come home when the problems start.

Perhaps it's because in war, everything is guided, structured, and compartmentalized. There's a routine. Everything is set up and regimented. For example, you don't have to cook; you just go to the dining hall. There are less decisions to make. And there is purpose to the routine. As a warrior, you are needed and important. The guys on your left and right need you to do your job, just as you need them to do theirs.

When I think of my deployments, at a moment's notice, I can still remember their smells, sights, sounds, feelings, and the roller-coaster ride of being in combat for a year. One time, I even volunteered to stay. As my unit headed back to Germany, I stayed in country and helped secure all the combat aircraft for shipment back to the home base, which meant taking off helicopter blades and packing every piece of equipment. At the time, Octoberfest was happening in Germany with endless beer and maybe even some R&R with friends in Amsterdam or Spain. Yet I volunteered to keep working. I'm not exactly sure why, but I think a part of me didn't want my importance to end or for regular life to begin. The Gulf War was the biggest thing going on in the world, and I wanted to remain a part of that.

This chapter will cover all the nuances a SOF member might experience when transitioning out of the military.

Culture Shock

On that day, at the end of June 1988, I was my job. When I was discharged, I could not separate me from what I did. I was a Navy SEAL operator. Then there was my addiction. Not only were their drugs (crystal meth, marijuana), but I was also smoking cigarettes, chewing tobacco, and consuming large quantities of alcohol, both beer and hard liquor. A crucial question that should be asked in the initial counseling session is: How are your finances? For me at that time, a separation check of $900 and some odd dollars was all that I had. As an operator, I was a rootin', tootin', shootin', parachutin', double-cap crimpin' frogman. Becoming a civilian was a cultural shock.

—Thomas J. LaGrave Jr., LCSW

The vast majority of those who join the military do so at a young age, either right out of high school for enlisted service members or upon college graduation for officers. All active-duty personnel go on to live in a military environment where the line between professional and personal life is blurred. Many active-duty service members live on or near the military base where they work, shop at the base's commissary (grocery store) and PX/BX (post-exchange/base-exchange general store), and so on. When deployed or at sea, they're on the job 24/7, living and working with their team or unit.

The longer a person serves and the higher rank they achieve, the more time and effort they give to their career, not just to do well but also to support and protect their subordinates, unit, and country.

As noted in the previous chapter on SOF culture, the military's rigid atmosphere, well-defined social norms, and distinct culture and subcultures are quite different from average civilian life. A service member who had an MOS (military occupational specialty) that doesn't translate well into the civilian world (for example, if they were a machine gunner or nuclear submarine technician) may have even more trouble adjusting to civilian life. Because of the immense amount of dedication to training and real-life missions, some SOF members have a very difficult time adjusting to a new civilian career and living in a world separate from the SOF lifestyle and teammates they used to know.

Now multiply that times ten and you have an idea of what some SOF members go through when their elite military career ends. SOF members are adrenaline junkies, and finding another job that replaces that adrenaline and sense of importance can be incredibly difficult. This is why many SOF members go on to work as government contractors, private security workers, first responders, or continue their work in the government alphabet agencies (like the CIA, DIA, NSA, NGA, and DNI). As the Green Beret quoted earlier says:

> I think the other thing is that people tell [us] to find something to replace what [we] were doing. I would love for you to show me a job where I can jump out of an aircraft at thirty thousand feet in [an] oxygen mask and glide across an international border into another country and land a small team of people in a swimming pool–size area, and then shoot at bad guys and perform surgery . . . Where? What? [How] are you going to do [that outside the Special Forces]? (S. Williams 2024)

Other SOF personnel, especially if they were a higher rank or an officer, may go into the corporate world as consultants, executives, or business owners, using their leadership skills to make more money sitting behind a desk or in a boardroom instead of in the field. Retired Navy SEAL Jocko Willink is a perfect example of someone who found success in this route. (For some reason, I've seen a lot of Navy SEALs go on to get their MBAs, more so than other SOF veterans.)

However, many SOF personnel, especially when dealing with mental health issues affecting their quality of life, may not be able or desire to go those routes. And success doesn't mean everything is okay. Many SOF veterans continue to succeed and push themselves, and continue to push away their problems, because moving forward is all they know. But most problems don't go away on their own; they eventually come to the surface.

SOF Transition Study

The Global SOF Foundation conducts surveys every few years on SOF members who have transitioned or are planning to transition out of the military. The latest survey results discussed in this chapter help illuminate the serious challenges SOF members face when their military careers end.

The SOF operators surveyed were from all branches of service from nearly all ranks and from twelve different countries. The majority of the *SOF for Life Survey Results 2020–2021* respondents were from the United States, male, white/Caucasian, and highly educated, with over 83 percent holding a college degree, and more than half (51 percent) holding a master's level degree (SOF For Life 2021, 3–5). Approximately 18 percent of the SOF members who took the survey were still on active duty (8–9).

Expectedly, most of the SOF members surveyed had extremely high rates of deployment: 65 percent reported deploying six or more times during their military service, and 17 percent reported deploying *sixteen* times or more (11)! The study's authors noted that a high number of shorter deployments can cause more mental health issues.

> Medical research conducted with Army soldiers showed "a significant association between number of deployments and mental health screening results" such that soldiers with two deployments showed greater odds of screening positive for post-traumatic stress disorder (PTSD). (10)

> Medical research has also shown that deployments with dwell time of less than 12 months was associated with significantly greater long-term PTSD symptoms than those deployed once or with dwell time greater than 12 months. Given the research showing that frequent, short deployments result in higher rates of PTSD, the fact that 65% of the respondents reported deploying six or more times should give the reader

pause and begs the question "what specific clinical and non–clinical studies are being conducted to better understand the mental distress of SOF?" (10)

More than half (62 percent) of respondents indicated they "experienced anxiety in the year prior to and leading up to the moment that they separated from military service." Fifty percent stated that their spouse also suffered from anxiety during the same time period (15). Additionally, "financial stress was identified as 'a large source of anxiety leading up to separation from military service' for 56 percent of the survey respondents" (15). The survey's authors also noted that "financial stress is the second leading cause of divorce (second only to infidelity) and increased financial stress along with a significant change in career puts a tremendous strain on relationships" (16).

Unfortunately, less than half of respondents agreed they had a thorough understanding of all their government and military health and financial benefits during or after their transition period (18). Almost a third (28 percent) "indicated they were uncomfortable going without a paycheck for any amount of time immediately after retirement," and "8% had no investments or savings at all" (19). Over a third (37 percent) said they were underemployed for over four months since leaving the service, and "almost half (46%) of the respondents agreed that they 'have felt more stressed or disconnected since they transitioned from service'" (33). Additionally, "despite feelings of stress after military separation [and despite the fact SOF operators usually pride themselves on being extremely physically fit], less than 60 percent of respondents indicated they maintained a regular fitness routine since their transition from military service" (35).

Just over half (54 percent) of respondents reported they were in their first marriage, 22 percent were in their second marriage, 10 percent were divorced, 7 percent were on their third marriage, 5 percent were never married, and 2 percent were on their fourth marriage or more. This means that divorce rates among the SOF members surveyed were 40 percent—astonishingly high when compared to around 3 percent for the active military force (38). The majority (over 81 percent) had one or more dependents (6–7).

Surprisingly, 96 percent of respondents said they were not medically discharged before twenty years of service (28), implying that most retired at normal military retirement age. While this should indicate most of the respondents could therefore better plan for their transition to civilian life, only 48 percent of respondents said they had created a comprehensive transition plan prior to leaving military service. This is a decrease by approximately 10 percent from those who responded to the *2017 SOF for Life Survey* (11).

While the majority of respondents were not medically discharged, almost 80 percent reported a disability rating of 50 percent or greater upon or after their retirement or discharge, and 37 percent reported a 100-percent disability rating (28). This is an increase over the *2017 SOF for Life Survey* of only 51 percent reporting that they were 50-percent or more disabled.

A majority (80 percent) of respondents indicated they experienced joint, back, or other orthopedic pain and/or headaches two to three times per week or more, and 65 percent experienced pain daily (29). A similar majority (83 percent) "indicated they 'experienced challenges with memory or concentration' with *more than half* (51%) having such experiences more than two times per week" (30). Sadly, almost all SOF members who responded to the survey (93 percent) indicated they "experienced challenges with sleep to include insomnia, sleep disruption, or obstructive sleep apnea" (31).

Only 64 percent of those surveyed agreed with the statement that "prior to separation or retirement from military service they had created a resume that translated their military knowledge, skills, and experiences so that non-military professionals could understand and appreciate what I could offer" (14). Even less (56 percent) agreed that they had developed appropriate interviewing skills prior to separation (14).

These findings reveal that many SOF members are not as prepared for a civilian career as they could be. Physical injuries and frequent pain along with mental, cognitive, and sleep difficulties increase the likelihood that this unique group of warriors might abuse drugs and alcohol and have difficulty with personal and professional relationships.

The military, VA, and us clinicians need to better understand, educate, and support SOF members and their loved ones before and during their transition to civilian life.

PEW Study on Re-Entry Difficulties

"Why do some veterans have a hard time readjusting to civilian life while others make the transition with little or no difficulty?" (Morin 2011, 1). Pew researchers attempted to answer that question by analyzing the attitudes, experiences, and demographic characteristics of 1,853 veterans. Through this study, they were able to identify factors that independently predict whether a service member will have an easy or difficult reentry experience. Their study does a great job revealing what many military and SOF veterans are dealing with and why those issues negatively disrupt their transition to civilian and home life. Part of the study is quoted below:

> Of the 18 variables in the model . . . four were positively associated with re-entry: being an officer; having a consistently clear understanding of the missions while in the service; being a college graduate; and, for post-9/11 veterans but not for those of other eras, attending religious services frequently. Six variables were associated with a *diminished probability* [emphasis added] that a veteran had an easy re-entry. They were: having a traumatic experience; being seriously injured; serving in the post-9/11 era; serving in a combat zone; serving with someone who was killed or injured; and, for post-9/11 veterans but not for those of other eras, being married while in the service (3).

While more than seven-in-ten veterans (72%) reported they had an easy time readjusting to civilian life, 27% say re-entry was difficult for them—a proportion that swells to 44% among veterans who served in the ten years since the Sept. 11, 2001 (1).

The lingering consequences of a psychological trauma are particularly striking: The probabilities of an easy re-entry drop from 82% for those who did not experience a traumatic event to 56% for those who did, a 26 percentage point decline and the largest change—positive or negative—recorded in this study (1).

Similarly, suffering a serious injury while serving reduces the probability of an easy re-entry by 19 percentage points, from 77% to 58%. (Morin, 4)

More than half (56 percent) of all veterans who experienced a traumatic event reported having experienced post-traumatic stress symptoms such as flashbacks and repeated distressing memories of the experience, and nearly half (46 percent) said they specifically suffered from post-traumatic stress (Morin, 4–5). Those who served in a combat zone, and especially those who knew someone who was killed or injured, also faced a more difficult re-entry (2).

A word of caution . . . Those in the post-9/11 era were interviewed relatively soon after they left the military, and their views could reflect the immediacy of their experience and could change over time . . . (Morin, 5)

This survey confirms what I've seen in my practice in relation to Special Forces operators. Most will be able to adjust to civilian life. But due to the op tempo of a post-9/11 world, those who have been on numerous deployments, those who have experienced trauma and/or severe injuries, and those struggling with a troubled marriage or dealing with divorce are more likely to find readjustment much more difficult. (It's also interesting the study mentioned religion being a factor for post 9/11 veterans, which I discuss in Chapter 9.)

Type of Discharge

> For those mental health professionals who are working directly with those who served, it is important to take into consideration why they left the military, as the exit process directly influences the transition period back into life as a civilian.
>
> —Jessica D. Garner (2018, 105)

The military has two discharge categories based on in-service conduct and performance: administrative (voluntary) discharges and punitive (involuntary) discharges. There are three main types of administrative discharges: honorable, general, and other than honorable. There are two main types of punitive discharges: bad conduct and dishonorable. Any service member who receives a punitive discharge, or any discharge other than honorable, even if it's administrative, may not be eligible for VA benefits. Those who receive a punitive discharge may also lose the right to veteran status and be ineligible for other federal programs and benefits.

The manner of military separation plays a large part in an SOF member's reintegration journey. Because a SOF member always tries to be the best of the best, any discharge other than honorable can cause psychological hardship and may be a catalyst for maladaptive behavior. Separating from the military without an honorable discharge can lead to feelings of shame, guilt, perceived failure, and/or organizational betrayal (where they feel they were wronged by the military), on top of other transition issues.

In my experience, the vast majority of SOF clients I had were kicked out of the military because of substance abuse and had received an other than honorable discharge. One consequence of this is that those with an honorable discharge are afforded some training and assistance on transitioning to civilian life before they leave. Those without an honorable discharge are not always eligible for that assistance, and they get no real guidance on what they could do as a civilian or how to get there.

Another type of administrative discharge SOF members may have is medical, when they are unable to continue serving in the military due to an illness or injury. As mentioned, due to the high level of training and hostile deployments SOF members take on, as well as the extreme physical nature of their jobs, SOF members are somewhat vulnerable to career-ending injuries. However, to get kicked out of the military for medical reasons usually means the injury or illness is significant.

SOF members are extremely fit and able to overcome many physical and psychological setbacks. Combine that with amazing advances in medical science and technology, and there have been service members, even at the SOF level, who have been injured and returned to active duty, even with prosthetics if they're missing an arm or a leg. However, other more "minor" injuries can result in a discharge. For instance, if a service member loses one eye, they no longer have the ability to fire a weapon accurately because they have lost depth perception. So when one SOF member is forced out on a medical discharge for an eye or back injury, while another SOF operator can stay in with a prosthetic leg, for example, the member who cannot continue their career may feel depressed when they compare themselves to others, however unfair or unrealistic those comparisons may be.

Not only does a medical discharge prematurely end a SOF member's career, but their injury and resulting disability often makes it harder for them to adjust to civilian life and limits their civilian job opportunities. Medical issues, especially chronic pain, can also cause a SOF member to self-medicate and use other maladaptive coping mechanisms.

When I suffered a career-ending spinal injury in law enforcement, I learned quickly that the guys and gals who were still working didn't know anything about what it's like to be forced to retire. Of course, this isn't something most of us want to think about, even in (especially in) high-risk careers. But that stigma meant that some of my former fellow officers thought I was like a broken toy, or at least that's how I felt, which made the transition to civilian life even harder. I had to come to terms with my disability while also figuring out what I could do, because I still needed an income beyond my disability pension, and I didn't want to sit around all day. I wanted to be useful and feel important again, as we all do. This led me to eventually become a psychotherapist helping military and law enforcement veterans, among other clients.

Loss of Identity

One of the first things people ask in social settings is, "What do you do?" What we do is part of our identity, especially for a SOF operator. Once that gets ripped away from them, it can be a dangerous road if they don't navigate it correctly. It can lead to maladaptive coping, which is usually alcohol and sometimes hard drugs. Then, generally speaking, that can lead to suicidal ideation. I've even talked to clients who had homicidal ideation, where they got to such a low point that they wanted to find and kill a supervisor who had reprimanded them. That may sound extreme, but it stems in part from the isolation many SOF veterans feel after being separated from their former team members and struggling in a "foreign" non-military environment. Jessica D. Garner authored a fascinating dissertation that I thought perfectly captured the difficulty of SOF re-entry:

> When soldiers go from active to veteran status . . . they feel misunderstood by others and experience a crisis of identity. Many veterans state that transitioning back home is often a difficult process because of the lack of structure . . . the inability to connect with civilians, and loss of purpose in their lives . . . Those who were able to [1] make sense of

their combat experiences, [2] found a sense of purpose as a civilian, and [3] integrate their post-combat perspectives into their daily lives, had smoother transitions and positive adjustment and integration. Those who did not, however, had more difficulty . . .

As [these] individuals move into their new roles, they may be marginalized as they transition into a different work environment. (Garner 2018, 54)

For a service member's entire military career, they have been addressed and respected by their rank and specific MOS. Other specialties and achievements are listed in every service member's personnel file, and some are shown on their uniforms as awards, badges, unit designations, and the like.

SOF members have quite a few more specialties and achievements than the average service member. Even if a SOF member doesn't have many awards or chooses not to wear them, just wearing a SOF unit patch indicates that they successfully completed many arduous and technically challenging specialty training or schools. Furthermore, SOF members develop a specific identity while working with a close team of like-minded and elite individuals. This identity can become lost in the transition of cultures and may lead to feelings of alienation and loss of connectedness with their civilian peers.

Everything someone does in the military stays with them in the military. Anyone who completed Ranger School or Pathfinder School in the Army, for instance, gets to wear those tabs/badges for the rest of their career, whether they're using those specialties in their current job or not. Even if a SOF member is no longer serving in a SOF unit, and even if they choose not to wear all of their badges, anyone with access to their personnel file will be able to see everything they've done, and everyone in the unit will hear about that person's tremendous amount of knowledge, skill, and experience even without that person saying anything.

Whenever I see a military person in the media, I always pay attention to their uniform. I can tell just from taking a screenshot and zooming in on a uniform if someone was in the Special Forces, if they were in combat, what specialty schools they completed, what awards they received, and so on. I'll notice if someone has a Purple Heart, or two stars for service in Southwest Asia, for example. The meaning of military badges, awards, and unit patches speaks volumes to those who understand. If nothing else, they look impressive to those who don't speak the language.

But once that SOF member leaves the military, all that goes away. No one knows that the guy they see buying milk at the grocery store parachuted out of airplanes in total darkness into hostile territory in a country few people know anything about. Once the uniform gets hung up and the SOF member puts on a business suit or a pair of overalls, it's as though all those accomplishments no longer exist. They often feel as though they're starting from scratch, no matter what they did in their former life. It's really a loss of identity, and a lot of people have a very hard time with transitioning because of that loss.

When I was in the military reserves, wearing a USASOC combat patch and airborne wings meant something. I would walk into a room and get instant respect because of what I'd done. But in the civilian world, no one knew about it, and if they did, they wouldn't know what any of it meant anyway. In the Army, I had fifteen people under my command and was in charge of maintaining aircraft worth $10 million each. My word could purchase a $100,000 helicopter rotor blade based off my expertise, and it would show up at our maintenance bay from a military depot a week later.

As a law enforcement officer, I was an emergency services unit member, EOD liaison, and a hostage negotiator. Not only did those jobs provide a lot of adrenaline rushes, but they also made me feel incredibly important. I had a pager on me at all times, and if I was paged a certain operational code, I knew I had to gear up and report to the department immediately, get debriefed on the situation, and grab my vehicle and respond to the scene. I still remember how amazing that felt.

When I went into the civilian world, I was no longer in charge of other people; some civilian was in charge of me. Even though my new boss had zero experience compared to what I had, I had to do whatever he said. That was a hard pill to swallow. Garner sums it up this way:

> After swearing to support and defend the constitution of the United States, and potentially sacrificing their lives, many Special Operators exit the military, feeling disenfranchised and expendable. [...] For some, this means living out the rest of their lives with a broken-down body full of chronic pain or tragic memories from lived experiences. (2018, 103)

Going from being an important figure who is called upon to accomplish uniquely challenging and dangerous missions to being just another face in the crowd where no one needs you is a really tough transition to make. It can really screw with someone psychologically. Even to this day, it's a bitter taste in my mouth. I'm fortunate that I was able to get my stuff together and figure out a way to stay relevant within the field of both military and first responders by becoming a specialized therapist.

Perceived Failure

Similar to feelings of guilt and shame and even survivor's guilt, perceived failure can occur when a SOF operator feels they haven't lived up to a certain set of standards. An operator on active duty may feel responsible for something bad that happened during a training exercise or a mission. They may also feel like a failure if they were unable to be promoted or get on a special team, or when comparing themselves to other SOF operators.

With SOF veterans, though, the most common reasons behind a client's perceived failure is either in their personal/home life, or perceived failure when integrating into civilian life. Since SOF veterans made it to such a high level in the military, there's an expectation that they will be the best in every area of their life and that they can do anything in the civilian world. So, when they find themselves struggling in their marriage or with their kids, or struggling with substance abuse or homelessness, or they find themselves struggling to get a job, or underemployed in a job in which they feel no one cares about what they previously accomplished, they can see themselves as a failure, especially if they received a medical or other than honorable discharge.

A SOF member probably had a Top Secret/Sensitive Compartmented Information (SCI) security clearance. This means they were briefed or "read-in" on highly secretive operational information and intel directly from the Pentagon and were doing crazy stuff in countries most people don't even know exist. To go from that to suddenly becoming a civilian, and a "broken" civilian at that, can cause a lot of depression. No one is expecting them to get up at four o'clock in the morning and do crazy stuff all day. No one is expecting them to travel the world. No one knows their backstory. They are only judged on how well they can do whatever job they have currently. Their past accomplishments don't necessarily matter anymore. I've had SOF clients tell me that they don't want to "beg for a job" or get told what to do by someone "dumber than a box of rocks."

Those who are struggling with various issues and aren't adjusting well may not get a job they find fulfilling or that takes into account their unique skills and experiences, which is when loss of identity and perceived failure really hit hard. They went from being the best the military has to the bottom of a low-wage job. To get and keep a job, they often have to go through all the hoops in the civilian sector to prove they can do menial tasks, attend trainings, and be a reliable employee. For example, they may not be able to use the office printer because they're not allowed to have the passcode until they're on the job for six months. That's a hard pill to swallow after being briefed by the Pentagon. It's simple stuff like that that's very hard to deal with, on top of everything else a SOF member is going through during their transition.

I've seen perceived failure most often during the transition phase, but sometimes a SOF member may have perceived failures from their time in the military as well. It could mean they didn't make the cut for a particular unit or get on a special team, or they feel they let their team down if they made a mistake, or if someone was killed in action or during a training exercise and they feel it's somehow their fault. But those types of perceived failures generally fit more into the realm of PTSD or moral injury, as will be discussed in later chapters. Perceived failure usually hits hardest when SOF members perceive themselves as failures due to their current situations in civilian life, which is so different from their former military lives.

Home Life

There's something to be said about SOF operators being able to go away for work and do what they love, having only a small amount of time at home, then suddenly being stuck at home dealing with depression and PTSD once their careers end. If they have a spouse or partner, it makes it really hard for those relationships to move forward smoothly unless they have been working on their relationship the entire time.

I've seen some really good examples of couples that hung in there through thick and thin and love each other to this day, but a lot will end up getting divorced.

It's the same for a spouse being home alone all the time, raising kids by themselves, worrying that their partners may not come home. Then when those partners are home all the time, they're not helping out or emotionally available. All of these things can wreck a marriage. A lot of the gentlemen I've worked with who had been married in the service got divorced after their service. Divorce is yet another stressor many SOF members deal with, which will be discussed more in the next chapter on families.

Isolation

Isolation can be caused by circumstances (geographical location, lack of transportation, etc.) or be self-imposed (not reaching out for help due to stigma, etc.). A Study by Dittrich et al. (2015) found that:

> Because higher proportions of veterans come from rural communities, access to care may be an issue when behavioral health care is needed. Although the Veterans Administration has expanded health services in rural areas, this has not always resulted in increased service utilization. This study examined the prevalence of depression and associated health service deficits (HSDs) for rural versus nonrural U.S. military veterans . . . analysis revealed that rural veterans had greater odds of having at least one HSD . . . [and] had higher odds of both current and lifetime depression than nonrural veterans when controlling for socioeconomic status and race/ethnicity. Additionally . . . rural veterans with current depression had higher odds of being Hispanic or Other/Multiracial than Caucasian, not employed for wages . . . , <65 years of age, and reported having at least one HSD.

Living in a rural area can negatively affect spouses and family members as well, due to a lack of employment opportunities, access to care, and so on.

However, self-isolation is also very common with those dealing with mental health issues, especially SOF members who struggle with the myth of uniqueness. Garner found in her research that many "veterans felt disconnected from their family and friends, as they did not share the same experience of military service" (2018, 55). This is something I experienced and have heard from many others. Garner also found that veterans felt social support treatment would be more effective "than traditional treatment programs including therapeutic groups and hospital programs" (85). However, Garner continues:

> Many veterans do not use their original support networks in times of stress because their *perception* of support is not existent; they have lower levels of trust, purposely avoid closeness with those around them (including intimate partners), and increased levels of suspicion toward others. (85)

> As you can see, this is why developing trust with veterans is so important, especially because a lot of veterans and SOF members don't open up easily unless they're around other veterans. To combat that isolation, it can also be immensely helpful for them to join a SOF or veterans' group, so they can regain some of that camaraderie.

John Lovell, a former Army Ranger (2nd Ranger Battalion) and founder of the Warrior Poet Society, provides a good way of looking at transition and connecting to those who aren't veterans:

> Improvise, adapt, overcome . . . that's the Special Operations mantra. [We need to] carry that into the civilian world. The civilian world is not going to change for you. You have to change to be able to integrate. And if you don't find a new mission and you don't find a new band of brothers, you're not going to make it. So whatever PTSD you have, it will be made worse over time because you do not have a new band of brothers and you didn't find a new mission. You just looked back. Live in the present and work toward a future that you are planning for. But you have to find a new mission, and you have to find a new band of brothers. And they're not going to look anything like your past band of brothers. But understand that they are better in some ways than your old band of brothers. It's going to be easy to spot how they're worse. They're going

to be worse in a bunch of different ways. [So you have to] find out how they're uniquely better. (Ryan 2023)

Reminding a SOF client how they were able to overcome obstacles, adapt to the unknown, and persevere through immense difficulty can help them gain a positive perspective on their current challenges, even cultural ones.

Positive Transition

[When] I'm around all of us [SOF] guys, I'm seeing, 'Oh my gosh. This is who I am. I don't have to be angry that I've lost it. I don't have to be angry that I'm not this anymore. It will always be a part of me. But now I'm going to adapt it. And also, these other badass bros, my other freaking Pararescue brothers and SEAL brothers and Royal Marine Commandos, they were all going through the same stuff I was. So I didn't feel alone.

—Rudy Reyes,
former Recon Marine and co-founder
of Force Blue (Ritland 2023)

A SOF operator might be able to strip a weapon in no time flat, set up a C-4 charge, or organize a covert mission, but tell them to write an essay or create an Excel spreadsheet and you'll get some weird looks. Unless they're planning to get hired as a mercenary, many of their skill sets are hard to translate to the civilian world, and without any government support, they can have a really hard time adjusting.

You as their therapist can help them understand what jobs they might find enjoyable and fulfilling, then assist them in developing a plan on researching job, networking, and/or educational opportunities. There are usually many career counselors, job placement services, and other resources available to veterans that you can research and suggest to your SOF clients.

As mentioned, it's equally important for SOF veterans to build a support system of family and friends who can provide emotional and practical support during their transition. They should know that they are not alone in their experiences, and there are many people who can understand and help them through this challenging time.

The best way to cope with job loss and shame is to try and get the client to stay positive and focus on the future. Let them know it's okay for them to take time to grieve their loss and accept that their situation is out of their control. Once they have done that, they can shift their focus on what they can do to find a new career and purpose in life. Garner (2018, 104) writes:

> For those who have a direct sense of purpose, whether it be an elite member of a unit, being a father, or provider of a household, this purpose can be directly tied to one's sense of self [. . .] For a successful identity transition, it is critical to have more than one identity present which can serve as a fluid shift from one to the other. This serves a dual purpose: if one identity is suddenly in crisis, as with an SOF who experiences a sudden career ending injury, there are other identities that can immediately take over; the second reason is to create a sense of balance in one's life.

When I went through my own transition, I thought of a million scenarios of what I could do. It can be helpful to talk with SOF clients about different job options and resources that might help them regain some of the identity they lost, and to join some of the SOF organizations mentioned in Appendix II.

What I'm doing now as a therapist, working with SOF members and, more recently, working with the Washoe County Sheriff's Office helping my brothers and sisters in law enforcement, helps fill that void for me. That's why I always push people to do whatever makes them happy, to fill that void, so they feel like a valuable member of society again.

When I was in the Army, I would never have guessed that I would become a cop. When I was a cop, there's no way I could see myself being a clinician. There are a million possibilities. Just because bad things happened or are happening, there are always next steps in life. You can help your client work toward the things they want in life and help them see that what they want is achievable.

I also try to understand what the SOF member does outside of work that can be healing for them, such as getting outdoors or doing something physical. Many of them still want to exercise and stay fit, even if they're physically disabled or have stopped exercising due to a mental health problem like depression. SOF members have been exercising for years and years, so they know how to work out and they understand the benefits. And on top of the health benefits of exercise that we all know as clinicians, it can remind them what they're capable of and who they are.

I may also suggest they go to a range and shoot some weapons, as long as whatever trauma they're dealing with doesn't involve weapons and they're not a threat to themselves or others. While this is probably outside the box of what most therapists would recommend, dealing with weapons can be therapeutic for SOF members. It can remind them of their technical proficiency while providing a way to relieve stress, and it may be an activity they can do with friends or in places where they may meet like-minded folks.

SOF members strive for perfection, so when they perceive themselves failing in so many areas of life during their transition, it's important to remind them that they're human—incredibly amazing humans who have accomplished more than most civilians could imagine, but human all the same. It's normal to have detours and setbacks. Remind them that they can overcome incredible odds. If they don't give up, they can find something that gives them purpose again. They can move from career loss to being a productive and proud civilian member of society.

PART II:

WORKING WITH SOF FAMILIES

5. FAMILY STRESS & RESILIENCE

"You can't change the world alone. You will need some help, and to truly get from your starting point to your destination it takes friends, colleagues, the good will of strangers, and a strong coxswain to guide them."

—William H. McRaven

This chapter will help you understand how a SOF member's lifestyle and subsequent transition to civilian life affects their immediate family members. Much of the information presented here is based on a qualitative study of resilience among Canadian Special Operations Forces Command (CANSOFCOM) families, which provides a unique window into the world SOF spouses live in. The research results, titled "Understanding Special Operations Forces Spouses Challenges and Resilience: A Mixed-Method Study," were published in 2022 and conducted by Richer, Frank, and Guérin. The authors combed through fifty-three studies on military and Special Operations Forces families, collected quantitative data through an online survey, and captured qualitative data by conducting semi-structured interviews and gathering responses from 159 CANSOFCOM spouses.

The majority of respondents were employed (83.5%) women (94.3%) between 19 and 34 years old (56.6%). 9.5% of respondents were active military personnel themselves. 65.9% reported living in an urban or suburban area (versus a rural area). Almost all participants (94.4%) reported being either legally married or in a common-law relationship with their SOF partner. A small proportion (2.5%) were either separated or divorced from their partner. Three quarters of surveyed spouses (75.5%) reported having children, and one third (38.4%) reported having at least one child under 3 years of age. (102)

Three quarters of participants (75.7%; 95% confidence intervals [CIs]: 68.9%, 82.5%) reported their mental health as good, though a large proportion of spouses reported that their partner's employment had created work-family issues (47.7% to 84.3% agreed or strongly agreed with scale items). Almost a third (30.4%) reported that their SOF partner had sustained a serious injury. (104)

A major potential risk factor identified in the study was that spouses felt their military partner's work interfered with family responsibilities. As parents who were often without their spouses, they were therefore left to "do it all" and lacked time for self-care (102).

As mentioned, you may not expect to see a SOF member in your office, but once they leave the military, they are often "hiding in plain sight." The same goes for their families.

Family Separation

SOF operators are often separated from their families due to ongoing deployments and training exercises. Many studies show that separation decreases military spouses' psychological and physical well-being as well as their marital and overall life satisfaction. Separation is also linked to decreased well-being among military children, and the negative impact on children's well-being has been shown to further increase with the number of deployments (Richer, Frank, and Guérin 2022, 100).

Studies on Special Operations Forces specifically show that SOF personnel experience stronger and unique stressors. SOF operators often deploy on secret, high-risk missions with little notice and for an unspecified amount of time. This causes SOF team members to routinely miss family milestones and commitments (101).

> Participants acknowledged that the high frequency of deployments put a strain on their families . . . Even when in garrison, participants reported feeling over-tasked, leaving them with little time to reconnect with their families and repair family bonds . . . A survey of the morale in CANSOF-COM units revealed particularly high levels of work-family conflict . . . Moreover, four of the six CANSOFCOM units are located in rural, semi-rural, or suburban locations, which can limit employment and career opportunities for CAN-SOFCOM spouses. (101)

> Many spouses discussed compounding fatigue from multiple years of high tempo—having to handle household chores and parenting alone with minimal personal time to recover—leading to exhaustion. Some spouses mentioned having had mental health issues (e.g., harmful drinking, panic attacks, severe anxiety, burnout, depression, sleep disorders) and attributed these issues to their partner's occupation and family demands.

> [Spouse interview:] "So I did have an anxiety attack, because he had to rush off and go, 'Okay. I don't know when I'll be back. I don't know where I'm going. I don't know anything.' 'Okay. Bye-bye.' It was rough." (106)

These unpredictable and dangerous deployments often leave SOF families with anxiety, stress, isolation, and a lack of support, especially in rural areas.

In order to best support these families, SOF units, military bases, and surrounding communities must ensure to provide them with access to mental health services, support networks, and educational and recreational activities as well as the most up-to-date information regarding the status of their loved ones and any changes in their deployment.

Supporting the Ill or Injured SOF Partner

The CANSOFCOM study details the types of injuries SOF personnel experience and how those injuries affect both the operators and their family members. Both physical and psychological injuries can cause additional strain on family members.

> Physical injuries—especially musculoskeletal injuries— appear to be prevalent among SOF personnel . . . A recent study showed a high prevalence of both acute and repetitive strain injuries among CANSOFCOM personnel . . . Conversely, research suggests that the prevalence of mental health disorders (e.g., depression, anxiety, post-traumatic stress disorder) is lower among SOF personnel than their counterparts in the conventional force. (101)

> When a [military] member is deployed, families often report being afraid the member will be seriously injured or that the member will not return home . . . Although death is relatively uncommon . . . both physical injuries and operational stress injuries (OSIs) are more common. (100–101)

> Participants described their involvement during their partner's recovery as being emotionally draining and heartbreaking, especially when their SOF partner was suffering from severe physical pain or psychological issues. Spouses

described the increased workload at home and some discussed the stress of being constantly vigilant and mindful of their partner's needs and constraints (e.g., avoiding crowded stores and social gatherings). (105)

[Spouse interview:] "I was taking care of three kids. So I had the two boys, and then I had my husband home. He could get up and use the bathroom, but he was not happy. He was in pain. He was suffering." (105)

It's important that the whole family gets the support and resources it needs to cope with an injured or ill SOF member. There are many veteran- and SOF-oriented nonprofits and organizations that may be able to help, even if the SOF member is ineligible for some VA benefits due to the nature of their discharge. Some of these are listed in Appendix II. Connecting the SOF member, spouse, and/or children to the right support networks can be a lifeline.

The Mistress

In law enforcement, there's a saying: "The job is your mistress." The same goes for Special Operations. That's because the job takes priority and precedence over everything else in the operator's life. This is another common paradox, because SOF units demand so much of their members. The dedication and time SOF members must give to their teams and missions affects their families, especially their spouses.

For example, a regular military member's schedule is generally going to be planned in advance. They may deploy, but their deployments are generally longer (six months to a year) and they're home for longer in between deployments compared to a SOF member's deployment cycle. And when they're "home" on base, their schedules are fairly predictable. Like other government employees, they have federal holidays off and ideally can spend more time with their families.

In special operations, especially in Tier 1 units with unique specialties, they need to be available on twenty-four hours' notice. This is comparable to when I was a law enforcement officer and, at various times, a hostage negotiator, emergency services unit member, and an EOD liaison. When I was on one of those special teams, I needed to be available at a moment's notice. There was no nine-to-five. When I got called up, I had to report for duty regardless of where I was or what I was doing. There were many times I had to abruptly leave family events. I missed anniversaries, kids' birthdays, and other important milestones. The job was the priority.

The higher up the chain a SOF member goes, the harder it is. The more rank and responsibility they have, and the more training they get, the more specialized they become, which means they're more in demand.

In the study by Richer, Frank, and Guérin, SOF spouses expressed anxiety and frustration over having an uncertain schedule, and that the high op tempo and unpredictability of their partner's schedule had significantly impacted their families. The study does a good job explaining what spouses go through, so I'll share a portion of the study here:

> Spouses described how frequent departures meant their partner not only missed out on milestones and family events, but also that they were not able to support their family through hard times. Some spouses also discussed how their SOF partner—even when in garrison—was so over-tasked and absorbed by their work that they were unable to be present and engage with the family. Some spouses also discussed the lack of support, communication, and recognition for family sacrifices from the SOF unit leadership, often leading to family interference and resentment. (104)

> Many spouses mentioned the weight of the SOF lifestyle challenges depended on the time in their life. Some

mentioned that the SOF lifestyle was especially difficult when their partner started their SOF career and when their family demands were greater—for instance, when their children were younger or they had less support available. (105)

[Spouse interview:] "And when we finally settled into our new little town, he was gone all the time. So I pretty much raised a newborn up until the age of three by myself, multiple deployments, missing birthdays, missing anniversaries. Because my son was a baby, new town, it was really hard to get out and meet people. I'd say the first three years of him being at that unit was the hardest. And because my husband really wasn't around to be able to help with that, it really was all on me." (105)

Not only are spouses often left to care for the rest of the family and the household duties by themselves with minimal outside support, but their own personal and professional lives often suffer as well.

Almost all spouses indicated that their partner's employment with SOF had impacted their own career path . . . Some spouses had decided to either put a hold on their career aspirations or become a stay-at-home parent to provide a stable environment for their children.

[Spouse interview:] "I had to stay home and raise the kids, and I know other members that are friends of ours that have the same thing . . . they either end up leaving or they end up divorcing. So for me, because I just knew, I just wanted to support him, so the only way I could was to create my own business." (105)

Many spouses also remarked that the SOF lifestyle involved other sacrifices, such as delaying major life events (e.g., pregnancies, travel, weddings), and a lack of time for personal

> development, hobbies, and a difficulty developing and main-
> taining social relationships. (105)

As is known by many studies—and military families themselves—military personnel and their families must periodically relocate to different duty stations, sometimes as often as every two to three years. These frequent moves have been associated with decreased life satisfaction due to increased unemployment among military spouses, decreased social support systems for spouses and children, and increased tensions at home (100).

Another issue with "the mistress" is that some SOF members use the high op tempo to ignore home and parenting duties, as some feel that home life is beneath them or something they shouldn't have to worry about. But when they transition to civilian life, especially if they don't have a full-time job right away, they're confronted with being a spouse and parent, and suddenly they're in a world they're not used to. They've been a master of the secretive warrior world, but they're not usually masters of the home life. And generally, the spouse and/or children will want the SOF member to be able to pick up some of the spouse and/or parenting duties, which some SOF members won't know how, or be willing, to handle. So even though SOF members and their families are probably eager to enjoy their new life and spend more time together, the transition phase can cause further familial issues.

The Secrecy Paradox

There are many contradictions or paradoxes that can cause difficulties for SOF families, especially between spouses. One paradox is secrecy.

Many spouses in the CANSOFCOM study described how operational secrecy (OPSEC) made it difficult for them to develop relationships and relate to those outside the SOF community, including military family services. They themselves don't know many details, and what they do know (e.g., position, unit, departures, challenges), they are reluctant to share for fear of breaching OPSEC.

Many spouses remarked that the secrecy of operations also negatively impacted their marital relationship because it created a distance between them and their partner and reduced their capacity to understand and accept the sacrifices the family has to make. (105)

"That's been one of the things we've noticed is [that] people [SOF spouses] are kind of reluctant to make friends because they're not sure what they can share and, as women, we tend to naturally want to have conversations, socialize and share stuff." (105)

One could say that the SOF member has two different lives: their secret SOF life and their family life.

"We can't communicate during the day. We don't share about his day. So there are two different worlds. He lives in one world, and I live in another, and we try and make them cross paths and work together, but he knows all about me, but I only know a part of him. That's honestly been one of the biggest struggles." (105)

Secrecy is part of the job for many military service members and their families. Assisting clients in personal and family communication skills can greatly enhance their ability to connect and create deeper relationships without breaking any OPSEC rules.

Families in Rural Areas

Earlier, I briefly mentioned that when veterans live in rural areas, the challenges they and their loved ones face can be aggravated by isolation and a lack of resources. Richer, Frank, and Guérin found the same in their research.

Living in a rural area is another factor related to poor mental health of SOF families. Qualitative findings suggest that this is, at least in part, due to the lack of career opportunities. Offering support for career and professional development for SOF spouses may therefore increase their well-being. (100)

Overall, SOF spouses appear to have a higher prevalence of poor mental health than their regular force counterparts, but the majority of SOF spouses reported having good mental health. Social support was associated with good mental health, while work-family conflict and living in a rural area were related to poor mental health. Qualitative findings suggest that living in a rural area appears to be linked to poor mental health due, in part, to the lack of career opportunities. Because families are key to members' readiness, SOF organizations must engage in efforts to foster family well-being and resilience. (109)

The researchers suggest that military units and military family services provide more resources for spouses and families, especially in rural areas (109). Of course, the reality may be different depending on where SOF members and their families are located. Many SOF veterans and their families may no longer be near or be able to access a VA or equivalent medical facility, or they may be unwilling seek care from one. Ensuring more mental health clinicians are culturally competent on the SOF lifestyle and transition difficulties can greatly help these families, no matter where they live.

Spouse Employment

SOF spouses' employment and careers are often interrupted, put on hold, or unattainable. SOF spouses are often left "holding down the fort" by themselves, taking care of the SOF member, home, children, and other duties. These demands, combined with living wherever their SOF member lives, can make it extremely difficult for SOF spouses to hold down a decent job, much less have a long-term career.

Cooke and Speirs (2005) found:

> Migration [military-mandated moves] is associated with a 10 percent decline in employment among all civilian wives and a four-hour decline in hours worked per week among civilian wives who remain employed. Migration is associated with a statistically insignificant but very similar 6 percent drop in employment among all civilian men and a five-hour decline in hours worked per week among civilian men who remain employed.
>
> The results provide solid evidence that being a tied migrant, irrespective of gender, is disruptive to both labor-market status and hours worked. Thus, the assumption that wives are harmed because of their disproportionate status as tied migrants is supported.

Richer, Frank, and Guérin noted that those spouses who had a strong relationship with their SOF spouse were more resilient and better able to keep or find employment, even during frequent moves or when living in rural areas.

> Many spouses spoke about the importance of their SOF partner's support and the importance of a quality relationship—including equality, partnership, mutual emotional support, and quality communication—as key to facing the challenges of the SOF lifestyle. (106)
>
> "We work really well together. I mean, my husband is my partner. He does laundry, he vacuums, he washes the floors, he changes diapers. He takes on more of that when he comes home, so that partnership again as opposed to one of us doing all of it. (106)
>
> Participants also discussed the importance of their partner's support for pursuing a career and achieving personal goals,

and some described how their partner had taken a step back at work or had delayed their career progression to better support the family. (107)

Many spouses who faced mental health issues because of burnout, anxiety, or depression, mentioned that their SOF partner had supported them and attended to the family's needs. (107)

Providing marriage/relationship and communication counseling can greatly help families overcome the difficulties of the SOF lifestyle and difficulties transitioning out of it. Employment and career assistance are also crucial, yet sometimes overlooked, resources for spouses of both active SOF members and SOF veterans.

SOF Family Support & Resilience

Because military spouses are often left to "do it all," Richer, Frank, and Guérin found that perceived support from one's social and organizational networks decreases stress and increases well-being. Strong social support also enhances the odds of positive adjustment following deployment by 24 percent (101). Positive post-deployment adaptation and overall resilience were also linked to perceived support from military leadership and access to resources provided by the military community, such as emergency childcare. Living near other military families additionally contributes to high levels of perceived community, as military families often share a common ideology and purpose and perceive themselves as part of the larger collective military community (102).

Almost all spouses had used the programs or services provided or referred to them by the SOF unit, Canadian Forces Health Services, or Military Family Services (MFS), and most described these as beneficial ... Spouses also mentioned using external services, such as a childcare provider or nanny, a cleaning service, or lawn/snow maintenance to help allevi-ate stress. (107)

Social support, and the support of the SOF community in particular, stood out as an important factor in SOF spouses' well-being. New families would greatly benefit from oppor-tunities to connect with other SOF families through orga-nized events or SOF family services. Having a military background or being a current service member was seen as a resilience factor because it provided greater knowledge of what to expect. (109)

While this chapter focuses on the issues SOF families face, many spouses in this study described the SOF community as welcoming and tight knit. They said they felt connected to and supported by their rela-tionships with other SOF spouses through a shared understanding of the SOF lifestyle. Both formal and informal social gatherings helped SOF members and spouses connect with other SOF families. These relationships served as support networks between spouses and between spouses and other SOF members when their partners were away, such as help with babysitting, lawn care, and snow removal (106).

Conversely, some spouses "mentioned feeling judged and criticized by family members and civilian friends for staying in a lifestyle involv-ing such hardships" (106). For those spouses who had support from their extended families, they described that support as critical, "espe-cially when they had young children" and "during their partner's pro-longed absences and periods of high stress" (107).

[Spouse interview:] "My husband was deployed when I was first pregnant, home for the summer, and deployed again right up until basically I gave birth. But then Mum came and she stayed with me for weeks on end . . . We [try] to make sure [that when] he is deploying or gone for a long period, we have family members that step in and help. That doesn't necessarily mean that things aren't stressful, but it helps us cope with it." (107)

Clinicians in the civilian sector can attempt to link their clients with SOF family services as well as military, veteran, or other volunteer family groups, such as the ones in Appendix II, to further help SOF families get the social support and connection they need.

Individual Strengths and Positive Coping

According to the multiple studies cited by Richer, Frank, and Guérin (2022), SOF spouses often use coping techniques associated with increased resilience, such as problem-solving skills, active distraction (i.e., avoiding thinking about the stressor, listening to music), and perceived mastery (i.e., the degree to which they feel in control of their lives) (101).

Many spouses spoke about their own military background—either as a serving member, being part of a military family, or having grown up near a military base—and how it contributed to their understanding of their partner's occupation and their being amenable to unpredictability and the sacrifices of the SOF lifestyle. Some spouses also discussed how having observed a parent navigate the military lifestyle had helped them to acquire effective coping mechanisms and useful parenting skills to support their own children. (106)

[Spouse interview:] "What you should know about both of our backgrounds is that we both come from military families. So I often kind of make light of it by saying it's a bit of a family business. We are very service-minded people, giving back, and I think sometimes understand that sacrifices have to be made. Maybe better than somebody who wouldn't have grown up or been exposed to this. I think to generally understand and accept the lifestyle. The changes that can happen last minute." (106)

Some spouses mentioned that their partner's joining SOF was a family decision. Many spouses were pleased to see their partner gain new opportunities and a sense of purpose, and see them fulfilled and happy with their work. Some felt this was worth the sacrifices . . .

"I'm extremely proud of my husband. Extremely proud of what he does, of the type of person he is, the commitment he brings to his work. And frankly of his skills and of his level of dedication to his job. So I'm very proud of that." (106)

As you can tell, it takes a special person to be a SOF spouse. It's therefore no surprise that many of the CANSOFCOM spouses interviewed described themselves as emotionally strong and independent. Some said these were personal character traits, while others said they had developed these traits over time as a SOF spouse. Some even mentioned appreciating the time they had on their own while their SOF partner was away and that the distance actually made their relationship with their SOF partner even stronger. One spouse put it this way: "I think you have to be a certain kind of person to be successful as a spouse in this type of environment. If you're not good with being on your own and doing your own thing, then you're not going to be happy." (106)

Many spouses mentioned using coping mechanisms to overcome the stress, such as finding time for self-care (e.g., beauty care, having a hobby), maintaining healthy eating habits and a fitness routine, good sleep hygiene, and ensuring they had proper time to recover from high op-tempo periods. (106)

Spouses who had a high degree of cultural competency in the military lifestyle prior to meeting their SOF partner or gained cultural competency during their relationship; was or learned how to be self-sufficient; had or gained healthy coping mechanisms; had or gained strong family support; had a community of supportive family organizations and/or other SOF spouses and were able to reach out to them, all greatly increased their personal and their family's well-being. Civilian mental health professionals can increase client well-being by teaching cultural competency, healthy coping mechanisms, and family and social communication skills.

6. SOF MARRIAGES & CHILDREN

Avoid negative sources, people, places, things, and habits. Believe in yourself. Consider things in every angle. Don't give up, and don't give in. Enjoy life today—yesterday is gone and tomorrow may never come. Family and friends are hidden treasures; seek them and enjoy their riches. Give more than you plan to. Hang on to your dream. Ignore those who try to discourage you. Just do it. Keep trying, no matter how hard it seems. It will get easier. Love yourself first and make it happen. Never lie, cheat, or steal. Always strike a fair deal. Open your eyes and see things as they really are. Practice what makes perfect. Quitters never win, and winners never quit. Read, study, and learn everything important in your life. Stop procrastinating. Take control of your own destiny. Understand yourself in order to better understand others. Visualize it. Want it more than anything. Exuberate your efforts. You are unique of all God's creations. Nothing can replace you. Zero in on your target and go for it.

—Danny Dietz

This chapter will discuss marriage issues in particular, then focus on SOF children as well as SOF members as parents.

Garner (2018, 53) writes:

> [A]fter returning home, veterans often come across four obstacles that impact smooth transitions: (1) renegotiating roles and household responsibilities with other family members, (2) managing strong emotions, (3) reducing their dependence on emotional suppression and creating emotional intimacy, and (4) creating shared meaning with other family members regarding the deployment. Each obstacle can be detrimental to the reintegration process, as it may cause a disruption in the familial support network and lead to feelings of loss and not being understood.

From the above information, the transition to civilian life is also accompanied by an equally difficult transition to home and family life. If the SOF family members are unable to successfully navigate these adjustments and difficulties, it can lead to the disintegration of the family unit, as well as worsen mental health issues any of the family members were already experiencing.

Infidelity & Divorce

As mentioned in the previous chapter, those spouses who had some military exposure or experience prior to marrying a SOF member have a better understanding of the demands and situations they might face. Therefore, they generally have more resilience and successful marriages. Furthermore, if the SOF member and their partner have a stronger relationship, they are more likely to stay together. I've often found that marriage issues and divorce happen more between those spouses who did not have a firm foundation when they married.

SOF members and spouses are not immune to infidelity. What is different is that SOF units have their own military compounds on military bases. They have their own barracks, chow halls, and gyms. The units are small and everyone knows each other and their families.

Everyone knows who has a wife and who has kids. Infidelity is not allowed in the military because of the stress it causes service members and units. It can therefore cause even more friction within a SOF unit or base than it might in a larger military unit.

Because SOF is a young man's game, and because of military culture in general, some SOF members end up getting involved with women they meet at a bar or club, think they're in love, and rush into marriage before they're off on their next deployment. Obviously, these types of relationships are not usually very sound. Neither the SOF member nor the spouse really know the other person or what they're getting into.

I've seen situations where the wife didn't know their SOF husband that well, and when he was off on deployment, she decided that another SOF guy was the one for her. Or she got married more for the military benefits—the basic housing allowance (BAH), tax-free shopping, the prestige of being married to a "stud," or, in the case of some foreign women living overseas, a chance to get a free ride to the United States. This is not to paint a negative picture of military or SOF spouses at all, but it does happen, especially when young people rush into relationships and marriage without taking time to get to know the other person.

Other times, the spouse realizes they're alone all the time, they may not be familiar enough with the unit to get the support they need, or they get burned out taking care of the home and children. When the SOF member can't be there to support them, the marriage starts to break apart. It's difficult to be married to someone you rarely see.

Unfortunately, it's not ideal to have a significant other in the military unless you are married. A romantic yet non-legal partner doesn't get any support or benefits from the government or SOF unit. When the SOF member is moved to a new duty station, the girlfriend gets left behind. If the SOF member dies, the girlfriend or boyfriend gets nothing. Basically, there's not much you can do if you're not married.

On the other hand, I've had to caution SOF members who thought getting married wouldn't have any consequences. Young men in the military generally don't have a lot of assets, so they think that if they end up divorced, it won't be a big deal. It's a convenient decision they make when they think they're in love, and they don't think about the long-term future.

It's important to inform the SOF member that any benefits they receive—either on active duty or as a veteran—may end up divided in half if they get divorced. Sometimes I tell clients about my situation where, after my career-ending injury in law enforcement, I had no job while my ex-wife got half of my disability. I needed that money for my medication, my doctors' visits, and for food and rent. I try to explain that marriage is a big deal and that they really need to take the time to get to know someone before they rush into it.

If a client is going through a divorce, I help them navigate that emotional and financial roller coaster so they can be resourceful. If the client is the SOF member, I remind them that they can use the skills they learned in SOF to overcome their issues and emerge more resilient, even if their life is a bit more complicated.

Due to the extreme nature of SOF, divorce does happen, even when couples got married for the right reasons. People grow apart and change, and the constant expectations on operators to be operational cannot be underestimated. SOF members and their families are human, and the same strategies on a civilian client going through divorce will most likely be appropriate for the SOF member or spouse. This is another reason why I don't have to know all the nitty-gritty details of a client's problems, because their problems are human problems.

Domestic Violence

I haven't found any research or statistics on domestic violence or abuse within SOF families, which would be hard information to gather, though no section of society is immune from these problems. Personally, I have not worked with any SOF members who admitted domestic violence. There were a few, however, who expressed they had explosive anger issues. My first thoughts in those cases were that the client could be suffering from traumatic brain injury (TBI), which will be covered later in this book. When a SOF member is struggling with substance abuse, PTSD, TBI, maladaptive coping mechanisms, and other issues, there's no doubt domestic violence can occur.

While SOF members try to remain emotionally detached from home life when they're on the job, many SOF members I've spoken to feel as though they haven't done enough for their families and feel guilty they weren't around more. These people made a difficult career choice, and as all choices in life, their decision has pros and cons. I help them deal with the consequences and try to get them back on track, in the here and now, so they can start being the spouse or parent they want to be. (As always, it is critical for you as the clinician to make it clear that if any domestic abuse is actively occurring, it will be reported for the safety of the client and their loved ones.)

Family Communication

Communication problems in relationships are universal. There's nothing necessarily special about SOF in this matter, and most people have a hard time with communication. However, military members and those who work as first responders, and especially SOF members, tend to be direct-style communicators. Whether this is their natural tendency or they learned it from their profession, SOF operators need to be short and to the point. In high-stress, life-threatening operations, only the most critical and useful information is shared as quickly and clearly as possible to avoid any mistakes or misunderstandings. The slightest miscommunication or delay might put the entire mission and team at risk.

Obviously, this communication style doesn't always translate well in the family or civilian environment. Direct-style communicators often feel frustrated when they don't understand the bottom line of a conversation, while the indirect conversationalist may feel misunderstood or that their partner simply doesn't listen to them.

What often is miscommunicated (if communicated at all) is how each spouse deals with stress. Everyone at times needs personal space and time to decompress, and we all do this in different ways. I teach clients about the arc of adrenaline and the adrenaline dump, stress-relief techniques, and how to be able to reach out and have that conversation with their partner, so they understand how their significant other deals with life's difficult moments. This can help both spouses recognize when the other is stressed and how to react appropriately, depending on each individual's communication style.

I've told folks to come up with a code word that tells the other spouse when they're stressed and that they need to destress, whatever that means for them. When one person says their code word, the other person knows that their spouse needs solitude, or needs to go to the gym or the gun range, because they don't want to talk about the shit day they had. Or it might be that they need to talk and vent, or they need affection or physical touch. It could be anything, but having that code word helps the other spouse know how to react in that moment so as not to inadvertently escalate the situation. It also helps the spouse understand why their significant other acts a certain way when they're upset.

Couples as well as parents and children need to have those heart-to-heart conversations with each other about how they see things and what their needs and wants are. They must be reciprocal to the other person's needs and wants if they're going to be successful, especially when one or both spouses are (or were) in a high-stress job.

SOF operators don't have a nine-to-five job; they're in a high-stress career that demands much of their life. In jobs like these, it's easy for the SOF member to bring their job home with them, so when they have a really shitty day and don't have healthy ways to de-stress, they often take it out on whoever is home: the spouse or the kids (or both). Over time, that breaks the family apart. But being a spouse and/or a parent is also not a nine-to-five job, and sometimes the SOF member (or any new spouse or parent) needs help understanding and dealing with those responsibilities as well.

The reason for most of the divorces I've seen was communication—or lack thereof—which meant there was no real understanding of what the other person was going through. That causes people to grow apart, because they never figured out how to handle stress together as a family unit. When each partner has a very different coping strategy, they're not connected to each other when "the shit hits the fan," which only causes more stress and friction.

When the SOF member is struggling, they're often not telling their spouse about their issues because they either don't know what to say, they don't know what's wrong, or they're not focused on the relationship and don't see that their maladaptive behaviors are causing real problems. They're used to the mission (or "mistress") always coming first, and it's hard for them to realize how their behaviors affect those around them. As a clinician, you can help families by giving them a better understanding of what's going on, why it's going on, and then providing helpful tools to help mitigate those issues.

All that being said, seeing a SOF member in couples therapy with their spouse or significant other is not very common. Most of the SOF members I've worked with say it was hard enough for them to come in and talk to me by themselves. They generally don't want anyone else to know they're in therapy. In their minds, they want to be able to fix whatever's wrong, become a better husband or father or whatever the case may be, and move on. They don't want their whole family involved with the issues they're dealing with.

That's not to say couples or family therapy wouldn't happen down the road once the SOF member feels comfortable with their therapist, but they must trust you as a clinician. They must understand that you won't "play sides" or "pick favorites" when other family members are involved in therapy sessions.

I may recommend couples or family therapy if I think it will be helpful to my client and if the SOF member is open to it. Otherwise, I will do my best in our one-on-one sessions to help the SOF member work out his/her relationship issues.

Love Languages

You've probably heard of *The 5 Love Languages* by Gary Chapman, and believe it or not, men—even SOF dudes—find that information very useful and don't mind talking about it. The term "love languages" may turn them off at first, but the five ways people receive and express love can really help people better understand and communicate with their partners. But the information isn't just for romantic relationships. It can be used to improve family relationships, friendships, and even work relationships. Gary Chapman's company now also addresses apology languages and how to better deal with anger. (Of course, there are many other relationship books and resources you can use and recommend to your clients.)

I've found the love languages especially helpful when SOF members are having a relationship or communication issue. I won't necessarily teach them all the five love languages or go into details, but I'll educate them on the concept, that there are different styles, and I'll often give them personal examples. I'm very open and transparent because I've been through a lot of the things they're going through. So, if it's relevant and not always about me, I'll share some of my own experiences.

For instance, I said to one gentleman, "My wife's love language is verbal engagement. That's how she lets me know she cares about me, by wanting to talk and engage with me. Mine is physical touch." I will explain to the client how that works on her side and then my side, how they're seen from the opposing sides, and how we work through that. And it *is* work. For my wife, it's helping her collect her thoughts into a more condensed delivery, as opposed to her "walking all over the park" with whatever she's talking about. For me, it's listening and engaging with her so she knows I appreciate being with her.

I might also share an anecdote, such as, "With my background in the military and law enforcement, I'm used to quickly dispensing only the most crucial data, like, 'Suspect, three o'clock!' whereas my wife might say, 'Well, I was looking over to my right, and there was this individual, and he kind of looked suspect,' and I'm thinking, *Oh my God, woman, get to the point!*" Usually, my clients understand what I mean. It gets them laughing, and that usually gets them talking, like, "Oh yeah, my wife does this," and that's what I want. The more that comes out of their mouth, the more I'm learning about them and thinking about the best approach.

Other Marriage Issues

The older way of thinking, which in a way fits the SOF lifestyle, is that a woman has her place and the man—the SOF member and "breadwinner"—has his. This may divide along gender lines but can also divide between the Type A partner (usually the service member or veteran) and the Type B partner (usually the civilian spouse, though not always). My experience has been that the person in the military is basically the top dog in the relationship, even if that person is female. They make the big decisions, take the reins, and get things done. Being in SOF demands leadership, perfectionism, attention to detail, motivation, and so forth. The SOF member has to make a lot of crucial decisions on a regular basis.

However, especially in SOF, when the SOF member is away training and deploying, it may be the civilian spouse at home who is in charge of the family and/or home life, and the military member takes a back seat in that regard.

Sometimes when the SOF member is home for an extended period of time, or when they transition to civilian life, they try to take over the home life. That often causes a lot of conflict with the spouse who has been in charge of that arena for so long. It can also cause conflict with the children who aren't used to the SOF parent's style of parenting or discipline. Some clients talked to me about the fact that divvying up the household duties with their spouse was causing World War III.

Sometimes it's the opposite, where the military veteran feels they have earned the right to do nothing. They're burned out, possibly dealing with physical or mental injuries and/or having trouble adjusting to civilian life, and they don't want to lift a finger if they don't have to. Certainly, SOF members deserve some downtime when they no longer have to get up at zero dark thirty every day. But doing nothing forever will kill a marriage.

One couple I knew had a child who was around six years old, and things needed to be done. The civilian spouse was really upset because her husband wasn't helping. She was prepping all the meals, making the doctors' appointments, doing the taxes, and everything else that had to do with the home and family. The veteran was still in the mindset of how things were in the military, when he didn't have to do any of it. He came home and the house was clean, the kid was taken care of, the car payment was made, and the meals were done. The SOF member had sacrificed a lot to serve at the highest echelons. But the wife had made sacrifices of her own, and now that her husband was finally home, she wanted him to lighten some of her load. And that was a problem for him.

Transitioning out of the military means the whole family has to make adjustments. The ones who are willing to adjust are the ones that survive as a family.

A factor to consider is that, similar to the SOF member, spouses who spend time in military culture, especially if they live on a military base, may develop some of the maladaptive coping skills that service members develop. A one-of-a-kind study in the UK by Gribble, Goodwin, and Fear (2019) found that military spouses had a "significantly higher prevalence of probable depression, hazardous alcohol consumption, and binge-drinking [when] compared to women in the general population."

Similar to SOF members themselves, many SOF spouses and children may face stigma and other barriers to seeking help. A survey conducted by Mailey et al. (2018) concluded that a main barrier to spouse self-care, such as physical activity, social connection, stress management, and healthy diet, was a lack of time. Other barriers SOF spouses noted for their self-care were financial concerns (especially in terms of eating healthy), parent/family responsibilities, the transient military lifestyle, deployments, and the necessity to "do it all." SOF spouses give new meaning to sacrificing themselves for their families, though it was noted that many participants exhibited rigid definitions of what "counts" as exercise or healthy eating.

Another issue can be when a SOF operator is dealing with emotional detachment, where they're so used to being a SOF operator that they don't know how to switch off. That's one of the worst things for a marriage. For example, when the spouse brings up an issue they think is urgent, like the dishwasher being broken or the garage door not closing, the SOF member can easily ignore or even lash out at the spouse for making a big deal of what they think is not a serious issue at all. The operator is still in the mindset of life-and-death missions. So the SOF member thinks, "The dishwasher is broken? So what? Figure it out and get it fixed. It's just a dishwasher! Why are you asking me to worry about it? I just came back from the 'real world.'"

I've heard things like that more than just about anything else when it comes to relationship issues with SOF members. SOF clients often complain to me about the frustration they have in dealing with "stupid shit" at home (their words, not mine), which is miniscule compared to what they're used to dealing with on a daily basis. And that's ended a lot of relationships, because the communication isn't there and the empathy isn't there. The spouse feels completely left out and has no idea why telling this person that the dishwasher broke completely set them into a rage. Working on communication is vital so that the spouse understands what the operator is going through and vice versa, and so that the operator can show some sort of compassion and understanding with the spouse.

I sometimes tell them to find a marker—say, a certain time before they go home, either from training or a deployment—that marks the time for them to start to unwind, switch gears, and prepare to deal with home life instead of work life. For example, on their drive home or the night before their redeployment, I'll tell them to start to think, "Okay, when I get home,

I'm gonna have to deal with my son and his behavior issues at school. I'm gonna have to deal with my wife and whatever's going on with her and and our son, or her job, or her lack of finding a job." I explain to the SOF member that they can't be G. I. Joe twenty-four hours a day. They have to show up and support their family just like they show up and support their SOF team. That family support is going to be very different from SOF support in a lot of ways, but it's needed all the same.

Successful Marriages

As a clinician, we often see people when things have gone wrong and they need help. So, when I see a successful couple that's doing well in spite of challenges or are still amicable after separating, I try to learn from them as much as I can.

Those who stay happily married seem to have found an equilibrium in their relational power dynamic. Rather than one spouse taking charge, both are able to give and take when necessary to keep the relationship going. Both people in the relationship need to be willing to discuss their problems, listen to each other, and be willing to adjust their behaviors based on the other's concerns and needs.

It's extremely important that both individuals have a hardcore truth and honesty session with each other. To create true change, they both need to lower their egos and be genuinely honest about what it is they want or need out of the relationship. This requires that they both listen to the other, and then it requires that they make changes to their own behaviors. Because if the other isn't willing to give what's wanted or needed, then a loving relationship isn't truly possible.

People in military relationships are required to make a lot of changes and sacrifices. At first, the civilian spouse must generally adjust their life and take a back seat to the military's demands, because the mission comes first. That's just the nature of the beast. Then, once the SOF member has transitioned, that veteran generally needs to shift to the reality of the fact they're no longer active in Special Operations Forces, and that is a hard transition to make.

Some veterans never really make that transition. Everything they talk about and who they want to be seen as is what they used to be. As discussed in the previous section, it's painful to have been so important and suddenly be just another face in the crowd. But the reality is, unless they're retired or on disability, they have to pay rent and get a job. And if they want to stay married, they have to be invested in their spouse and family life.

Some of the SOF members I've worked with who fell into that category—who were locked into who they were—did end up making the changes they needed to make. What finally broke them was the fracturing of their family unit. That fracturing forced the SOF member to make a choice: either do something different or lose those family relationships forever. Unfortunately, it takes those tough times to force some people to make better choices.

When I question clients about their marriages, I'm generally able to determine the strength of the relationship's foundation by learning about how they first met and how well they knew each other when they got married. Did they meet at a bar or at a church? Did they date for two weeks or two years? Did the non-military spouse know about the SOF lifestyle she was entering into? If the foundation wasn't there and the couple never got to truly know each other, they are unlikely to last.

SOF Children

Children of SOF personnel often experience unique challenges associated with the lifestyle of their parents, such as: frequent military moves; the absence of the SOF parent due to deployments, training, and other demands; and the lack of knowing exactly what the SOF parent does, when they will be gone, and for how long. Support from military units, schools, and communities is essential in helping special operations children and their families cope with the challenges they face.

The high SOF op tempo can lead to significant disruptions in family life, causing SOF children feelings of instability and anxiety. The high-stress, high-risk, and secretive nature of special ops often compounds this stress, as children may fear for their parent's safety and live in an environment of constant uncertainty. This may additionally cause SOF children to have trouble understanding the world around them and their own identity.

A study by Bullock and Skomorovsky (2017) examined the impact of deployment on the well-being of school-age children from Canadian Armed Forces families. Results "showed that deployment negatively impacted children's well-being, routines, and family dynamics. Active distraction and social support seeking served as the most effective protective factors against deployment stress." The absence of a parent due to multiple training requirements and deployments not only shifts family dynamics but often places additional responsibilities on children, such as taking care of younger siblings or assuming more household duties. Older children, in particular, might take on roles that are beyond their age, which can lead to premature maturity and, in some cases, resentment.

Additionally, the unpredictable schedule and long absences can disrupt parental bonding and normal family routines, making it difficult for children to develop secure attachments or cope with the emotional strain. These factors can manifest in children as academic difficulties, social withdrawal, behavioral problems, and emotional distress.

If a SOF member or spouse is experiencing acute stress or hypervigilance or other issues, it can cause the whole family to be in a constant, heightened state of fear and worry—a dynamic that can psychologically affect children even if the adults in the family try to hide their concerns.

The lack of a stable parent figure during critical developmental periods can also impact long-term emotional and psychological growth. Addressing these challenges often requires targeted support systems, including counseling services tailored to military families, support groups for children, and educational programs that help them understand and cope with the unique aspects of their family dynamics.

The transitory nature of military life means that children often move from one community to another, losing contact with friends and repeatedly adjusting to new schools and social environments. This can hinder the development of deep, lasting friendships and lead to feelings of isolation and loneliness. These frequent changes can make it difficult for children to feel a sense of belonging, impacting their social development and self-esteem. This lack of stability can lead to increased anxiety, which can manifest as mood swings, irritability, or depression. Conversely, some children adapt to changing environments by learning how to be more social and make friends more easily, which has more positive effects on their well-being. Helping children find ways to connect to new people can help them navigate transitional difficulties.

Each move can also bring a change in educational settings, curricula, and expectations, complicating academic achievement. Children may face difficulties in adapting to new school systems, catching up with different academic standards, or coping with gaps in their education due to relocation.

Children are also affected by the aftermath of their parents' experiences in the field. Parents who return with physical injuries or psychological trauma can alter the parent-child dynamic significantly. Children may find themselves in caregiving roles or may struggle with the changed behavior or emotional unavailability of their parent.

A study by Hisle-Gorman, Susi, and Gorman (2019) found that parental injuries and illnesses affect child and family life in a negative way:

> Children with injured parents had decreased rates of preventive care visits and increased rates of visits for injuries, maltreatment, and mental health care, as well as increased psychiatric medication use, following their parent's injury. Across all categories of care, children of parents with post-traumatic stress disorder (PTSD), both alone and with traumatic brain injury, appeared to have more pronounced changes in care patterns. Parental injury and illness are associated with changes in children's health care use, and PTSD in a parent increases the effect.

However, not to minimize what SOF families got through, but psychologically speaking, there's a common thread among children who have one or both parents working high-stress jobs, especially one that keeps the parent away for unpredictable and unforeseen amounts of time. The parent misses holidays, birthdays, and other special moments. The child may have feelings of abandonment or anger toward that parent for not being there, or they may have the idea that the parent doesn't care about them or doesn't love them. Children often lack an understanding of the bigger picture, that the parent is putting themselves in harm's way to make the world a better place, or at the least, providing for the family.

Supporting SOF children, as with any child, can involve helping them communicate their wants and needs with others their age and with adults, teaching them ways to deal with and express their emotions, educating them on healthy coping skills, and helping them identify stable support systems they can use for continuity through changes and difficult times. Family services within the military or veteran communities can offer coping strategies for dealing with parental absence and trauma, and they may have social groups where children in similar situations can connect and form healthy friendships.

Erikson's Developmental Stages for SOF Children

Understanding the psychosocial challenges that SOF children face through the lens of Erikson's developmental stages can help clinicians provide tailored support and emotional and psychological development despite the challenges of military family life. Below are just some examples.

1. Trust vs. Mistrust (Infancy)

SOF parents are often absent due to deployments and training, which can make it difficult for infants to develop a consistent sense of trust. Ensuring consistent caregiving from the other parent and/or family members can help mitigate feelings of uncertainty and foster a sense of trust in their environment. It's also important to ensure the caregiving family members have adequate support as well.

2. Autonomy vs. Shame and Doubt (Toddlerhood)

Frequent relocations and changes can disrupt toddlers' routines, which are crucial for developing autonomy and confidence. Maintaining consistent routines as much as possible and encouraging self-directed play can help toddlers develop a sense of autonomy and confidence.

3. Initiative vs. Guilt (Early Childhood)

Children may feel guilty or anxious about their desires for independence or may struggle with fears of causing harm due to stories or stress from the SOF parent's job. Providing safe opportunities for play and interaction with other children in similar circumstances can help mitigate feelings of guilt and bolster initiative.

4. Industry vs. Inferiority (School Age)

School-age children may face difficulties in feeling competent and self-assured due to frequent school changes and the absence of a parent. Encouraging involvement in consistent extracurricular activities can provide a sense of achievement and belonging.

5. Identity vs. Role Confusion (Adolescence)

Adolescents might struggle with their identity as they reconcile the values of their SOF family with external expectations and their personal ambitions. Open communication about their experiences and feelings and connecting them with mentorship programs within the military community can support healthy identity development.

6. Intimacy vs. Isolation (Young Adulthood)

Early adulthood might bring challenges in forming deep relationships due to the transient nature of their upbringing and potential emotional guardedness inherited from their environment. Encouraging young adults to engage in social groups outside the military circle and pursuing higher education can help them form diverse relationships and reduce feelings of isolation.

While SOF children face unique challenges, the strength and situation of each child's family obviously plays an important role in the child's ability to deal with stress. When treating SOF children, it may help to ensure the child understands their SOF parent's profession and how that affects the family unit.

Parent Regret

Because SOF is a young man's game, it's not very common that a service member would have started a family before going through the pipeline. The majority of SOF members start families while they're serving in a SOF unit. Unfortunately, as mentioned previously, some of the dating habits for a lot of the men in the military is where things go wrong, and SOF operators are no exception. When couples marry without a firm foundation or marry in response to a pregnancy, neither partner may fully understand the work required to stay together in the SOF environment, especially if they have a child together.

When the SOF member leaves the military and has more time to spend with their family, they often realize how much they missed and may have feelings of regret. Many parents pride themselves on having a close relationship with their children, but often the SOF member didn't have the same opportunities to develop those relationships—especially if the family unit is broken due to a divorce or separation of some kind. I've talked with many SOF members who felt bad because they didn't know what their kid's favorite movie was or how to comfort their child when they were sad or scared.

I've also met a lot of folks that, while they didn't say it, probably resented having those parental responsibilities. Sometimes ego gets involved, and the SOF member feels that changing diapers and grocery shopping is beneath them, or at least isn't something they want to spend time on while fighting to be the best of the best, or while they're adjusting to civilian life.

Continuing Erikson's stages of psychosocial development, it's important to note how SOF parents might feel when juggling the dual demands of being a parent and a SOF operator or veteran.

7. Generativity vs. Stagnation (Middle Adulthood)

A SOF parent may struggle with balancing the needs of their own careers, physical and mental health, and aging with the needs of their children. It's important to help the SOF member find ways to get involved in their children's lives and in the community supporting their children, which can also benefit the SOF member in their recovery and/or transition.

8. Integrity vs. Despair (Older Age)

Reflecting on a life that was dominated by the demands of special operations can lead a SOF parent to have regrets or despair over missed family experiences. Facilitating life review processes and creating legacies through storytelling or memoirs can help older adults develop a sense of fulfillment and integrity. Helping the SOF parent reconnect with their children can be beneficial at any age, as mentioned above.

Garner (2018, 93) writes:

> In addition to possible physical and psychological wounds, the former operators are now faced with looking for and establishing a new career and developing new relationships with others, including focusing on intimate partners and establishing and supporting their own family. According to Erikson, this stage usually takes place between the ages of 19–40, suggesting that operators are slightly behind the civilian population when it comes to completing this life stage of identity development.

The above quote shows how the military, especially the SOF life-style, can make veterans better at some areas of life (i.e., functioning well in emergencies) and lacking at other areas when compared to civilians.

Helping SOF members become better parents is similar to helping them become better spouses. SOF parents can learn improved communication techniques and develop bonding routines with their children. It's important to ensure the SOF member has realistic expectations, as this may take time, especially if those bonds were broken due to divorce or separation.

Family Treatment Tactics

If you work with couples, children, or families, you are probably familiar with some of the modalities that are beneficial for these groups, such as attachment-based therapy, family systems, the Gottman method, play therapy, pragmatic/experiential therapy (PET), structural therapy, trauma-focused cognitive behavioral therapy (TF-CBT), and trust-based relational intervention (TBRI), as well as interpersonal therapy (IPT) and relational therapy and more (Mental Health Match, 2024).

It's best to be proficient in several different modalities so you can adjust as needed based on the clients you're serving and their specific issues and personalities. As mentioned, communication is key, and understanding family dynamics, personalities, and even love languages can especially help SOF members better connect with others and repair familial bonds.

PART III:

COMMON PRESENTING PROBLEMS

7. SOF ISSUES

Danny Dietz died right there in my arms. I don't know how quickly hearts break, but that nearly broke mine . . . I had to leave him or else die out there with him. But I knew one thing was certain: I still had my rifle, and I was not alone, and neither was Danny, a devout Roman Catholic. I left him with God.

—Marcus Luttrell,
retired Navy SEAL and lone survivor
of Operation Red Wings

Two books on SOF issues are worth mentioning. One is *Operator Syndrome* by Chris Frueh, PhD. The other is *Warrior Syndrome* by T. M. Johnson, MD. Both books hypothesize that "warriors," such as first responders, and specifically SOF operators, often have multiple issues at once. For example, a SOF veteran may be simultaneously suffering from traumatic brain injury (TBI), post-traumatic stress disorder (PTSD), a spinal injury, chronic pain, and depression. This prevalence of comorbidity in people who have experienced repeated and prolonged physical, mental, emotional, and spiritual trauma is what these authors refer to as operator syndrome or warrior syndrome.

I mostly agree with this hypothesis, though every client is different. Sometimes it is only one issue. But more often than not, what I've seen in my SOF clients is that they are suffering from two or more issues at once, and those issues may have different causes and therefore require different treatments. Some issues may not be mental at all, yet the issues they're dealing with compound and negatively influence their mental health.

That's why it's important to understand all the issues SOF members may face and how to treat them simultaneously, which means keeping an open mind, being flexible, and learning about many different modalities and techniques.

Post-Deployment Issues

Special Operations Forces personnel often face unique challenges when they return from combat deployments. Common post-deployment problems can include:

- Reintegration with family and social life
  - Difficulty adjusting to the relative calm of home life after the high tempo of operations
  - Changes in family dynamics or roles that occurred during deployment
  - Feeling disconnected from friends and family who may not understand their experiences
- Physical health issues
  - Chronic pain or injuries sustained during deployment
  - Sleep disturbances, fatigue, or other health issues exacerbated by operational demands
  - Potential exposure to hazardous materials or conditions impacting long-term health
- Mental health challenges
  - Post-traumatic stress disorder (PTSD) stemming from traumatic experiences during missions

- o Depression, anxiety, or other mood disorders
- o Substance abuse as a coping mechanism for stress or mental health issues
- o Maladaptive behaviors meant to replace the adrenaline rush of deployments
- Stigma and reluctance to seek help
  - o Cultural stigma within military and SOF communities regarding seeking help for mental health issues and perceptions of weakness
  - o Concerns about the impact of seeking help on career progression
- Cognitive effects and emotional regulation
  - o Difficulties with memory, concentration, or decision-making
  - o Challenges in managing emotions or coping with anger, frustration, or irritability
  - o Challenges due to traumatic brain injury (TBI)
- Relationship and marital issues
  - o Strain on relationships due to prolonged absence, communication gaps, or stress
  - o Challenges in reconnecting with partners or adjusting to changes in relationships
- Loss and grief
  - o Processing the loss of colleagues or dealing with survivor's guilt
  - o Coping with injuries or disabilities, whether personal or among fellow service members
- Identity and existential issues
  - o Questions about personal identity, purpose, or future direction after intense experiences
  - o Reconciling personal values or beliefs with experiences during deployment

While these issues may surface after deployments, they tend to worsen when the SOF member's military career ends and they are transitioning into civilian life, as discussed in detail in Chapter 4.

Physical Injuries

SOF members often suffer from physical injuries throughout their careers. Many SOF members are forced into retirement due to injuries that cause mobility issues or chronic pain conditions. The impact of these traumas can affect their mental health and also extend to their families, leading to stress, anxiety, depression, substance abuse, and other issues.

Garner (2018, 92) writes:

> Because the typical career of a Special Operator lasts until they are in their late 30's, the warrior is now involuntarily transitioned back to civilian life with many years to live and many challenges before him. Physical injuries may now prevent the operator from utilizing their specialized skillsset developed and honed-in the military and utilized in the civilian sector. If severely injured, the operator may be deemed potentially disabled and/or unemployable. For many operators, this change in status is difficult to accept, as they were once the top of their profession and are no longer performing at the highest levels.

It is critical for the clinician working with SOF operators to get a full list of their health problems. Because of the constant, high-level physical and mental grind that SOF operators go through, clearly listing their history of physical, biological, emotional, and social issues can be helpful in determining the problems they're dealing with and potential root causes. Not all issues are purely psychological.

For those who are young and accustomed to being at the top of their game, it's hard to think of being injured to the point of no return—i.e., to have a career-ending or even life-altering injury. Because of this, those who do experience career-ending injuries may lose a lot of team-mates. Part of this may be because those still serving are not able to keep in touch due to various time and geographical constraints. Part of this may also be due to the stigma toward those who are not opera-tional, as discussed in previous chapters.

It's important to get an injured SOF client thinking about life beyond the injury in all facets of their life, to include their career, new ways to stay in shape, hobbies, and so on. Ensuring they have adequate social support can be a lifesaver, especially if they're able to connect with other SOF members, veterans, or even civilian groups with shared activities or interests.

While serving as a law enforcement officer, I suffered a debilitat-ing back injury. I had also been a part-time Army reservist and, using my combined active duty and reserve time, was hoping to retire from the Army as well as from law enforcement. My spinal injury ended both careers at the same time. After that injury, I ended up living with my mother for a period of time (which was nice, because she's a good listener). On top of my career loss and transition, I was going through a divorce and was raising my two kids as a single parent. Half of my disability retirement from law enforcement was being sent to my ex-wife during the four-year legal battle. I was dealing with an avalanche of issues.

Going through that whole experience is what led me to become a therapist. I bring this up sometimes to my clients in hopes that they can see there is always a way forward, even if they can't see it yet.

Special Operations Exhaustion Syndrome

Special operations exhaustion syndrome (SOES), or special opera-tions burnout, is a term used to describe the psychological and physical exhaustion experienced by individuals engaged in high-stress, highly specialized military operations. It is a form of post-traumatic stress disorder (PTSD) that has been identified in SOF members. SOES is characterized by physical, mental, and emotional exhaustion that can persist long after the SOF member has returned from a combat mission or other high-stress situation. Special operations burnout can be caused by a variety of factors, including high operational tempo, lack of adequate rest and recovery, and the psychological and physical effects of extended deployments.

Exhaustion syndrome, or combat fatigue, can and does happen to service members in combat. Lt. Col. Dave Grossman points out various theories and research over many decades in his book *On Killing*. He determines that exhaustion can be caused by many different factors, often more than one at the same time. These factors are primarily:

- Physiological exhaustion caused by a continual fight-or-flight arousal condition
- Lack of sleep
- Lack of food
- Impact of the elements (cold, heat, wind, rain, dark of night, etc.)
- Impact of the senses (witnessing destruction and others wounded, dying, or dead)
- The wind of hate (knowing another human hates you enough to want to kill you even if you have never met)
- Guilt (i.e., moral injury) at having taken another human life

Grossman writes:

Many authorities speak and write of emotional stamina on the battlefield as a finite resource. I have termed this the Well of Fortitude. Faced with the soldier's encounters with horror, guilt, fear, exhaustion, and hate, each man draws steadily from his own private reservoir of inner strength and fortitude until finally the well runs dry. And then he becomes just another statistic. I believe that this metaphor of the well is an excellent one for understanding why at least 98 percent of all soldiers in close combat will ultimately become psychiatric casualties. (2009, 82)

This understanding of exhaustion also helps explain the extreme training and long pipeline service members must endure to become an elite SOF operator. By design, their Well of Fortitude runs much deeper than the average service member's.

Even so, when a SOF operator is not deployed, they're training. And when they're not training, they're deployed. The training never ends, and that definitely lends to the burnout rate—and why so many don't (or can't) make it a full-time career. It's extremely rare for someone to be a lifetime SOF combat operator and retire from the Special Forces, especially for enlisted members (as opposed to officers, who may be present within teams but not doing as much physical activity as their team members).

Symptoms of SOES can include fatigue, difficulty sleeping, memory problems, irritability, depression, anxiety, difficulty concentrating, and decreased performance. Treatment for SOES typically includes counseling, psychotherapy, stress management techniques, medication, and lifestyle changes.

Combatting Combat Fatigue

For many people, the first thought on combatting burnout is to slow down and take time off work. But for SOF folks, being that they're usually very driven, Type A people, that's not always going to resonate with them. In fact, just lounging around could cause an operator a lot of stress. They don't want to just sit around. It makes them feel as though they're wasting time. They need to feel useful and productive in some way at all times.

What I normally recommend is for them to redirect their energy. If they're dealing with exhaustion syndrome from their job, I work with them on alternative activities during whatever free time they have, and I have them set up a new routine or hobby. Often, I will suggest doing physical activities, especially outside, whether it's swimming, kayaking, archery, or even metal detecting. It all depends on the person. I feed off of the individual and what likes and dislikes they express, and I try to get them planning and scheduling activities that will be a healthy outlet for them.

A lot of SOF personnel enjoy weapons, so I might encourage them to look into a local gun or archery club. I might also encourage them to get out jogging or hunting deer or hiking mountains or whatever, as long as it's not work and especially if it's something they used to do. We as clinicians know the benefits of being in nature, and a lot of SOF members already enjoy outdoor physical activities; it was part of the draw to the military. Getting outdoors, doing fun activities for themselves without the stress of work, is one of the many things that can get them out of their autopilot exhaustion.

When an individual is dealing with exhaustion syndrome, their brain isn't working at full capacity. Their mind tends to glaze over, and they're just going through the muscle memory and routine of their work and home life. I try to break them out of that shell and switch it up, change their direction, and get them engaged in a non-work activity. This then gives their brain the reset it needs, because their focus has shifted.

Myth of Uniqueness

When you have a SOF client sitting before you, it will become apparent that these individuals are inundated with the myth of uniqueness, as discussed in Chapter 2. For example, some of my past Naval Special Warfare (NSW/SEAL) clients shared a common mythos. They have multiple sayings that they live by, such as "Quitters never win and winners never quit" and "We are rooting, tooting, shooting, looting, double-cap crimping frogmen, no sea too deep, no sky too high, and no muff too tough." It's true that these individuals are unique in many ways and served in elite units. But their myth of uniqueness can make it harder for them to understand why they're dealing with "regular" life problems and how to cope with those issues. That's where those mental health metaphors come in handy, to bring them back down to earth and realize that they need a checkup every once in a while, just like their car or their weapon.

They must realize that while they have years of training and experience being a SOF operator, they probably don't have much (if any) training or proficiency in marriage, parenting, familial communication, going through the Twelve Step program, or whatever the case may be.

Yet, while they may not be invincible, the strengths that allowed them to become a SOF operator can be used in other ways. A good clinician will help them see how they can apply the lessons and skills they learned as operators to other areas of their life and help them solve their problems with the healthy coping mechanisms they already have.

Incident Envy

Incident envy, also known as "compare and despair," refers to the tendency to compare oneself unfavorably to others and to feel envious or resentful of their successes or achievements, as mentioned in Chapter 2.

During my experience working with SOF members in therapy, I've seen incident envy quite a bit, because everybody in SOF is an alpha trying to be the best. When one individual has "only" two deployments, and another individual has seven deployments, but the two-deployment person is having problems, they compare themselves to the operator who has seven deployments who looks like they're doing just fine. Of course, they don't actually know how that person is doing, but they think that person isn't affected by anything. It's a sense of, "Why am I screwed up? Why am I having these problems? Why do I have to see a therapist? What's wrong with me?" Some of these folks have done more in a few years than most humans will ever do in a lifetime. But they judge themselves against their peers.

As mentioned, it's important to remind them that they're human. They're putting themselves in harm's way on a regular basis, deploying at a moment's notice to who-knows-where, and seeing others in difficult situations. These experiences, if not processed appropriately and in a timely manner, can manifest themselves in other ways. And just because they don't *see* other SOF members suffering doesn't mean they're not, or that they haven't had issues in the past or won't have issues in the future. And the more they know now, the more they can also help their teammates in the future, though that comes after the healing process.

Of course, each person is unique, with their own set of values and experiences. So even when a SOF member compares their situation to other SOF members, they still need to understand how their experiences correlate to their own beliefs and background, which, in turn, can help them understand why they're having issues and how to overcome them.

Other ways you can help SOF clients experiencing incident envy may include having them set realistic goals and expectations, plan a healthy path to self-improvement and a new sense of purpose, practice gratitude, focus on their own strengths and accomplishments, and seek support from friends and family.

Hypervigilance

Maintaining high levels of vigilance can be demanding and can lead to mental and physical fatigue over time. Hypervigilance is a normal response to stress and danger, but it can also be debilitating and can interfere with a SOF member's ability to function in daily life. A key in distinguishing between vigilance and hypervigilance is simply acknowledging this dynamic.

Some of the symptoms of hypervigilance include the following: excessive awareness of surroundings; constant scanning of their environment for possible threats; reacting strongly to sudden noises or movements; difficulty sleeping or restless sleep due to nightmares or flashbacks; strong feelings of anxiety or unease in crowded or unfamiliar places; and increased heart rate or sweating in response to triggers or reminders of combat experiences.

Some treatments that can help SOF members regain a sense of normalcy and reduce symptoms include therapy, medication,

EMDR, and cognitive-behavioral techniques that assist SOF members in managing anxiety and reactions to triggers. Recently, many SOF veterans have also benefited from psychedelic-assisted therapy, though most psychedelics are not legally available for treatment yet in the United States.

Panic Disorder

Similar to hypervigilance but even more serious is panic disorder. Panic disorder is characterized by sudden and repeated episodes of intense fear or discomfort, known as panic attacks, which can include symptoms such as heart palpitations, chest pain, shortness of breath, dizziness, and feelings of unreality or detachment. It's not uncommon for individuals with panic disorder to also develop intense anxiety about when the next attack will occur, which can lead to avoidance of certain situations or environments.

I don't see panic disorder very often in SOF clients, but there are some combat-related stressors that can carry over into civilian life, which can cause a veteran to have panic attacks. For instance, veterans often find it difficult to be around large groups of people. When in the military, and especially in a SOF unit and/or combat operations, service members become accustomed to being around the same group of people for months or years at a time. Any time they venture out in a combat situation, any person they see is a potential enemy and could be a deadly threat. This makes returning to the civilian world a challenge, because suddenly they're around a bunch of strangers. They don't have their team, they don't have their weapon or protective gear, and they don't know who is around them.

Those with combat experience tend to avoid crowds for other reasons as well. There is a sense of a lack of mission and a lack of order to daily civilian life that's unsettling. Americans and Westerners have the luxury of an easy lifestyle when compared to those living in poverty and war-torn countries, and also when compared to the military—especially SOF—which can be an isolating and frustrating experience.

Many veterans find it easier to be alone or with close family and friends rather than go out and socialize a lot. Part of this also has to do with the fact that once someone has served, especially in combat, it's very hard for others to understand what they've been through, and it's even harder for those veterans to explain it. This is even more true with SOF veterans who often operate in complete secrecy.

Trusting civilians can also cause panic when a SOF client doesn't want to share their innermost thoughts or problems, even to their therapist. Once, I had a client who panicked after he told me his introductory story, because he suddenly felt he had shared too much too soon, and he felt really vulnerable. Most clients don't want to divulge everything and be totally transparent right away, which is understandable. Especially because, even though we're clinicians, we are also strangers. We're certainly not like their "band of brothers" they served with.

In this particular case, I felt it was appropriate to put some skin in the game and self-disclose a bit of my history with the client. This was just what he needed to feel more comfortable working with me. As our sessions went on, he became less concerned with how much he had said and focused more on the issues.

Treatment for panic disorder typically involves psychotherapy, medication, or a combination of both. CBT is particularly effective for panic disorder, as it helps individuals understand and manage their fears. Stress reduction techniques such as mindfulness, meditation, and relaxation exercises can also be beneficial in managing anxiety and reducing the frequency or intensity of panic attacks. Regular physical activity can help in managing overall stress and anxiety levels, which can also reduce the occurrence of panic attacks. And it's important that the SOF client has, or finds/creates, a supportive environment and/or network where they feel safe.

Perfectionism

Excessive perfectionism can lead to a range of negative feelings, such as inadequacy and self-doubt, anxiety, and depression, as well as physical health problems such as sleep disturbances, digestive problems, and headaches. It can also hinder an individual's ability to form and maintain healthy relationships, as it can lead to a tendency to be overly critical of themselves and others.

Obviously, SOF members strive for perfection in all that they do. One mistake in their profession can lead to death and/or mission failure. Therefore, it's important for SOF members to recognize when perfectionism is negatively affecting their daily life and take steps to manage it in a healthy way. It may also help them to understand that perfectionism is not as common in civilian life, that situations are often not as life-threatening, and that civilians may not understand or be accustomed to the need for such a high level of perfection. This is not necessarily better or worse than SOF; it's just different.

Treatments may include setting more realistic goals, practicing self-compassion and self-acceptance, and seeking support from friends and family. It may also be helpful to engage in activities that can reduce stress and promote balance, such as exercise, relaxation techniques, and hobbies.

Emotional Detachment

You may run across some SOF members who have become cynical, numb, or emotionally detached. Their job requires them to make quick decisions in chaotic and dangerous environments and to sometimes use deadly force to eliminate serious threats and neutralize enemies. Over time, this can create emotional detachment. This may make it harder for the individual to deal with and process difficult or traumatic memories. It can also negatively affect the operator's personal life, family life, and work life, as they may be less able to connect with others. This often turns into isolation, which then often turns into substance use, depression, and other maladaptive behaviors.

Keep in mind that emotional detachment does not mean an individual is antisocial. Generally, SOF combat units are oozing with alpha masculinity, but in a good way—they are made up of individuals who strive to be the best, work together as a team, and want to right the wrongs of the world. However, this can mean there's little tolerance for operators who have a mental issue. While not every unit or leader may react negatively toward a person who appears overtly upset or nervous, and hopefully instead will render support and try to figure out what's going on, there is a risk of a lot of stigma against an operator who's not mentally at 100 percent, especially if they're a leader. At the very least, the operator would fear being taken "out of the fight" and put on leave, which is the last thing they want. Weakness is not tolerated, and a SOF operator is hardest on himself.

I've seen emotional detachment affect how individuals compartmentalize traumatic incidents. If one of their teammates was killed or injured, or they accidentally bombed civilians who were with the enemy target, it can start to become a numbers game. It's just numbers, a part of their job. They're numb to it. They don't feel either way about it, good or bad. They are completely turned on mentally and physically, doing what they have to do, but there's no real emotional attachment during operational events. This then starts to affect the rest of their life outside of work, because if part of their emotional brain is numb, it tends to stay numb and keep those emotions locked away so the operator can keep operating.

The best way I've found to reach a SOF member who is emotionally detached and to get them to open up is to first and foremost establish some type of trust. Without trust, you have nothing. But if you're open and honest with them, and show your expertise and confidence without a know-it-all attitude, and show them you really want to understand them and help, maybe a little bit of what they're dealing with will come out.

When I run across someone who is detached, I try to establish some rapport and get them to open up, even if just a little. Sometimes the fact I'm a veteran establishes a connection between us and shows that I have some cultural competency. But whatever it is, if I can get them talking, maybe they'll start ranting, and I'll let that person get it out for a little while. For me, a little bit of their honesty is all I need. Once I have an idea of what they're dealing with, I can pick that out and hold on to it. When they're done, I circle back and talk about the things that came out.

For emotional detachment or a SOF member you're having trouble connecting with, it's best to start with very small activities. You might have to start in the office as opposed to giving them homework. Since SOF members may be dealing with serious trauma or other issues like addiction, and because they may not have had much experience in therapy before, having them leave a session and suddenly do a bunch of scary shit on their own without a therapist present can be very unhealthy.

I usually start in the office and just take tiny baby steps exploring what things in that operator's life matter to them. What matters to them are what I call "hooks." Hooks are things the individual cares about that you can utilize in therapy to get them to open up and talk more, or to get them motivated to do better. Usually, if they have a family, their hook is their family. They may not be treating their family the best, but it's still the most important thing to them (in addition to their career as a SOF member). If that's their hook, you can work with them on what will help them be a better parent or spouse.

Instead of focusing on what may happen to the individual if they don't change their behavior or actions, I focus on what's best for their family or what will happen to their kid without a solid parent in their child's life, for example. That often changes their perspective and gets them motivated.

Guilt & Shame

Guilt and shame are very common emotions when things go wrong, especially for SOF members because of their perfectionism. They really pride themselves on being the best—having the best intelligence, the highest skill sets, and undertaking missions at the "tip of the spear." So, when something really bad happens—say, a team member dies or innocent people are killed—it's a hard pill for those folks to swallow.

For example, a mortarman in the regular military might say they "chew dirt" and blow everything up using phrases like "Kill 'em all and let God sort 'em out." That's not what Special Forces do.

SOF members are the opposite of that approach. They're the scalpel, not the chainsaw. They pride themselves on being able to accomplish the mission unseen and unheard. They don't go in shooting everybody and dropping bombs unless something bad happens. And it's when something bad happens that you can get all kinds of trauma.

Everyone on a SOF team has a role to play and an important job to do. Almost everyone is a leader in some way, even if they're not an officer or a higher rank. They're in charge of certain equipment, or personnel, or a certain aspect of the mission. So, when something goes wrong, there's a chance that team member feels personally responsible. Furthermore, if a SOF member gets injured and has to leave a mission, unit, or even military service altogether, there may be feelings of guilt and/or shame that they had to leave while others carried on.

No one is perfect and mistakes happen, and often things happen that are outside of their control, especially in combat or during high-intense training. But SOF members take a lot of pride in being operational with a SOF combat unit. Once there, anything that takes an operator away from their team can cause a lot of guilt and shame, as well as survivor's guilt and anger, as discussed next.

Survivor's Guilt

Survivor's guilt (or survivor guilt) is another common issue that veterans deal with. The US Department of Veterans Affairs (2025b) says that "some Veterans feel guilt or remorse because of something that happened in their military experience, such as an injury to a buddy in their unit, friendly fire, or civilian deaths. Survivor guilt can include feeling guilty about surviving when others did not, wishing that you had died instead of others, or thinking you didn't deserve to survive."

Similar to feelings of guilt or shame, survivor's guilt can take a toll on the veteran and cause other issues such as stress, anxiety, and depression. The veteran may feel responsible for the negative situation they experienced or witnessed, and they may even feel unworthy to be alive. A common feeling many veterans have is, "It should have been me. I shouldn't be here."

Survivor's guilt often follows a veteran home, sometimes resulting in PTSD that makes it almost impossible to live a normal, healthy life. Veterans may deal with nightmares and/or flashbacks where they relive the traumatic event that resulted in their fellow service members losing their lives.

Probably the biggest example of this in SOF is retired Navy SEAL Marcus Luttrell. His story became widely known after he wrote the book *Lone Survivor*, which was turned into a movie of the same name. As part of Operation Red Wings, a four-man reconnaissance and surveillance group from SEAL Team 10 were inserted near a Taliban militia group in Afghanistan in 2005. They were compromised by some locals and retreated to a fallback position, where they were soon attacked. Luttrell was the only one who survived. Unconscious and seriously injured, he was rescued by a local who took him into hiding.

A rescue mission was organized with other members of SEAL Team 10, Marines, and 160th SOAR aviators. As several helicopters approached, one of them (an MH-47 Chinook special operations aircraft) was hit with an RPG-7 rocket-propelled grenade. All eight 160th SOAR aviators and all eight Navy SEALs on board were killed. Bad weather forced the rest of the helicopters to abandon the mission. Other rescue missions followed, until Air Force Pararescuemen (PJs) were finally able to recover Luttrell and the bodies of the rest of the teams. So, not only did Luttrell's team die, but more SOF operators also died trying to rescue him. That can put an amazing amount of strain and stress on someone.

Luttrell was medically retired from the Navy and deals with physical and psychological wounds still today:

Marcus Luttrell says part of himself died on the Afghanistan mountain where his three Navy SEAL teammates perished. Each year during the June anniversary of Operation Red Wings, Luttrell goes on a "blackout week" where he doesn't communicate with the world. "It's a mourning period that whole week," says his wife. "It just feels wrong to continue with everyday life that week. So he stops, reflects, prays and pays his respects to the guys that died that day and the families they left." (Alexander 2013)

Luttrell himself talked about some of his healing process in an interview with *Men's Journal* (Sullivan 2018):

My wife, Melanie, helped me step back and say, "I'm not a SEAL anymore." I had to learn how to calm down and let myself heal. We bought a 200-acre ranch in Texas a few years ago, and nowadays chopping trees, mending fences, and walking the property is a big part of my workout . . . I don't try to be perfect at anything anymore, especially when it comes to my body. I've seen what that can do. You'll drive yourself crazy and miss out on a whole lot of life.

It's incredibly difficult to move on when others can't. Similar to a parent who loses a child, a veteran often feels like losing one of their teammates is like losing a family member, and they often feel somehow responsible. Therefore, similar to any client dealing with a traumatic, sudden death of a loved one, it's important to help SOF clients gain perspective, navigate their grief, and find new ways to live full, meaningful lives.

Anger & Irritability

SOF members may become angry when they feel threatened, harmed, or powerless. Some veterans are more likely to feel anger in everyday situations because of a traumatic event from past military experience, such as combat, physical or sexual abuse, injury, or the loss of a team member. Others may experience anger because of the cumulative stress of such life events, either personal or professional, and sometimes a combination of both (US Department of Veterans Affairs, 2024a). Additionally, some veterans, especially SOF veterans, may deal with anger issues after years of intense training and back-to-back deployments, especially when dealing with home or family issues or when trying to adjust to civilian life after service.

When someone is accustomed to the regimented lifestyle, camaraderie, and other aspects of military culture, dealing with civilians who have completely different ways of operating can cause frustration and anger on the part of the SOF member, especially when compounded by stressors and mental health issues.

A recent study found that increased anger and decreased ability to control its expression "is a common and serious problem in veterans who have served in a warzone," no matter what war or era they served in (Shea et al. 2021, 274). Sixty-seven percent of Army soldiers and 57 percent of combat veterans receiving VA medical care said they had problems with anger and aggression following a deployment. A sizable number specifically reported acts of aggression, including threats of, and actual, physical violence. Some "consequences of anger and aggression in veterans include marital problems and divorce, parenting problems, domestic violence, and job instability . . . as well as increased suicidal ideation . . . and poorer response to treatment for posttraumatic stress disorder (PTSD)" (Shea et al. 2021, 274–275).

Several explanations for the frequency of anger and aggression in combat veterans were proposed: hyperarousal symptoms (i.e., hypervigilance), which are common in combat veterans both with and without PTSD; military training that focuses on aggression as a means of survival in combat experiences; and the fight or flight "survival mode," which preempts all other cognitive processing. The fight or flight mode results in an impaired ability to regulate responses to threats, as well as excessive anger and aggression in situations perceived as threatening, even where there is no real threat (Shea et al. 2021, 275).

Unfortunately, the study found that there are no clear guidelines for treating anger and aggression in veterans, especially as some may have PTSD while others do not. The researchers suggested that more controlled studies of treatments in veterans should be conducted. However, the researchers concluded that "CBI [cognitive behavioral intervention] is an effective treatment for OEF [Operation Enduring Freedom]/OIF [Operation Iraqi Freedom]/OND [Operation New Dawn] veterans with anger problems following deployment, regardless of PTSD diagnosis" (Shea et al. 2021, 274).

Other treatments can include helping the client identify their triggers and warning signs, teaching relaxation techniques and mindfulness, helping them channel their anger to positive endeavors as opposed to dwelling on past situations, restructuring negative thoughts and all-or-nothing thinking, teaching various coping skills, and improving communication skills.

Due to the sensitive nature of therapy, especially for someone dealing with anger and irritability, this is where I suggest taking into account the uniqueness of your client. Try to determine what will work best for them, ensuring they understand you're willing to be flexible and adjust based on their feedback. This willingness to meet your client where they are and listen to their concerns will help gain essential trust and make the therapy sessions more productive for both of you.

8. TRAUMA PTSD & TBI

The great events in our lives are physical. Childbirth. Sex. Combat. Death. Not poetry, or music, or the thoughts of great men will flash across the transom of our minds at the moment of dying. We will remember only the moments when we felt the fibers of our body sing. Bloodily. Messily. Ecstatically.

—Natasha Mostert

T he presenting problems discussed in this chapter are often overlooked and therefore misdiagnosed. This is especially true for traumatic brain injury (TBI), which shares many symptoms with other problems like post-traumatic stress disorder (PTSD) but must be treated differently.

Many clinicians may not ever deal with TBI, severe PTSD, or suicidal ideation in their practice. But when you deal with combat veterans and first responders, you're more than likely going to see those issues. It's important not to overreact and prescribe some outside intervention such as medication, residential treatment, or involuntary commitment right away. In fact, it's common for any human who has dealt with extreme stress and traumatic events to have these issues.

159

Importance of Accurate Diagnoses

It hurts when I hear about a SOF member who finally mustered up enough courage to ask for help, and the first clinician they see just throws out a PTSD diagnosis so they get paid without truly understanding what the client is dealing with. This also means the clinician has no understanding of how a diagnosis could end up on their client's employer insurance records, hurting their ability to keep a job. Most importantly, it shows that the clinician didn't understand—or didn't care—that the treatments and prescribed medicines could end up doing much more harm than good and even cost that veteran their life.

I wish our medical system didn't require a diagnosis for people to get mental health care, which would greatly decrease a major stigma and barrier to getting help, especially for SOF members. But since this is not the case (for now), I simply ask that you read this book, do your homework, and get to know your clients before putting any labels on them. I know most therapists are overworked and underpaid, and unfortunately, insurance companies are not easy to work with. But you must avoid diagnosing someone just to start a payment process.

This is especially important if a client is seeing you as part of an employer-based insurance plan or due to an employer- or court-ordered assessment. A PTSD or other diagnosis can put them at risk of losing their security clearance, a promotion, or even their job. Plus, the emotional stigma of being tagged as someone who has a mental illness can further aggravate a client's unwillingness to open up or seek help.

A diagnosis on an individual's employee or legal record stays with them for the rest of their life. It doesn't go away. I've suggested to some clients not to go through their EAP program or workers' comp, because they will get tagged with a diagnosis that they will then have to declare on every job application from then on. I often recommend they go outside of their network and pay out of pocket, because then they can get help and not have to worry that the treatment is recorded in their employee file. Unless they're too mentally ill to work, which is rare, having a permanent label and losing their paycheck can do a lot more harm than good.

I also give SOF clients a list of resources available for this specific group of individuals, many of which are listed in Appendix II. I also make sure I know local clinicians and resources who can help these types of clients, because just like with cops, if they go to the wrong person and don't get the right help, they may think there's no one who can help and they will never go back. Just reaching out and talking to someone is such a hard thing for a lot of them to do.

Rather than only looking at the symptoms, ensure you understand what your client has been through, narrow down the possible causes, and if necessary, suggest other types of tests, such as a sleep study or neuropsych evaluation, to ensure you know what's going on so you can make an accurate diagnosis if needed. Of course, some people may require a more specific diagnosis if they're a danger to themselves or others or if they need more serious care. But in general, we shouldn't be considered mentally handicapped just because we had a duration of depression, especially given situations like divorce, combat, transitioning to civilian life, and so forth. All of that can be easily explained.

Traumatic Brain Injury

Traumatic brain injury (TBI) is surprisingly common in SOF members and, as we're learning, it's more common in sports and other activities than we previously realized. We often use the term "concussion." Athletes use the terminology CTE (chronic traumatic encephalopathy). No matter what it's called, it's the same thing. Doctors refer to any bump, blow, or jolt to the head that disrupts normal brain function as a TBI. That term encompasses everything from a sports collision that benches a youngster for a few games to severe head trauma requiring hospitalization and rehab (El Camino Health 2023).

The Cleveland Clinic (2024) says that TBIs are a leading cause of disability and death in the United States. Signs of a TBI include the following: behavior or mood changes; confusion or memory problems;

convulsions or seizures; dilated pupils or blurred vision; dizziness, fainting, or fatigue; headaches; nausea and vomiting; restlessness or agitation; sensitivity to light and smell; sleeping too much or too little; and slurred speech.

According to Garner (2018, 62), "the Defense and Veterans Brain Injury Center (DVBIC) report that since 2000, there have been 333,169 service members diagnosed with a TBI . . . [Another study] found that approximately 22% of all OEF/OIF military personnel have suffered a TBI."

Many combat veterans were exposed to tremendous blast waves from improvised explosive devices (IEDs), vehicle-borne improvised explosive devices (VBIEDs), mortars, rocket-propelled grenades (RPGs) and AT4s (anti-tank launchers), hand grenades, breaching charges, howitzers, and more. SOF members are especially at risk because they routinely use explosives to do their job. During operations, they often need to breach a door or wall, remove an obstacle, destroy mines, or throw grenades—and they train for these scenarios over and over again. Even repeated, small blasts have effects over time. SOF members don't need to be in the military very long or deploy much to suffer from TBI. Depending on their SOF MOS (military occupational specialty), they may have had several concussive events in a very short amount of time.

If someone is the breacher on a team, or even one of the individuals on a "stack" behind the breacher who is fifteen feet away from a C-4 charge, they will still get those blast waves. Those teams may retrain with explosives three or four times a day. That's not including when someone encounters an IED blast during combat, for example.

A lot of SOF members go undiagnosed with TBI because they don't know the physical effects of what they've been through, and because clinicians often forget to think about physical injuries and focus only on mental and emotional problems.

One of the ways I rule out TBI, or any issue, is by asking certain questions. First, I want to know if they're dealing with a personal/

home problem or a professional/work/military problem. Those things can overlap, but it gives me a starting point to better understand the core issue. If their problems seem to be caused by their military service, I'll try to find out about their military job and experience, if they were exposed to explosives (outgoing or incoming), or if they had any concussions. If they were in Special Forces, or if they were around explosives or large weapon systems like howitzers, I know TBI may be an issue. Then I can determine if they have the right symptoms for TBI, and if so, I'll refer them to a neurologist for further testing.

As a good therapist, it's important to know where a client could go to get a neuropsych evaluation or visit a neurologist who specializes in TBI, and how that facility works with the VA or clients who may not have insurance. Those tests can be costly, but they can save the client's life.

Regular therapy will not work on TBI. TBI needs to be dealt with neurologically, and newer therapies like electroconvulsive therapy (ECT) and psychedelic therapy have been shown to be beneficial.

The effects of TBI can be catastrophic, because it's not anything the person can control or get away from. It's twenty-four hours a day, seven days a week, 365 days a year. It's probably one of the most common reasons SOF members become suicidal. But there are operators who have found ways to thrive in life with TBI—so long as they get the proper diagnosis and treatment.

TBI vs. PTSD

Many TBI symptoms can mimic or overlap with PTSD, such as fatigue, irritability, night terrors/insomnia, difficulty concentrating, headaches, vision impairment, loss of balance, difficulties with memory, depression, anger, and irritability. Symptom checklists, neuropsychological testing, and computerized brain scans may help determine an exact diagnosis.

If a client is suffering from PTSD, they'll be upset about their marriage or their job, or they'll have recurring thoughts of situations in combat—something tangible you can usually identify. But TBI sufferers don't understand why they're having fits of rage or lucid horror dreams several times a week. The symptoms are random. They could be in the middle of the grocery store and have a full-on rage, ready to physically fight another patron because they were standing too close to them in the milk aisle. Sometimes during a rage, they will destroy property or vehicles. TBI sufferers often have relationship issues where they return from a deployment and everything seems fine, then out of nowhere, they start beating their spouse or threatening to kill people.

Of course, some SOF members may be experiencing both PTSD and TBI at the same time. So, it's important to dig a little deeper and find out if that person was ever around blast waves from any type of explosive weapons or if they experienced incoming rocket blasts or IED blasts in close proximity.

For example, I was in combat aviation, so you wouldn't think I would have any exposure to that. However, our FOB (forward operating base) got hit by FROG missiles on a routine basis. While taking cover inside the sandbag bunkers, I could feel the blast waves ripple through my body and heart. Everybody on the base was exposed to that, no matter their job.

Unfortunately, TBI symptoms are usually out of the person's control. They can't talk themselves out of them or do deep breathing techniques. TBI just comes and goes, and when it comes, sometimes it completely takes over. So, it's important that TBI is properly diagnosed so the client gets the help they need as soon as possible.

Treatment for TBI is covered throughout Part IV (Chapters 11–14).

Past Abuse

Abuse within SOF units is not something I've encountered with my clients. I've seen clients from the regular military who experienced sexual harassment and sexual assault, and other types of harassment or abuse. But in SOF combat units, this seems to be rare. Perhaps that's because once those service members get to that level and work on those small teams, there is a level of camaraderie and trust that generally prevents those other problems.

In one case, a woman in the regular military was sexually assaulted by her superior. Because he was her superior, she pushed it down in the "psychological trash compactor" and kept going as if nothing had happened. Of course, it blew up later in life, which was why she was being seen. But that term adequately describes how people in general deal with extremely distressing experiences like child abuse or sexual assault. They can't handle it at the time, so it goes in the psychological trash compactor but never really gets thrown away. It's compacted, down in the psyche somewhere, and eventually, it starts to stink and cause problems and has to be dealt with.

Past abuse is what I've seen most from SOF clients. Past child and domestic abuse is not necessarily related to a client's military service, but I've been surprised at how often it has come up in sessions with SOF members. I wouldn't say it comes up very often, but when it does, I'm shocked because I'm usually the first person they've ever told. Since so many SOF members have generally not done much regular mental health therapy and only do so when they feel they have no choice, those sessions can bring out a lot of stuff they've never dealt with or mentioned to anyone before.

I've had decorated combat veterans, almost all men, tell me that a babysitter or a family member fondled them or that they experienced sexual assault, that an uncle sexually abused them for years starting when they were thirteen years old, or whatever the case may be. For them, it's usually those earlier situations in life that tend to manifest into problems later as an adult. And the perpetrator is usually a family member, because family members have easy access and are usually trusted. And if the child does say something about it, they aren't always believed.

A lot of times, this is the reason folks go into the military, Special Forces, or law enforcement: They don't want to feel helpless. When someone goes through a difficult and traumatic childhood, it can be a catalyst for them to overcome incredible odds later in life. They push themselves extra hard to ensure they get out of their situation and never go back, and to protect others from the same. It often gives them a deep desire to make the world a better place and right the wrongs they witnessed and experienced when they were young. At the same time, they have built up an incredible tolerance of hardship and a resilience that allows them to excel.

Even so, child abuse is obviously incredibly difficult to deal with. I wish I knew the perfect answer for how to help these clients, but I don't think there is one, though there are plenty of other books and materials specifically about that topic. My advice is to do your best not to overreact and not to overdramatize it. A pity party is the last thing they want. At this point, this person has not only lived through it, but they've also gone on to have a career and often a family of their own, and they've accomplished a lot. The best method I've found is to focus on the positive—the fact that they survived and were able to make a good life for themselves and for others. A lot of these folks are wonderful parents and would never do anything that was done to them. In a way, their desire to make the world a better place was something they achieved, and I get them to focus on that.

Trauma in SOF

> Many medical diagnoses such as TBI are often accompanied with trauma-related symptoms and depression. Therefore, it is imperative that military personnel are receiving a holistic, trauma-informed approach to treatment and not just treating one thing at a time . . . Healing both the physical and emotional wounds from war can have a drastic impact on both the individual and the military.
>
> —Jessica D. Garner (2018, 65)

SOF members may experience various types of trauma during their service, including combat-related trauma, physical injury, and other traumatic events that can cause long-term psychological and physical effects. Combat-related trauma, such as seeing a fellow operator killed or severely injured, losing a limb or experiencing other personal injuries, and exposure to enemy fire or explosions, can leave visible and invisible wounds. These traumatic experiences can cause flashbacks, nightmares, and hyperarousal, leading to PTSD, depression, and anxiety.

Lt. Col. Dave Grossman expertly analyzes the psychological cost of killing other human beings in his book *On Killing*. However, there are some differences I've seen between SOF members and other combat vets, the main one being the trauma around killing itself.

Most SOF operators I've seen as a clinician are not bothered by what they've done in combat. Because SOF units operate at a precise level, they generally have more specific missions and targets than the regular military. For instance, they had to kill or capture a high-level al-Qaeda or ISIS operative, or they had to kill insurgents (i.e., known combatants) who were holding fellow service members hostage. For them, when "dealing" with a target or an adversary, that's their job. They don't feel bad about those things. If anything, they're glad they could rid the world of terrorists who are actively killing Americans and allies.

Possibly because SOF kills are easier to rationalize, they are not as traumatizing for SOF members. Their ultrarealistic and constant training also plays a role in their ability to execute their missions without hesitation. As stated, most SOF members have a strong desire to make the world a better place, and they do that by strategically getting rid of bad guys. That's not to say some SOF members don't have regrets later on, especially if their combat situations and memories are more complex.

Trauma that occurs more often for SOF members is when things didn't go according to plan—when a team member was killed, or they inadvertently killed civilians (noncombatants), or they were unable to rescue other service members, or when they're having trouble in their home/personal life and it starts affecting the rest of their life and they no longer feel in control.

Grossman (2009, 52) writes that studies "indicate that fear of death and injury is not the primary cause of psychiatric casualties on the battle-field . . . it is instead the fear of not being able to meet the terrible obligations of combat that weighs more heavily on the minds of combat soldiers."

While they were in special operations doing all these amazing things around the world, they could also have collected a lot of demons, or as I like to put it, collected rocks in their rucksack. Maybe they already have a demon of abuse from childhood. Then, if in combat they accidentally kill a child or see torture, those would be the big rocks. Then, if they can't get a job after service or their spouse is threatening to leave, those are more rocks. And you can only carry so much weight. Certainly, SOF members are able to carry much more weight than most people, but at some point, their rucksack is going to overflow, and that's usually when they fall apart and have a hard time functioning.

Post-Traumatic Stress Disorder (PTSD)

Maybe PTSD really is triggered by a single incident, a stressor, as it's known in the psychiatric community, and maybe the attack at Al-Waleed was that stressor for me, but as I have learned in the intervening years, I was not damaged by that moment alone. In fact, while there are specific memories that resurface with some frequency, like the suicide bomber in Sinjar or the order riot at Al-Waleed, I find myself most traumatized by the overall experience of being in a combat zone like Iraq, where you are always surrounded by war but rarely aware of when or how violence will arrive. Like so many of my fellow veterans, I understand now that it is the daily adrenaline rush of a war without front lines or uniforms, rather than the infrequent bursts of bloody violence, that ultimately damages the modern warrior's mind.

—Luis Carlos Montalván, author of *Until Tuesday: A Wounded Warrior and the Golden Retriever Who Saved Him*

When reading this quote from Montalván, it becomes apparent that many psychological problems can be caused by prolonged exposure to war for those with lengthy or multiple tours in combat rather than just one traumatic incident, though certain incidents also play a destructive role on an individual's psyche.

PTSD has long been a common diagnosis for veterans who saw combat or who lost fellow service members during training or service. PTSD causes veterans to endure intense flashbacks, nightmares, and other uncontrollable, disturbing thoughts and emotions related to the trauma they experienced that make the sufferer feel as though they are experiencing the event all over again. While some of these intense memories, thoughts, and emotions occur without an obvious trigger, certain people, situations, sounds, sights, and smells can trigger them as well.

According to the Veterans Help Group (2024), some common triggers include:

- Television shows related to their trauma, war, or other similar traumatic events
- Certain conversation topics
- Disputes or anger, often unrelated to the trauma
- Crowded events or areas, such as large social events, games, or concerts
- Noises, especially those that remind them of the trauma
- Unexpected or unwanted touches

Aside from reliving traumatic events and painful memories, DAV (2024) asserts that other symptoms of PTSD can include:

- Avoidance of situations and conversations that remind them of the event, as well as avoidance of overstimulating experiences like crowded places

- Overwhelming and persistent negative emotions such as guilt, shame, and remorse
- Difficulty establishing trust
- Disinterest in previously enjoyable activities or difficulty feeling happy
- Hypervigilance (hyperarousal) when the sufferer is constantly on alert and uneasy in unfamiliar situations or finds it difficult to sleep or relax
- Anger or irritability
- Alcohol or substance abuse as a coping mechanism

It's important to understand the symptoms related to your client's PTSD and what the root causes are in order to provide adequate care. Remember that everyone is different, that PTSD symptoms can be similar to other issues like TBI, and that PTSD can co-occur with other problems.

9. MORAL INJURY & SUICIDE

How do professional problem-solvers become so over-whelmed by their own problems that hopelessness and sui-cide is a daily state of mind?

—Unknown

This chapter covers some of the psychological wounds elite warriors deal with that many clinicians may not be as familiar or experienced with: organizational betrayal, moral injury, religion in therapy, sleep issues, depression, and suicide.

Organizational Betrayal

Organizational betrayal refers to actions or behaviors within an organization that an employee perceives as being unethical, dishonest, or untrustworthy and that cause harm or distress to employees or other stakeholders. Organizational betrayal can take many forms, including unethical or illegal practices, discrimination or harassment, and violations of trust or confidentiality. If you imagine working in a company your whole career and get laid off right before you're eligible for retirement, that would be a civilian example of organizational betrayal.

Feelings of organizational betrayal and a lack of trust are some of the reasons why so many veterans don't want to go to the VA for help.

Organizational betrayal can also cause a distrust of authority in general, another reason why some people are reluctant to see a therapist or seek mental health care.

Organizational betrayal can cause loss of trust and credibility, decreased morale and motivation, and increased risk of legal and financial consequences for individuals and organizations. It can also lead to negative mental and physical health outcomes for individuals.

An example of this is when one of my friends, who is a clinician and former Navy SEAL, told me he had been caught taking performance-enhancing drugs and was discharged from the Navy. Even though performance-enhancing drugs are prohibited in the military, it's actually quite common in special operations for individuals to try and gain any competitive edge. They do whatever it takes to stay in the fight and not be the weak link. Everyone's trying to physically push themselves over their limits.

In this case, he said there was no effort from the command staff to retain him or rehabilitate him after the positive urinalysis. He was discharged, and nobody wanted to talk to him after that, which completely ruined his life. He felt so abandoned by his "brothers," a lone wolf out in the world, that he didn't know what to do. He started drinking heavily and eventually ended up passed out by himself somewhere down in Baja, Mexico, with no idea what had happened.

I also find organizational betrayal a lot with my law enforcement clients, because it seems you're either in or you're out. And if you're out, old buddies don't keep in touch. That's what happened to me after fourteen years in law enforcement. It felt like I was discarded, as though everything I had done and all the sacrifices I had made for the betterment of the organization and the population didn't mean anything anymore.

Another personal example is when I tried to apply for VA disability benefits. One of the reasons I applied was because I had been involved in a helicopter crash in Iraq. However, I was denied benefits, and not because I didn't meet the criteria. It was because they didn't have my paperwork. The Army's personnel command had somehow lost or destroyed countless service members' records. I got a letter saying my claim couldn't be processed because they didn't have some pertinent documentation from my active-duty personnel file. It pissed me off so much that I just gave up and moved on. It wasn't until many years later, with my wife's encouragement, that I went through the VA process again and was approved for 60 percent service-connected disability. A lot of veterans don't trust the VA because of situations like that, and then they miss out on opportunities for treatment and health benefits.

You can see the theme that organizational betrayal happens frequently when someone's career prematurely ends. Since special operations is a young man's profession, this happens a lot.

A way to combat feelings of organizational betrayal is to help the client see their experience as just one experience with just certain individuals that may not represent the whole organization or every experience or person with that organization. After all, organizations are made up of people, and people are imperfect. Other therapeutic techniques mentioned throughout this book can be helpful as well.

Moral Injury

Moral injury refers to the emotional, psychological, and spiritual distress that occurs when someone's deeply held ethical beliefs, values, or moral codes are violated, leading to what is often called a "soul wound." In special operations, this concept takes on a unique significance due to the nature of the job. Operators are regularly placed in situations where their actions, or lack thereof, may conflict with their personal morals.

For example, say a SOF team took heavy fire from a building and were pinned down, so a team member called in fire support. A five-hundred-pound JDAM (joint direct attack munition) bomb was dropped on the building and neutralized the threat. But later, locals brought the SOF team some children who had been in the area and were wounded in the blast. The team had to help those innocent casualties that they hadn't known were in the area. Anyone on the team could be shaken up by that, especially the member who called in the air strike, even though he did it to save his own team. Another example could be if an operator shoots an unarmed civilian in a high-stress situation, like mistaking a cell phone for a gun. The realization that they took an innocent life can lead to immense guilt and internal conflict, especially when reflecting on their oath to protect the oppressed. These are examples of action-based moral injury (or mistaken-action), because the client did something they feel was wrong.

Moral injury can also be caused by a failure to act—when the client did not do something they feel they should have done. Using the above example, say the locals came to the SOF team with injured children, but the team leader decided they didn't have time to help the children or that it was unsafe to stay in the area, and so he ordered the team to leave without helping. Later he wonders if this was the right decision and feels bad for not staying to help. Another example could be when an operator sees a colleague or leader doing something wrong but fails to speak up for fear of retaliation.

A third type of moral injury can happen when someone witnesses something they have no control over but the incident still injures their spirit. For example, if an operator sees the aftermath of a suicide bomber and has to wrestle with the fact that a terrorist killed and injured innocent people for no reason, and that messes with their idea of right and wrong. One of my clients said he teared up while watching a baby food commercial and he didn't know why. It turned out he was dealing with moral injury, because he had seen something bad happen to a child and it was coming up to haunt him later. Even though he didn't do anything to the child himself, he still witnessed it, and it affected him.

A fourth type of moral injury is betrayal, which is similar to (or can coincide with) organizational betrayal but could also be a personal betrayal. An example of this could be when an operator wants to help some injured children, but the team leader decides it's best to leave the area instead. The operator can feel betrayed by his team leader and the unit as a whole after witnessing others' actions or inactions that go against their personal and/or the unit's values, standards, and moral codes. Vietnam veterans often suffer from moral betrayal, for example if they were drafted into combat and forced by the military to do things they didn't want to do, or because of the public criticism and prejudice they received from society when they returned home. Both are examples of when another person, organization, or community has betrayed an individual's sense of trust or moral fabric.

Moral injury can be a complex and confusing experience that can have a profound impact on a person's mental and emotional well-being. Symptoms of moral injury may include feelings of guilt, shame, and self-condemnation; difficulty trusting others; strained relationships and isolation; burnout; reduced job performance; career dissatisfaction or early retirement; and difficulty finding meaning and purpose in life. Sometimes it also leads to the individual committing ethical violations, as repeated exposure to moral dilemmas can cause operators to "bend the rules" themselves and act unethically, contributing to further guilt and moral injury.

Strategies to help clients heal from moral injury include talk therapy and journaling, reframing the narrative, self-compassion and forgiveness, and building supportive connections. Peer support groups, faith communities, and programs like the All Secure Foundation, run by Tom and Jen Satterly, or the TARA Mind organization run, by Marcus Capone, can offer operators a space to share their experiences without judgment. This sense of belonging can be vital in the healing process.

Moral Injury vs. PTSD

The symptoms of moral injury and PTSD can overlap a lot, but in general they are caused by different issues. PTSD is caused by a stressor or multiple stressors that happened to the individual. Perhaps the person was involved in a car accident, was injured by an IED, or lost a battle buddy, and now they're dealing with the physical and psychological repercussions of those incidents.

Moral injury happens when someone experiences something that goes against their inner moral compass, whether it happened to them personally or not. There may be times a client is dealing with both from the same incident. For example, if a SOF operator lost a team member in a battle they fought in together, the operator could have PTSD from the battle itself and also have a moral injury from an aspect of the experience that they feel isn't right. Say their battle buddy was married with young children and should not have died in a just world, or they feel somehow responsible for their colleague's death. Regular encounters with violence, death, and suffering can take a toll.

It's important to listen carefully to know what the client is dealing with. It's easy to think, "This guy has seen dead bodies. He's been in combat. He has PTSD." But I know plenty of guys who killed over ten people and are perfectly fine with it. But one time, they had to call in fire support and bomb a target. When they sifted through the rubble, they saw teddy bears and children's shoes. They hadn't known there were children in the building. That wasn't supposed to happen. It's things like that they're dealing with, and that's moral injury.

Of course, everyone is different. Five people could be involved in the same incident or see the exact same thing, and two of them might develop PTSD or moral injury from it but the other three are fine. You never know. I always assume that if someone is reaching out to me for help, there's something wrong, and I want to accurately identify it as quickly as possible. Sometimes it is PTSD, but more often in my personal experience with SOF clients, it's moral injury, or it's all the bad stuff that an operator saw and dealt with throughout their career that builds up over time, not just one incident.

Religion in Therapy

> We [worked with an Iraqi family] for a month, and they never sold us out. So I asked them, "What do you need? Do you need money?" [The husband and wife] said, "Our kids

get really sick from all the dust from the dirt road. Do you think you could pave the road?" That's all they wanted . . . And in the end, I left them. After two of their kids were killed and half of their home was blown up . . . and I'm talking to the command, "We need to get these people out of here!" [Command said,] "Sergeant Reyes, it's not your problem. Return to base." [. . .] They were all eventually killed. Ah, the moral injury I got from that made me turn my back on God, made me turn my back on everything.

—Rudy Reyes (Lyon 2023)

The story above is an example of organizational betrayal, moral injury, and a crisis of faith, all at the same time. These things often go hand in hand.

Moral injury is an injury of the spirit—a tearing of the fabric that connects a person to their moral compass, their core values, and their idea of right versus wrong. And for many people, their religion is their moral compass.

In our training to become clinicians, we're often told not to touch religion, but that's not realistic. Religion will come up with some of your clients, especially when it pertains to moral injury. A lot of SOF operators are deeply religious. A key element to addressing a moral injury can be found in the individual's spirituality.

The other thing I heard a lot during school was "Fake it till you make it," which as I've said before, is also bad advice, especially when working with SOF members. If you don't know anything about someone's religion, don't act like you do, but don't brush off the topic either. Many SOF members have a religious background and believe in right and wrong in the world, so if this is an important topic to them and it's causing them distress, they will expect you to address it in some way.

One of my clients who had a Christian background told me he felt like a piece of shit and that God had already judged him for the things he'd done. That was a hard one for me. I'm not religious, so dealing with the spiritual has never been my strong suit. But I learned over time that religion and spirituality cannot be taboo topics, because some clients will need help in that area. While I'm not qualified as a religious leader, I have learned what to say and certainly what not to say when religion is brought up in session. My advice is to tread with caution and not be too forceful with any of your own opinions or beliefs, but don't be aloof either.

I've had people in my office flat out say, "I'm going to hell." Instead of pushing back and saying, "That's ridiculous," or "There's no such thing as hell," or "That's not true because God loves everyone," I say, "Okay, tell me more about that. Why do you think you're going to hell? What makes you believe that?" And then we can work on those beliefs from there.

While Special Forces operations are often supposed to be surgical, in-and-out, nobody-knew-they-were-there type missions, in counterterrorism and urban warfare environments, civilians are often casualties of war despite the precautions taken. And when innocent people are killed or injured, that can be hard for SOF members to deal with, because that's not supposed to happen. That can tear their connection to their moral compass. They may feel farther away from God, that they've sinned in some way and maybe can't be forgiven or won't be accepted into heaven. Their action, no matter the circumstances, caused a conflict within their psyche that they're unable to rationalize.

There is a lot of self-hatred involved with moral injury, which is why suicidal ideation is often very prevalent in these cases. Lessening that self-hatred is important. You're not going to sprinkle magic dust on a horrible situation your client had and make it good. But you can help that individual not beat themselves up for something they had little to no control over.

A lot of my SOF and law enforcement clients were beating the hell out of themselves before they came to see me or another therapist, either through substance abuse or alcoholism, torching every relationship they have, or not allowing themselves to be happy. Deep down, they felt they didn't deserve to feel good.

First, as delicately as possible, I try to understand their memory of the event and make sure it's accurate without forcing them to relive it too much. Reliving it could be retraumatizing, and it would be difficult regardless since they're often dealing with shame and guilt. Then I try to remind them what the situation was, what was going through their minds at the time, and that they made the best decision they could.

Often, we find ourselves in circumstances where we acted in a way counter to how we wanted to act. SOF operators often find themselves in extreme circumstances where they have to make life-or-death decisions. It's one thing to look back on our past with a civilian perspective—as they say, hindsight is twenty-twenty—but we often forget what we were dealing with and what was going through our minds at the time. We all do the best we can, and comparing ourselves to our twenty-twenty hindsight, or to others, is a good way to leave out our own humanity and compassion toward ourselves.

You should research local religious leaders so you can refer clients to them when needed. Most religious leaders have a good grasp of moral injury and how to deal with it, and also how to bring someone down from depression and suicidal ideation. You can ask local law enforcement departments, fire departments, hospitals, and other first responder agencies if they have a chaplain on staff, because those chaplains are usually good at dealing with those issues. You may even learn something from them on how to help your patients. And more importantly, you'll have extra resources to refer clients to when needed. Personally, I've never had any practitioner say no to a referral.

Sleep

Sleep issues can also be misdiagnosed as PTSD or can co-occur with other mental illnesses. If the client is having a hard time sleeping, complaining about night terrors, having vivid dreams, waking up every two hours, having trouble going back to sleep, complaining of feeling constantly lethargic and tired, especially when they're not used to feeling like that, or experiencing any anomalies with sleep or energy, I often suggest a sleep study, because they might have sleep apnea or another sleep-specific issue. Unless the SOF member gets a sleep study, you often can't definitively say what's going on with that veteran, unless there's a clear connection to a traumatic event or other problem.

If their sleep issues are directly related to other issues such as PTSD and depression, teaching them good sleep hygiene while tackling the root causes of their core problems may be enough to help them gain better sleep, though it may take time for those core issues to resolve. Obviously, sleep is crucially important for overall health and well-being, especially mental health. Conversely, bad sleep can greatly compound mental health issues. A good therapist will understand the correlation between various issues and how they affect sleep. More tips on helping clients with sleep and nightmares can be found in Chapter 12.

Depression

Depression can be the cause or the result of the other problems listed in this chapter. Often, people suffering from one problem have related issues, such as depression and anxiety, or depression and PTSD or moral injury. As the Department of Veterans Affairs (2024c) describes, depression is characterized by feelings of sadness, hopelessness, irritability, and low energy. While these are common, occasional feelings, those suffering from depression can find it hard to do everyday activities for a prolonged period of time and have trouble seeing the positive. They also don't feel pleasure in doing activities or spending time with people they used to enjoy. This may cause their professional and/or personal relationships to suffer. Depression "is a common but serious problem that affects people in different ways. It affects not only your mood but also your body, actions, and thoughts" (US Department of Veterans Affairs, 2024c).

For the depressed SOF member, there may be additional feelings of guilt and/or shame at being depressed, since they're accustomed to operating at such a high level. They may wonder why they can no longer function at the level they once did.

It's helpful to determine what might be causing the depression and if it's co-occurring with other mental or physical problems. Helping the client design ways to cope and move forward while treating other core issues will greatly ease depression when the depression itself is a symptom of other issues.

When dealing with depression-related triggers, it's important to work with the client on reestablishing schedules and healthy routines. Many former SOF members have expressed a loss of pleasure in activities they used to enjoy. Some are unable to exercise or stick to a daily routine due to mental or physical injuries sustained during service. This is where the clinician needs to think outside the box and explore options that would be engaging for the client as well as fit into their physical and mental capabilities.

Suicide

Some of our veteran brothers say that if you kill yourself, you're weak, you're a quitter, you're a coward. I know from my personal experience that when you've hit so low, and you don't have anybody in your life that really cares about you . . . I started drinking because I could never sleep. Then I started doing hard drugs, because I believe I like to feel pain, to feel that I'm even existing. I was at the bottom. I lost my son [in court]. Shoot, I got out of the courthouse in St. Louis, did a couple of lines [of coke] in my car . . . I had probably been up already for two days . . . And I had my pistol, I had my weapons. I was very close to taking my life because I really felt like a letdown. I felt like I let down my son . . . Me being an orphan and growing up without a father, I know what that did to me. And that I was somebody before—I've got a freaking chest full of medals and I'm a Recon Marine, you know . . . and yet, I didn't have nothing together . . . I called my brother . . . I told him to come to the house, take all my guns. [I] flushed my freaking cocaine down the toilet . . . And I started that long walk back home, to myself.

—Rudy Reyes (Ritland 2023)

All therapists have been trained in suicide prevention, but not all therapists have dealt with a client who was dealing with suicidal ideation. As I mentioned before, when a SOF member seeks therapy, it's usually because they're in serious need of help, so you must be prepared to deal with this topic. It will make you a better clinician overall if you are able to do so.

Because I've been counseling cops for so many years, I understand that just talking about suicide is not a code red. It's something to be concerned about, but generally speaking, the worst thing you can do as a clinician is go completely nuclear and get authorities involved right away. It's important to take your time and find out what's going through their mind and how close they are to carrying out their ideation. Do they have a plan? Have they ever attempted suicide before? What social factors at home could be contributing? Is it work related? Just thinking about suicide is okay, because every cop I've ever known who has worked more than ten or fifteen years has thought about it. It's not that they wanted to or that they were going to, but they thought about what it would be like if they didn't exist.

If your client has an imminent, specific plan, then of course you should inform them that you are a mandated reporter and you want to ensure their safety, and that it's better they go to a hospital or psychiatric treatment facility than carry out their plan.

Either way, when someone tells you about their suicidal thoughts, it actually shows trust. When an officer or an operator exposes that much, it shows that this person actually trusts you enough to tell you their deepest, darkest thoughts, even knowing that you're a mandated reporter.

Sometimes, it might just be to see what you're about as a therapist, how you will react, if you will overreact, or how you will take care of them. Of all the stigmas around mental health, suicide probably carries the most stigma within the military, as it overwhelms all levels of the command structure and carries over to the individual's family.

It's hard to understand how an individual who has gone through a process of arduous and lengthy physical, tactical, mental, and emotional training, as well as a rigorous psychological screening, can want to commit suicide. There are probably as many answers as to why a Special Forces operator would kill themselves as there are operators themselves.

Information that I found extremely helpful comes from Edwin S. Shneidman's book *The Suicidal Mind*, where he describes ten commonalities of suicide:

1. The common purpose of suicide is to seek a solution.
2. The common goal of suicide is the cessation of consciousness.
3. The common stimulus of suicide is intolerable psychological pain.
4. The common stressor of suicide is frustrated psychological needs.
5. The common emotion in suicide is hopelessness/helplessness.
6. The common cognitive state in suicide is ambivalence.
7. The common perceptual state in suicide is constriction.
8. The common action in suicide is escape.
9. The common interpersonal act in suicide is communication of intention.
10. The common consistency in suicide is with lifelong styles of coping.

Shneidman did a lifelong study on suicidal individuals, and when I read that book, it really resonated with me when I started thinking about everyone I have worked with who had suicidal ideation.

Going through these steps backward, as an example:

(10) The client has a lack of effective coping mechanisms. Partially by their own design (possibly due to stigma), they block out a lot of resources they may have and shut themselves off from family and friends. They don't want to talk to other people because they feel embarrassed or unworthy of attention or help, or don't want to be a burden on others, or don't feel anyone can help them.

(9) This isolation and other actions, such as giving away their assets or money, can be an indication of suicidal ideation.

(8) Suicidal ideation is a result of wanting to escape what they see as a hopeless situation and the intolerable psychological pain they find themselves in.

(7) Their perceptual state is that they feel constricted. They feel that there's no way out and that they're out of options and unable to make any changes. They have tunnel vision. They're blinded by their problems and depression to the point of ambivalence, (6) where they no longer desire to participate in life. They go numb instead of feeling pain, and they detach from loved ones.

(5) Because they feel like there's no way out of their situation, they feel hopeless.

(4) Their hopelessness is compounded by their inability to fulfill their psychological needs. They lack social connection and love.

(3) They don't know how else to ease their psychological pain other than to (2) suspend consciousness.

(1) Therefore, suicide is the only solution in their state of mind.

Fortunately, there are people who can help, there is a way to change that state of mind, and people do reach the other side of that and enjoy life again.

I've heard a lot of clients say things like, "I've got financial bills I can't pay, my wife is cheating on me, my kids hate me because I'm never around, and life would be so much better if I just weren't here." But they're afraid to say anything, when that's exactly what they need to talk about. This is why developing trust with your client is so important.

Garner (2018, 77) writes:

> From [a] qualitative study on suicide risk screening, they found that those soldiers experiencing suicidal ideation or even just admitting thoughts of wanting to kill themselves was a difficult task . . . The soldiers in their study felt as though they should be able to effectively manage suicidal ideation on their own because they were taught to do so. Because of the stigmatizing nature of suicide, however, many soldiers were concerned that if they admitted having mental health difficulties, they would incur harmful repercussions including a delay in returning home or invalidation from upper command.

One of the best things about the residential program for first responders where I used to work is that we had a private critical incident stress debriefing space we jokingly called the "rubber room." It was a detached building all by itself where people could talk about the things they would never talk to anybody else about, and none of it was documented. All our clinician notes were shredded as soon as the session was done. The whole point was to make sure nothing went into the client's files, since most of them were being sent to the program by their employer. Of course, if anyone had severe suicidal or homicidal ideations, we took the appropriate steps to make sure that person was safe and got the assistance they needed.

SOF members, as perfectionists, may be hard on themselves when they run into difficulties, whether that be in their career or their marriage or their finances. Of course, those setbacks do not define who they are, and they can still get back on track.

Suicidal ideation is often different than "assisted suicide," when a patient is seeking to end their life because they're dealing with a terminal illness, severe chronic pain, or something of that nature. It's important to keep in mind that every person and every situation is different. But most people dealing with suicidal ideation have a long, wonderful life ahead of them if they can overcome those commonalities—that dark tunnel vision—and get the help they need.

(Buddha Said) Let That Shit Go

Humans can withstand almost inconceivable stress—and you can too. So that is your first step: Gain perspective. And to do that you must do something critical in many situations: Detach. Whatever problems or stress you are experiencing, detach from them. Stress is generally caused by what you can't control. The worst thing about incoming artillery fire is you can't control it. It is happening and you just have to accept it. Don't stress about things you can't control. [. . .] Embrace it. [. . .] I couldn't control the chaos of combat. I had to embrace it. I had to figure out a way to take advantage of it. [. . .] So. Don't fight stress. Embrace it. Turn it on itself. Use it to make yourself sharper and more alert. Use it to make you think and learn and get better and smarter and more effective. Use the stress to make you a better you.

—Jocko Willink,
retired Navy SEAL and
author of *Discipline Equals Freedom* (2020, 19–20)

A lot of moral injury and PTSD is a result of things that were out of an operator's control or at least are out of their control now, because what happened is in the past and cannot be changed. This is part of the mental anguish, because SOF operators want to be in control. Often, anyone who has a traumatic memory wishes they just could have done things differently so the event didn't take place or there was a better outcome. One way to help clients heal is to get them to recognize what is outside their control and therefore isn't worth obsessing over. It's no use to blame yourself for something you can't change.

This is what retired Navy SEAL Jocko Willink means in the quote above. We must detach ourselves from trying to control what we can't and instead embrace it and try to take back control in another way, by using the experience to motivate change, for example. That doesn't mean burying negative emotions under the rug and not dealing with them—quite the opposite. It's dealing with them in a new way and gaining perspective on the fact that even SOF operators are not super-heroes, or at least not in the sense that everything they do and encounter will be perfect.

I like to compare detaching to a scene in the movie *Contact*, starring Jodie Foster. Foster's character, Dr. Ellie Arroway, is selected to travel through space inside a one-man machine. For her safety, she is strapped to a chair that is bolted to the craft. While the spaceship travels rapidly through various wormholes, the chair begins to vibrate, becoming more and more intolerable. Dr. Arroway notices her necklace floating in front of her, weightless, and she decides to release her straps. As she floats away, the chair continues to vibrate violently until the bolts come loose and the chair is destroyed.

It's a great metaphor for the fact that we're not designed to hang on to the things we can't control. At some point in time, you have to let it go and float away from destruction.

The Bull & The Matador

> For many years, I struggled with a feeling of not being good enough. To combat this feeling of inadequacy, I did the opposite of what I wanted to do. Instead of avoiding failure and rejection, I ran toward it. I figured that if I faced the big, scary monster, I could defeat it. I used ambition, drive, and determination as a way of coping with my fear. Yet with every achievement, I felt worse.
>
> It wasn't until I dug into my past and realized that my trauma made me better that I started to become proud of who I am. You will never stop fearing rejection until you stop rejecting yourself. Once you have embraced yourself, nobody can reject you ever again. If you have already given yourself permission to be great, you don't need anyone else to do it for you. As children we can be rejected or thrown away by our parents, guardians, or peers. As adults, the only person who determines if we are good enough is us.
>
> —Sean J. Rogers,
> former Green Beret and author of *Better Broken: The Hidden Advantage of a Challenging Life* (2024, 63)

For the exhausted, stressed, suffering client, therapy can be overwhelming. It can be especially overwhelming for those, like most SOF clients, who have never been in therapy before. One of my Navy SEAL clients put it this way: I mentioned in session about him dealing with his demons, and he said that sometimes he fights with them and sometimes they cuddle. In other words, sometimes his demons got the better of him, sometimes he was able to fight them off, and sometimes they were in harmony and he was able to work with them.

No one can fight forever. Even SOF members have to take breaks and change their focus away from their problems and their therapy every once in a while.

Many SOF members have studied, or still practice, martial arts. Martial arts can be a great way to heal from trauma, depression, and other issues. While yoga seems to be the go-to recommendation in the civilian sector, I would say martial arts is the SOF equivalent.

Martial arts is about more than learning self-defense and hand-to-hand combat. The various disciplines each have their own philosophies, which exercise the spirit, along with exercising both body and mind when learning various pattens of movement, not to mention the benefits of social interaction and the boosts in confidence from learning new techniques.

One technique in many martial arts is to utilize the momentum of the attacker to your advantage. One way to do this is to simply step out of the line of attack, just like a bullfighter tempts a bull with a red cape, then smoothly steps aside as the bull charges.

As clients learn more about themselves, they can learn to sidestep and redirect negative onslaughts in a way that keeps them mentally and physically intact. Instead of pushing back and getting completely rid of negative thoughts all at once, the client learns to deal with them until they slowly diminish and can be managed, just like the bull and the matador.

10. ADDICTIONS & MALADAPTIVE COPING

I am a former Navy SEAL, and on a personal note, have been in recovery from addiction for 28 years. I'm living proof that hope exists. During the most challenging times of my personal journey, I examined my years as a SEAL and recalled the conditioning and mindset, and that led me to want to beat my addiction. My personal and professional experience has taught me that addiction can be conquered by accepting—at times embracing—a range of emotions, including emotional pain. Now working as an LCSW and MFLC (Military and Family Life Counselor), I have observed the commonalities between PTSD, substance abuse, stress, conflict, depression, and anxiety.

—Thomas J. LaGrave Jr.

Addictions are the soft underbelly of the special operations arena. They cross the spectrum from alcohol and drugs (both legal and illegal) to recklessness, thrill-seeking, sex, and more. Of course, individuals can become addicted to any number of things according to their issues, experiences, and personality. In the military's work hard, play hard attitude, alcohol is a big part of the "play" culture. Addiction is problematic within the SOF community in part due to the op tempo and the constant need for training when not on deployment, which takes a toll on the mind and body.

Furthermore, pain is an ongoing issue for SOF members. Each operator has been through countless training scenarios that tested their physical limitations. No team member wants to be off duty because of an injury or illness, and they often "chew" non-prescription painkillers like candy to keep going. On top of physical injuries, substance abuse can be a maladaptive coping strategy when dealing with mental hardship as well.

Tobacco use is common (though discouraged by military doctors) due to the fact that nicotine both calms and stimulates one's nerves. This makes it a useful drug when stressed and fatigued on the battlefield and during training exercises. Off duty (and at some formal functions), alcohol is often used as a way to de-stress. Painkillers and performance-enhancing substances, such as steroids and even methamphetamines, are used to help operators endure the constant need to be 110 percent.

Special Forces usually know ahead of time when urinalyses are going to happen, unlike in the regular military where it's purposely kept secret, which helps operators keep an unhealthy habit.

When SOF members find themselves alone after a stressful deployment, or worse, dealing with issues on top of a difficult transition after their SOF career ends, they often turn to the habits and coping mechanisms they developed in the service, which generally involves drinking and other behaviors that lead to more problems.

Maladaptive Coping Strategies

Maladaptive coping strategies are ways of dealing with stress or difficult situations that are unhealthy or unhelpful. They may provide temporary relief or avoidance of an issue, but ultimately, they don't address the underlying problem and can lead to more negative consequences in the long run. Examples of maladaptive coping strategies include:

- Avoidance (of a problem or difficult emotion)
- Denial
- Procrastination
- Over- or under-eating
- Substance abuse
- Sexual recklessness
- Thrill-seeking

Maladaptive coping behaviors generally add problems that the client then has to deal with on top of the original problem, since they can be harmful and can interfere with an individual's ability to effectively deal with stress and difficult situations.

Garner (2018, 28) states, "When SOF veterans are no longer in military combat zones and exposed to high-risk situations, it is common for veterans to engage in high-risk activities" to replace the adrenaline rush of combat missions:

> When veterans who have had these intense experiences over long periods of time return back to civilian life, everyday life experiences are mundane and unmeaningful . . . Research indicates that many veterans take up hobbies such as skydiving, mountain climbing, reckless driving, or other high-adrenaline rush sports in an attempt to reach previous physiological arousal states . . . In addition, it is also common for veterans to engage in other addictive behaviors including gambling and substance use . . . Further, although many veterans try and utilize their already-acquired skill sets from their military training, many veterans find themselves in other high-risk positions including law enforcement, firefighters, paramedics, and other government jobs (i.e. military contractors, special agents).

Maladaptive behaviors can be positive or negative, depending on the situation. It may be a good coping mechanism to avoid certain situations that the client has identified as troubling. But this can mean they're avoiding things that they normally enjoyed or that are necessary to live a normal life.

I had one client suffering from PTSD who was having a lot of trouble being in crowds. He was very sensitive to a lot of stimuli, so a lot of people and loud noises triggered him. Luckily, though unfortunately, he was collecting enough military disability that he didn't have to go to work, but he still had to find ways to get his food and anything else he needed at different, smaller stores, and at times when they weren't crowded. This limited his ability to participate in society and be social when he wanted to.

I learned he enjoyed country music, so one day, I suggested he bring his noise-canceling headphones with a playlist of his favorite country songs. I explained my thought process and he agreed. The next time he arrived, with headphones in hand, we left the clinic and walked around the block, where there were some stores and a café. I gave him a clicker counter, and I had him click it every time he started to feel uncomfortable. This was so I could map out what his triggers were and what environments they happened in so we could tailor a plan for him to work on. By the time we stopped working together, he was doing it on his own.It's important for individuals to recognize when they are using maladaptive coping strategies and to seek healthier, more adaptive ways of dealing with stress and challenges. These may include seeking support from friends and family, practicing relaxation techniques, or engaging in healthy activities such as exercise or hobbies. Obviously, if the client has an addiction, that will also need to be addressed. With SOF folks, redirecting their negative energy toward healthy things they enjoy (like martial arts, competitive sports, or hunting) can help them through the healing process.

Counterphobic Behavior

While maladaptive coping strategies generally involve behaviors that try to avoid, ignore, or alleviate issues, counterphobic behavior instead is when someone seeks to confront their problems or phobias head on. An example would be someone with a fear of heights deciding to bungee jump or skydive. Counterphobic behavior may provide temporary or even permanent relief from anxiety or fear, but in some situations, it does not address the underlying issues and therefore can lead to negative consequences.

SOF members have told me that when doing freefall jumps (high altitude parachuting), especially when carrying heavy equipment, it's possible they begin rotating to the point where they lose consciousness. Their parachutes are set to open automatically by altitude sensors (altimeters) or other technology, but this is obviously an unsettling experience. When this happens during training, the answer is to do it again. And again. And again. Basically, SOF use counterphobic training to overcome their mistakes and their fears.

This can be effective in training. But when a SOF member is dealing with mental issues, especially comorbidity of several mental and/ or physical, emotional, and spiritual problems at once, counterphobic behavior may not produce the results they're looking for. Their issues may need to be resolved in other ways, or they may be confronting one issue but ignoring (either consciously or subconsciously) deeper issues. The counterphobic behavior itself may become problematic if it's reckless, obsessive, or interferes with other areas of their life.

It is important for individuals to recognize when they are engaging in counterphobic behavior and to seek healthy ways to cope with fear and anxiety. This may include seeking support, practicing relaxation techniques, or facing fears in a more gradual and controlled way. It's also important to address the underlying causes of anxiety and fear and to work toward finding healthy and adaptive ways to cope with difficult emotions and situations. This is where you need to be flexible and address the needs of your individual client.

Isolation

When SOF members are tired and rundown or dealing with various issues, they tend to isolate. The National Veterans Homeless Support (NVHS) organization says that research has identified three factors that commonly affect feelings of loneliness and isolation for veterans: (1) losing touch with friends from service; (2) physical or mental health issues; and (3) difficulty relating to civilians (McElhinny 2021).

NVHS continues to say that social isolation and poor mental health are long-standing issues that are linked to the fact that, in general, members of the veteran community are at a higher risk of homelessness than non-veterans. And for those who do experience homelessness, social isolation and lack of a social support network are correlated with a longer duration of homelessness and more chronic homelessness. (McElhinny, 2021). SOF members may especially suffer from isolation when transitioning to civilian life due to the many factors previously mentioned, such as physical injuries that limit their mobility, geographic location, lack of willingness or ability to connect with their SOF teammates or to connect with other veterans, feelings of rejection/organizational betrayal/moral injury, and the loss of a spouse and/or children in the case of divorce or separation.

Helping SOF members reconnect with other SOF members, such as reaching out to some of the resources listed in Appendix II (among other strategies and therapeutic techniques mentioned throughout), can go a long way in reducing maladaptive coping mechanisms, as well as preventing homelessness and suicide.

Alcohol Abuse

The naval term of "rum rations" in its day was considered payment for laudable service. Historically rum rations originated in the Navy, but alcohol is synonymous with military service in all branches. It's a lubricant that relieves stress, overcomes monotony, and allows for relaxation and bonding between not only friends but enemies alike. However, drugs are not acceptable, especially since 1980 when Ronald Reagan attempted a strategy called "zero tolerance."

—Thomas J. LaGrave Jr.

As mentioned, alcohol and pain medication play a big role in many SOF members' lives. Many service members drank alcohol throughout their military career because that was the thing to do, which is why it's a very common substance abuse problem. After the military, when they run into hardships and are dealing with mental issues, they go straight to what they know. Before, they would go out and have drinks after work and socialize with their buddies. But when they're suddenly sitting at home all day, every hour is happy hour. This is when I've seen a lot of SOF members go off the deep end. They're depressed, so they drink, which keeps adding to the depression, and the alcoholism gets worse and worse.

Many times, that's when their marriages run into serious trouble. Then housing becomes questionable. And the more serious issues a SOF member is dealing with, the more barriers they have to seeking treatment and even applying to civilian jobs.

Most of us clinicians have learned about addiction to some degree, so it's important to ensure a client suffering from any type of addiction gets the appropriate assistance and care. Hopefully the information you've learned here will help you gain a SOF client's trust so you can convince them to seek help. Alcohol often worsens mental health issues like PTSD and aggravates their symptoms, making it harder to cope with them and increasing the risk of developing other health issues.

Pain Medication

The treatment of chronic pain has changed considerably in the past thirty years. Beginning in the 1990s, the number of prescriptions for opioids began to increase in the US. But as opioid use gradually increased, the risks of opioid use became clearer, and opioid overdose deaths increased steadily over time.

Unfortunately, the military and the VA can be good at prescribing people medications instead of fixing core problems. The use of Motrin, ibuprofen, and Tylenol is extremely common throughout the military. Once you get into special operations, those medical specialists have access to a plethora of narcotic substances they can prescribe for pain management. Likewise, SOF operators are aware of the different medications and what works best, and they will sometimes advocate for those harder narcotics.

When someone says they got dropped out of an aircraft at twelve thousand feet and their main parachute didn't open, and with their secondary (smaller) parachute they hit trees at so-many-feet per second, you can imagine they're dealing with some chronic pain. Because SOF members train even harder than they fight, they get a lot of injuries, especially to their joints like their knees, elbows, shoulders, and back. It's much more acceptable for medical professionals to prescribe class two or three narcotics to someone with severe and chronic injuries. For these reasons, the SOF veteran is all the more likely to get addicted to prescription pain medication.

If something's hurt or broken, we generally need to take time out and heal as opposed to getting back in the fight. But SOF members want to stay in the fight as long as possible. Quitting is not an option. Taking time off could be detrimental to their careers. Some of the clients I've seen told me that their substance abuse started after they were injured during training and got hooked on pills. And when they got discharged, the pills turned into heroin and other substances.

Performance-Enhancing Substances

In addition to painkillers, performing-enhancing substances are very common for SOF members, even though they are unauthorized and, in many cases, illegal. While not talked about and generally frowned upon, many SOF operators do what it takes to operate at their best, to earn and keep a place on a coveted SOF combat team, to keep going past their physical limits, and to persevere even when injured or sick. This can definitely lead to maladaptive behavior later on, especially when combined with physical injuries and other substance abuse.

Performance-enhancing substances, such as anabolic steroids, androstenedione, somatotropin, or erythropoietin (human growth hormones), all have various risks and side effects, especially if taken over time, and in some cases can be addictive.

But "performance-enhancing" could also mean other legal and illegal drugs and even supplements, such as vitamins, protein powders, creatine, caffeine, or other stimulants. Continual usage of these substances in high doses can also lead to substance abuse and/or physical damage, which can lead to other maladaptive behaviors over time. While not all of these substances are necessarily harmful or addicting, since many performance enhancing substances are illegal (and therefore not very well researched), and legal supplements are not regulated by the FDA, there is not much information regarding long-term effects.

Sex Addiction

Not all addictions are to alcohol or drugs. Sex addiction, better known as compulsive sexual behavior disorder (CSBD), is a condition marked by obsessive thoughts and compulsive actions related to sex that are unwanted and uncontrollable. While CSBD is not officially categorized as an addiction in many diagnostic manuals, the behaviors associated with it can lead to significant distress, impaired functioning, and negative consequences in various aspects of life, including work.

Studies suggest that sex addiction may be a common issue among US military veterans returning from deployment. Sex addiction is associated with significant negative health markers, especially in men. One study published in 2014 "suggests that CSB is prevalent amongst veterans returning from combat and is associated with childhood trauma and PTSD, particularly re-experiencing" (Smith et al., 214).

Another study published in 2017 looked specifically at those who used digital social media to find sexual partners, abbreviated as DSMSP (Turban et al.). The researchers found that engaging in anonymous or casual sex multiple times per month, whether or not one is married, and a self-described "problematic" use of pornography were the most common forms of compulsive sexual behavior. They also found ties between such behavior and gambling, PTSD, insomnia, depression, hypersexuality, suicidal ideation, and sexually transmitted infections (STIs) (Richman 2017).

In the context of SOF, the high-stress environment, frequent deployments, and the intense nature of the work can exacerbate or contribute to CSBD, though it's important to note that sex addiction is a complex issue that can affect individuals in any profession or walk of life.

SOF members with sexual addiction may engage in risky sexual behaviors, such as unprotected sex with multiple partners, which may lead to STIs and unwanted pregnancies. Furthermore, sexual addiction in the SOF community can have significant consequences for the individual's career and personal life, such as loss of security clearance or dishonorable discharge, damage to one's reputation, and strained relationships.

A study conducted by the US Army Special Operations Command (USASOC) in 2021 found that sexual harassment is an ongoing issue in SOF units. Nearly every female soldier who participated in focus groups for the study reported experiencing some degree of sexual harassment while serving in USASOC (primarily in support roles). Seventy percent of the women who had been harassed said they were *not* comfortable reporting it. Among the lowest ranking soldiers (E-1 to E-4), 86 percent were uncomfortable reporting sexual harassment. The top five barriers to reporting sexual harassment were found to be fear of reprisal (90 percent), trust in the system (72 percent), fear of retaliation (70 percent), confidentiality concerns (67 percent), and trust in the command (64 percent).

Helping SOF members overcome sex addiction is one way to decrease sexual harassment and assault in SOF units, as well as in civilian environments when SOF members are off duty or past their SOF careers.

There is a growing recognition of the importance of addressing compulsive sexual behavior in the military and in the SOF community, though more research is needed. Addressing the complex issue of sex addiction requires a multifaceted approach that can include confidentiality, prevention and early intervention, a supportive environment, professional treatment and counseling, education and awareness, and family support. It's crucial that any measures addressing sex addiction be handled with the utmost discretion and professionalism with respect to the privacy and dignity of all individuals involved.

Residential Treatment for SOF Members

In some cases, you may feel it's in your client's best interests for them to attend a residential treatment program, especially in the cases of addiction. Unfortunately, many current or former SOF members are resistant to seeking treatment that requires a residential component. There may be an array of reasons for this. The stigma against them from their peers, command staff, or civilian supervisors is a real concern. Many fear being seen as not strong enough to "get over" their addiction or issue. They also fear that participation in treatment may lead to forms of administrative reprisal such as a denial of promotion, loss of security clearance, and even the loss of their job.

Some of the reasons past SOF clients told me they didn't want to go to a residential program included a perception that traditional mental health treatment centers are not equipped to provide adequate care for their level of training and wartime experiences. This is partially due to the top-secret operations they participated in and are not allowed to discuss, thereby restricting the clinician's ability to address their traumatic experiences. Additionally, most SOF members will not want to be clumped in treatment with civilians, especially street-level addicts with possible criminal histories.

The Veterans Affairs Administration has inpatient and outpatient centers for drug rehabilitation that might be options for some SOF members, though some may be unwilling to seek help from the VA for various reasons as already discussed. It's important to know the facilities in your region, which ones work with what insurance providers, and which ones work with veterans and people who don't have insurance or who need financial assistance.

There are various treatment facilities around the world. Recently, I visited two inpatient wellness centers for first responders. One was in Kansas City, Missouri, and the other was in Los Angeles, California—and they could not have been more different. The one in Kansas City was like Carhartt central. It had a down-to-earth and outdoorsy vibe. The one in LA was stereotypically all palm trees and acupuncture and yoga. If I were to recommend one of those treatment centers to a client, I would want to know that client's background and personality so I could recommend the place that was best suited for them as an individual. Both facilities do the same job, but not everyone will get the same result. If I have a client who is "countryfied," I'd need to send them to somewhere like Kansas City. If my client is more "metro," maybe LA's where they would feel more comfortable. These are all the things you have to consider, because every client is different.

PTSD & Substance Abuse

I don't know why some of our [SOF] guys go straight to Stanford, become doctors . . . it's unbelievable. And it's not the guys you [would] think. Then we got guys who get out, and something happens to them, and they get stuck in that dark place by themselves. And it's the guys you wouldn't think would do that—that's one of the problems. It's like, "Oh, he's good. He wouldn't go there." Those are the guys you gotta worry about—yes they would! If a team guy can get into something, he will. He just will. Because he just gets bored. It's simple boredom.

—Retired Navy SEAL Marcus Luttrell (2024)

According to the National Center for PTSD (2022), studies show having PTSD increases the risk for drinking problems, and that drinking problems increase the risk for traumatic events that could lead to, or worsen, PTSD. Up to three-quarters of people who survived abuse or violent traumatic events reported drinking problems. Those traumatic events included severe accidents, illnesses, and disasters. People were also more likely to report drinking problems if they had ongoing health problems or pain.

A study that specifically collected data from US Army Special Operations Forces also found a link between traumatic experiences and alcohol misuse. Skipper et al. (2014) anonymously surveyed 1,323 SOF soldiers regarding their combat experiences and mental health over a five-year period from three to six months after their return from a deployment to Iraq or Afghanistan. Combat experiences and mental health markers were independently analyzed and placed into the following categories: (1) fighting, (2) killing, (3) threat to oneself, (4) death/injury of others, and (5) atrocities. Alcohol misuse was measured using the Alcohol Use Disorders Identification Test–Consumption (AUDIT-C).

The researchers found that 15 percent of the soldiers sampled screened positive for alcohol misuse. While combat experiences relating to fighting, threat to oneself, and atrocities were significantly related to alcohol misuse when analyzed individually, combat experiences in the fighting category were significantly associated with a positive screen for alcohol misuse when analyzed simultaneously. The researchers concluded that soldiers belonging to certain elite combat units are significantly more likely to misuse alcohol if they are exposed to specific types of combat experiences versus other types of combat exposure.

According to a paper published in *Depression and Anxiety*, about 20 percent of people who suffer from PTSD self-medicate with substances in order to deal with its symptoms and their past trauma, which results in a lower quality of mental health and increases the risks of suicidal ideations and attempts (American Addiction Centers 2024).

People with PTSD report using central nervous system depressants, such as alcohol, opioids, or benzodiazepines, which help to acutely relieve their PTSD symptoms. These depressants can reinforce the "self-medication" approach and perpetuate a cycle of continued substance abuse (Mosel 2024).

Informing clients that their self-medication is actually worsening their problems can be the first step to helping them quit bad habits and find healthier ones that will help them in the long run, especially as they slowly deal with the root causes of their PTSD or other health issues.

PART IV:

SOF TREATMENT TACTICS

11. RX TREATMENTS

There's a temptation for all of us to blame failures on factors outside our control: "the enemy was ten feet tall," "we weren't treated fairly," or "it was an impossible task to begin with." There is also comfort in "doubling down" on proven processes, regardless of their efficacy. Few of us are criticized if we faithfully do what has worked many times before. But feeling comfortable or dodging criticism should not be our measure of success. There's likely a place in paradise for people who tried hard, but what really matters is succeeding. If that requires you to change, that's your mission.

—Stanley McChrystal,
former Joint Special Operations Command (JSOC)
commander

Medications can be effective depending on the client and their issues, including some medications many clinicians may not be as familiar with, which will be discussed in this chapter.

Resistance to Medication
It's important to understand many SOF members will likely be resistant to taking prescription psychological medications, even if you

believe medication will help them. This is due to the many different barriers to treatment as previously described, such as the military's strict anti-drug policies; unwillingness on the client's part to be "drugged" or suffer side effects that would make them less than 100 percent effective (even when their issues are hindering their ability to function); fears that side effects will hinder their work performance and/or make them feel even worse; fears that if a prescription for mental illness is disclosed or otherwise found out by their employer it could hinder their ability to work; not wanting to admit mental illness (i.e., "weakness," even to themselves) by needing a prescription drug, and so on.

These fears are not without merit and should be considered when talking to any client about possible medications. This is especially true if a client has a history of addiction. Additionally, some military, private, and (especially) VA doctors and psychiatrists have been known to prescribe multiple medications for varying ailments without always thoroughly cross-checking the client's background or current medications, resulting in clients being over-medicated to an unhealthy level.

Garner (2018, 61) writes:

> Nearly all veterans with psychiatric diagnoses will be placed on multiple psychiatric drugs from VA, often worsening their condition . . . According to a prominent Harvard psychiatrist who has done seminal work on the negative effects of psychotropic medications for over 40 years, he suggests that psychotropic medications make people more violent and suicidal.

It's important to recognize that resistance to medication is not unique to SOF. However, specific aspects of their training and operational environment, and cultural factors within the SOF community, can influence their attitudes and responses to medication.

First, there are physiological factors to consider. SOF personnel undergo rigorous physical training and often operate in extreme conditions, which can sometimes lead to a higher tolerance for pain and discomfort, potentially influencing their response to certain medications, such as painkillers. Additionally, their bodies may metabolize medications differently due to their high levels of fitness and unique physiological stressors. So, while a SOF member may take a prescribed medication, it may not have the desired effect as it would on someone similar due to their body's own uniqueness.

Then there is a myriad of psychological, social, and cultural factors that play a role in SOF members resisting medication. SOF operators are not allowed to be actively working while taking any medication that would affect their central nervous system, cognition, or judgment. Just like airline pilots, for example, due to the operator's need to make precise, split-second decisions in dangerous environments, if they are prescribed anything that would inhibit those abilities, they would have to take time off from work, which of course no SOF operator wants to do.

What this means is that, aside from strong painkillers and social alcohol use, many SOF members have little desire to be medicated and are extremely reluctant to take any psychiatric pills. This resistance also stems from a desire to remain fully alert and operational, fears of becoming reliant on medication, or concerns about side effects that could impact performance.

Many people are reluctant to take antidepressants and antianxiety medications, because medicine is not always a quick fix. It often takes several weeks for the individual to get used to a drug to see if it's effective and what any side effects (if any) they experience. If the side effects are too much or the drug doesn't work, they have to start over and try another medication. Those who have had experiences with psychiatric drugs already, especially negative experiences, can become disillusioned or exhausted of this trial and error. Or they may stop taking an effective drug once they feel better, due to the side effects or the stigma of needing a drug to function, and stopping too early can cause more problems and medication resistance later on.

Overcoming RX Resistance

Due to physiological and psychological resistance to conventional medication, some SOF members might turn to self-medication with over-the-counter drugs, alcohol, or even illicit substances. Others may seek alternative treatments that are perceived as more natural or less likely to interfere with their operational readiness.

Emphasizing a holistic approach to health that integrates physical fitness, nutrition, mental health, medication, and medical care can be more acceptable to SOF personnel. This approach can help in presenting medication as one part of a comprehensive health strategy. It can also be a way to give SOF members a chance to try natural solutions before trying traditional prescriptions. In fact, natural and holistic health care resources, such as physical therapists, chiropractors, and even acupuncturists, are available to some active-duty SOF units today around the clock, similar to the support a professional sports team may receive. All of this is an effort by those units to prevent SOF operators from resorting to performance-enhancing drugs or narcotics and to prolong their often short careers. Millions of dollars are spent training these elite warriors, so it's in the military's best interests to keep them as healthy as possible.

Addressing psychological, social, and cultural resistance to medication requires effective communication about the benefits and risks of medication and why you think a certain medication or psychiatrist's visit might be beneficial. You must explain that finding the right drug may take time, and you must also address myths and misconceptions. Educating SOF personnel about how specific medications work, their side effects, and their impact on performance is essential. Remember, they expect you to be honest and transparent and to guide them on the right path while listening to their concerns.

Antidepressants & PTSD

Research shows that PTSD may be related to changes in the brain that are linked to our ability to manage stress. People with PTSD appear to have different amounts of certain chemicals (neurotransmitters) in the brain than people without PTSD have. This may be why certain antidepressants have been shown to reduce PTSD symptoms in many patients, because they put these brain chemicals back in balance (Ursano et al. 2004).

Currently, the recommended antidepressants for PTSD are:

- Fluoxetine (Prozac)—SSRI
- Paroxetine (Paxil)—SSRI
- Sertraline (Zoloft)—SSRI
- Venlafaxine (Effexor)—SNRI

Of course, there are many psychiatric medications to consider according to each of your clients' needs and situations. Regular monitoring and follow-ups can help ensure that medications are working as intended and that any side effects are managed appropriately. This also provides an opportunity to adjust treatment plans as needed. It's also imperative to discuss concerns about confidentiality and privacy. You must ensure that SOF personnel have confidential access to medical and psychological care and that they know how to access their confidential medical and mental health records.

Psychedelic-Assisted Treatment

Psychedelic therapy is a type of therapy that uses psychedelic drugs such as ketamine, LSD, psilocybin, MDMA, ayahuasca/DMT, and ibogaine to help treat mental health conditions such as depression, anxiety, PTSD, and addiction. These drugs are often used in conjunction with other therapies such as psychotherapy, cognitive-behavioral therapy, and mindfulness to help a person in treatment gain insight into their mental health issues. Psychedelic therapy is still considered experimental and is not widely accepted or used by many psychotherapists. However, psychedelic-assisted therapy has recently shown a lot of promise, especially for combat veterans. This is especially true for those suffering from traumatic brain injury, which is encouraging since TBI is not treatable through regular psychological intervention.

Psychedelic treatments are becoming more known in the SOF community, thanks to several SOF veterans who have been outspoken on their personal positive experiences—like former Navy SEAL Marcus Capone and former Delta Force soldier Tom Satterly. Satterly founded the All Secure Foundation, which aims to help SOF members and their families heal from PTSD. Then there's Marcus Capone, former Navy SEAL and co-founder and CEO of TARA Mind, which aims to expand access to psychedelic-assisted therapy for anyone struggling with a mental health condition. He is also the chairman and co-founder of the nonprofit Veterans Exploring Treatment Solutions, or VETS. (All of these organizations are listed in Appendix II.)

Both Marcus Luttrell (the lone survivor of Operation Red Wings) and his twin brother Morgan (also a medically retired Navy SEAL) credit psychedelic therapy for saving their lives. Morgan Luttrell, now a representative in Congress, said, "I can honestly stand in front of all of you and the American public and say I was reborn. [Psychedelic drug treatment] changed my life. It saved my marriage. It is one of the greatest things that ever happened to me" (Laco 2023).

Studies indicate that around half of people diagnosed with PTSD do not respond to SSRIs or psychotherapy, and about a third of people diagnosed with major depressive disorder don't improve with treatment. Many recent studies suggest that psychedelics are beneficial for many of those resistant to more traditional mental health treatments and could help those suffering from other issues and comorbidity, such as substance abuse, obsessive-compulsive disorder, and even racial trauma. Additionally, evidence is mounting that psychedelic-assisted therapy often provides more immediate and longer-lasting relief from mental health issues than traditional treatment options (Stringer 2024). Chronic mental health conditions can damage brain circuits in the prefrontal cortex, which SSRIs may repair over time. Research suggests that psychedelics strengthen or even regrow lost synapses much faster than traditional psychiatric drugs.

A team of Stanford Medicine researchers studied thirty SOF veterans who had TBI and were experiencing clinically severe psychiatric symptoms and functional disabilities (Cherian et al. 2024). The veterans had independently scheduled themselves for psychedelic therapy at a clinic in Mexico, where they were administered ibogaine along with magnesium. Magnesium appears to prevent ibogaine's adverse side effects versus if it's taken alone (S. C. P. Williams 2024).

On average, one treatment of ibogaine immediately led to significant improvements in functioning, and those effects persisted until at least one month after treatment—the endpoint of the study. The study reports that "before treatment, the veterans had an average disability rating of 30.2 on the disability assessment scale, equivalent to mild to moderate disability. One month after treatment, that rating improved to 5.1, indicating no disability" (S. C. P. Williams 2024). The participants also experienced over an 80 percent reduction of PTSD, depression, and anxiety.

Another study on ibogaine concluded that "a single ibogaine treatment reduced opioid withdrawal symptoms and achieved opioid cessation or sustained reduced use in dependent individuals as measured over 12 months" (Noller et al. 2017).

Marcus Capone (the former Navy SEAL and CEO of TARA Mind previously mentioned) said that he knows individuals who have been in talk therapy for ten, fifteen, and even twenty years and haven't gotten any better. He said:

> Research shows it could take years to trust your therapist, where psychedelic therapy, the molecule itself can really get in there and open you up almost instantaneously . . . And then of course, like everything else . . . you do need to put in the work afterwards. But you're able to open up. (Your Next Mission, 2024)

Because of new, positive research on psychedelic treatment and the testimonials from so many influential SOF members, you may have a SOF member come into your office and ask about psychedelic treatment. They may even know someone personally who was successfully treated with it. For your client's benefit, it's important to be familiar with this treatment, what options may be available to them, and whether they can get a treatment in the US or if they have travel to a treatment facility in South or Central America.

Despite the promising research and extraordinary testimonials from SOF members, studies on psychedelic treatments are ongoing. In one survey of over 2,300 people who tried psilocybin, 11 percent reported persisting negative effects for weeks or even months after using the drug (Stringer, 2024, 50). It's also crucial that a trained therapist is available before, during, and after a client takes a psychedelic drug, especially because the trips can last many hours and clients may need help processing everything they saw and experienced. Stringer (2024, 50) notes that "psychedelics are also not recommended for people who have a predisposition to or family history of psychotic disorders or bipolar mood. The drugs, which can increase heart rate and blood pressure, are also contraindicated for people with cardiovascular conditions."

Personally, I saw some really bad stuff with people who were on various kinds of hallucinogens during my years in law enforcement, so it blows me away that so many people are receiving positive treatment from those types of drugs. But enough of my clients have told me their personal success stories that I know, in the right settings and the right dosage, psychedelics can transform lives. After all, these treatments might be new to us in the developed world, but many psychedelics have been used for a variety of reasons around the world for thousands of years.

But while studies continue, most psychedelics are still illegal in the United States, classified as Schedule I substances. However, as of late 2022, Oregon and Colorado have legalized psilocybin for mental health treatment under supervision, and Colorado has done the same for ayahuasca/DMT (Fleming and Nelson 2022).

There are specialized treatment facilities in other countries, especially in Latin America, that have been using these substances long enough to understand their benefits and how to properly use them—by administering microdoses under the care of specialists. Many SOF veterans have taken it upon themselves to visit these facilities when they don't get any relief from regular treatment.

Luckily, the VA and other government agencies are starting to notice the compelling research. In 2024, Congress authorized the VA to start conducting nationwide trials of various psychedelic therapies (Perez 2024).

Ketamine is the one psychedelic substance to date that is legal throughout the United States for medical use. An article in *Harvard Health Publishing* states that ketamine "reliably produces pain control, forgetfulness, intoxication, disassociation, and euphoria . . . Originally derived from PCP, or 'angel dust,' ketamine has been used . . . as an anesthetic for decades. It's also been cited as a drug of misuse under the moniker 'special K'" (Grinspoon 2024).

The dosing sessions for ketamine are much shorter than for other psychedelic drugs, generally lasting around two hours. Studies show that patients usually need multiple doses, along with continued psychotherapy, to prevent relapses and ensure long-term improvement (Stringer 2024).

Several SOF clients I've worked with have looked for alternative treatments outside the VA's "mega pack of pills." They're looking for genuine relief from their issues, not just masking the symptoms. I believe a lot of traditional talk therapy and medicine may not be able to tackle the severe trauma and all the experiences a SOF member goes through, but psychedelics are a totally different realm. I don't know why they've been so incredibly effective for so many people; I just know what I've heard from clients and that the studies so far are clinically significant.

Better Overnight

I had a SOF client who had worked in intelligence and did a lot of enhanced interrogation, such as waterboarding. After leaving the military, he went into law enforcement and unfortunately encountered many incidents that involved gunshot wounds. The worst incident was when he shot an armed suspect in the head, only to find out it was a juvenile around fourteen years old. The client discussed trying to hold both holes on either side of the juvenile's head because the brain matter was starting to come out with the blood. That's when his night terrors started.

When we met, he told me he was having night terrors and recurring dreams of specific incidents that were "kicking his ass," especially the juvenile incident. I worked with him for months during COVID via telehealth on the night terrors and insomnia, but the sessions were providing little improvement, and he described feeling somewhat helpless.

One day, I got a call from him, and to my surprise, he told me he was in a psychedelic-assisted treatment center in Peru! He had done the research and arranged the trip himself. The client was then assigned to a trained Peruvian clinician who administered the psilocybin in a guided process. It was done at a facility where medical staff were present on site on a twenty-four-hour basis if needed, during and after his treatment. He said that after his first treatment, his night terrors had stopped overnight. He explained that he had finished three rounds of treatment, and he was noticeably more focused. I was amazed at the difference in his emotional state and that he expressed a sense of determination to overcome his condition, which had not been present during many of our sessions. He seemed to have a renewed drive for overcoming his issues. Up until this point, he says he has not had night terrors since that experience.

He still saw me after his Peruvian trip, and we still worked on other issues, but his positive transformation blew my mind.

This and other accounts by SOF members who have engaged in psychedelic-assisted treatment therapy make me believe there are some beneficial aspects to it, and I hope the VA will continue to research the efficacy of this treatment modality.

12. PSYCHOLOGICAL TREATMENT TACTICS

Because emotion and logic will both reach their limitations. And when one fails, you need to rely on the other. When it just doesn't make any logical sense to go on, that's when you use your emotion, your anger, your frustration, your fear, to push further, to push you to say one thing: I don't stop.

—Jocko Willink (2020, 23)

This chapter covers the basic techniques of psychotherapy and how SOF clients may—or may not—receive benefits from each. As with any client, as you learn what your SOF client is dealing with, the root causes, and their personality, you should be able to gauge which treatment tactics are working and which ones aren't. Forcing a client through unhelpful treatment can aggravate symptoms and could deter a SOF client from every seeking therapy again, leaving them in a dangerously vulnerable state.

When you're an experienced clinician, you should be able to tell in the first few minutes with a new client roughly what you're dealing with, whether it's a professional or personal or family issue, whether it's trauma related or substance abuse, and so on.

Psychotherapies

> During the morning lecture Joel ... launches into the descrip-
> tion of certain states of consciousness and their correspond-
> ing powers. He uses the case of certain Tibetan yogis who
> can raise their body heat so high they are able to withstand
> the Himalayan cold with nothing on. Partway through his
> description all the men begin to hum loudly the theme song
> from "The Twilight Zone" ... We're all laughing. The joke is
> on us, but it's more than a joke. They don't want tales of the
> supernatural, they want applications.
>
> —Richard Strozzi-Heckler (2007, 44)

There are a variety of psychotherapies (talk therapies) that may or may
not be helpful for SOF individuals, depending on the individual's situation and personality. These include cognitive behavioral therapy (CBT),
cognitive processing therapy (CPT), compassion-focused therapy
(CFT), constructivist therapy, depth therapy, dialectical behavior therapy (DBT), narrative therapy, positive psychotherapy (PPT), psycho-
analysis, and rational emotive behavior therapy (REBT), among others
(Mental Health Match 2024).

Psychotherapy modalities focus on the process of verbal exchange
and analysis with the individual to break the connections between the
self, the emotions, and the behaviors. Each modality does this in different ways, but the general focus is on distancing, challenging, or changing one's negative thoughts and thought processes. By reconsidering or
"rewriting" their thoughts, feelings, and experiences, the client learns
to combat negative behaviors and support desired behaviors.

Sometimes these modalities are helpful for someone who's had
severe trauma and internalized a negative story about themselves and/
or the event. I might use CBT with a combat vet who has gone into
depression because they feel as though they let their team down or that
the trauma was somehow their fault. I usually describe this as "magical

thinking," where they think that if they had been faster or stronger or smarter or whatever, they could have saved whoever was injured or killed, for example. But usually, the reality is that they couldn't have done anything differently. But they have internalized the experience to mean that they're "ineffective" or "worthless." It's important to separate the person from those emotions, because how you think is how you feel, and how you feel is how you behave.

Once, I counseled a law enforcement officer who felt like he "was a piece of shit" because he was unable to resuscitate a person. Because of that incident, he had piled on all these negative images of himself. But when we actually went through the experience step-by-step, like a courtroom—just the facts of what should and shouldn't happen in those scenarios—it allowed him to see that he didn't do anything wrong, and in fact that he had done everything he was supposed to and could do for that person. This also allowed him to see that he had been beating himself up like a self-inflicted gunshot wound over and over again for no reason.

Because of the myth of uniqueness and perfectionism described earlier, and the fact that SOF operators train as hard or harder than they fight, they often berate themselves when things go wrong or when they make a mistake, especially when people's lives are on the line. By walking individuals through what happened, they realize they don't have a red cape or an "S" on their chest. From personal experience, I know it's easy to feel that way when you're called upon at a moment's notice to go save the innocent, get the bad guys, and "save the world." But SOF operators are human (and even Superman has his weaknesses and flaws). It helps to remember that and put those traumatic experiences into perspective.

Other psychotherapies to consider might be goal-oriented therapies, such as accelerated experiential dynamic psychotherapy (AEDP) (for moving past a specific trauma), Adlerian therapy (for addiction/OCD), neuro-linguistic programming (NLP), radically open dialectical behavior therapy (RO DBT), solution-focused brief therapy

(SFBT), expressive trauma integration, logotherapy, mindfulness, polyvagal theory, and reality therapy (Mental Health Match 2024).

Furthermore, acceptance and commitment therapy (ACT), choice theory, and integral psychotherapy (IP) are modalities that focus on better understanding one's own background, values, and desires, and how to make choices that align with one's true self.

It's important to note that most SOF members generally don't want to talk about their feelings or sit in their trauma for too long. They want to get to the bottom of their problems as quickly as possible, and they expect you as the therapist to take charge and use your expertise to guide them out of their suffering. Because of this, modalities such as client-centered therapy, collaborative therapy, emotion-focused therapy, exposure therapy, and motivational interviewing are *not* methods I typically use, as they either put the client in charge and not the therapist, or they focus too much on emotions and/or the trauma and not enough on what the client can do to get better.

The strategies you use depend on the individual you're working with and the level and type of trauma they have. I've seen a lot of tough, alpha operators who would instantly shut down and turn off if I said anything that sounded too touchy-feely, or if I said something like, "And how do you think you could do better?" which they would find condescending. I've had others, usually officers who had a higher level of education and possibly more life experience outside of the military, who were more open to discussing their feelings—to a point.

It's vital to be proficient in several different modalities and to be a well-rounded, experienced professional when dealing with SOF members. This enables you to better judge your client's personality, core issues, and what modalities will work best for them. It's especially important to do this in the first session, so you can start somewhere and give the individual a reason to come back and keep working on their issues. Of course, you must be flexible and adjust as time goes on, but taking those bold first steps will help develop trust between you and your client, which is crucial for success.

Prolonged Exposure Therapy

Prolonged exposure (PE) therapy, also called narrative exposure, is a type of cognitive-behavioral therapy primarily used to treat individuals with post-traumatic stress disorder (PTSD). The therapy focuses on helping clients confront and cope with their traumatic experiences by facing (re-experiencing) those traumatic memories and feelings in a safe and controlled setting to reduce the fear and anxiety they have associated with their memories. The therapy also encourages individuals to practice new coping skills that can help them to manage the distress they experience in their daily lives.

Sometimes a traumatic experience gets encoded in the brain incorrectly. Prolonged exposure can help the client decode their memory and see what's factual and what is emotional, and it can help them to make sure their chronological understanding of what happened is accurate. If their memory seems to be accurate, you can move on and work on the underlying trauma. If it's not, PE can help the client rewrite the incident into a more realistic and less emotional memory, which for some can be very beneficial. This may be especially helpful for those dealing with only one singular issue.

However, for some people, prolonged exposure can be retraumatizing and harmful. The reason PE is discussed specifically is because it's a technique to use with great caution. I've seen people shut down and dissociate because it's too intense for them to revisit their traumatic experience for a prolonged period of time; they're just going through the motions at that point. My experience working with former SOF members utilizing PE has been limited due to the fact many of my clients were not interested in continually reactivating their traumatic experiences. For the most part, they have been working through those memories for many years, sometimes on a daily basis.

I believe many are dealing with a moral injury based on what they have seen. Treatments for moral injury can involve revisiting their moral ideals and/or religion during their upbringing, rather than revisiting only the trauma. I treat it like we're in court: It's just the facts. That resonates with SOF members by helping them gain new perspectives without forcing them to relive every detail.

Another problem with prolonged exposure is that when clients start digging into one trauma, that process tends to trigger other traumas. This is very possible for many SOF personnel who may be in therapy for the first time and haven't opened up their can of worms yet in a therapeutic setting. If prolonged exposure starts bringing up other issues, it's best to change tactics, because that can be overwhelming. And in my experience, PE isn't the right method for dealing with multiple traumatic experiences at once.

In some scenarios, such as in combat, the mind can behave in strange ways. I was involved in several shootings as a law enforcement officer, and it was always interesting when we compared notes during the critical incident stress debriefings. Other officers remembered details I had no idea had happened, because sometimes everything flew by, but then there were moments I had tunnel vision and everything happened in slow motion, just like a movie. Later, I could recall all kinds of minutia about my surroundings and what the suspect was doing. With those kinds of memories, the client may not have *all* the facts, but they don't have the facts wrong either. If anything, they remember more than they want to.

I've found that when dealing with SOF clients, as well as other combat veterans and first responders, a lot of the trauma they experienced is very cut and dry. There's no scrambling of facts. The person understands exactly what happened, and they did what they were supposed to do. Continually reactivating that trauma to get them to work through it and forget it won't happen, because they'll never forget it. Once you've seen something like that, the memory will never completely go away—especially when the trauma deals with children, which is what I've heard from most of my SOF and law enforcement clients. And when they have children themselves, that trauma really messes with them.

This can be the same for sexual assault and abuse survivors. While they may have encoded certain things incorrectly or forgotten many details, they don't need to remember everything. They know they were assaulted, and that's what needs to be worked through more than their specific memory of the event. And once you start working on it in therapy, they'll likely start remembering other details of the incident. As I mentioned, the process will trigger other traumas, because it's not something they'll ever forget.

When PE isn't the best choice, it's better to try coping strategies and other techniques that help the client move forward, as opposed to letting them marinate in the worst day of their life. They've probably already been marinating in those bad memories for a while, which is why they finally decided to seek help. PTSD, moral injury, and a lot of the other issues discussed in this book often force those bad memories to surface over and over again, and they're looking for relief from that.

Unfortunately, narrative therapy, as well as cognitive behavioral therapy and any other form of talk therapy, can feel like prolonged exposure for many people. But if you're good at these modalities, they can be beneficial. They offer ways to walk the client through their experiences and reframe the situation rather quickly (when compared to PE), allowing the client to see the situation from a new, less emotional, personal, and/or negative viewpoint. But I would be careful with any talk therapy when dealing with trauma to ensure you gauge the client's well-being and avoid retraumatizing them.

The most important thing is to know your client and understand what they want out of treatment and sessions. Because SOF clients will be looking at you to guide them, if you say PE is the best way forward, they will probably do it and try to push through it until it becomes unbearable, just as they pushed themselves through the pipeline to become special operators. So, it's incumbent on you to get to know who you're working with in a short period of time. If you decide to use PE, it's vital to check in with your client and make sure they're feeling benefits and progress. If not, try something else before PE becomes overwhelming.

You have to read your audience and be able to make quick assessments on the fly, especially when you're just getting to know your client and might only have a thirty-minute initial session. A lot of this ability to make quick assessments comes with experience. You want to make sure you're a good fit for this person, that you're culturally competent, and that you know how to treat whatever might be going on. You must also communicate to them your therapeutic modalities and treatment ideas for them, as well as the business side of everything (cost per session), and consider their feedback and reactions.

Psychoeducation

Part of establishing trust with your client is explaining modalities and psychological concepts so they understand what you're doing and why, which can give an opportunity for the client to express their questions and concerns. Explaining how our minds work and how that impacts other areas of our lives can help individuals understand what they're going through. It's good to know what your client understands and what they don't. If it's their first time in therapy (which is likely for SOF members), they will probably appreciate some psychoeducation, which also helps establish your expertise, as long as you don't talk down to them or go too much into the weeds. For example, I mentioned understanding the love languages can really help SOF members communicate better with their spouses and family members.

Peer Support Groups

Peer support can be vital to SOF members, especially if they are isolated from other veterans. Creating a peer support element within your practice, potentially made up of like-minded folks such as combat vets and first responders, can be extremely beneficial as part of a SOF member's long-term treatment plan, as team members are often best suited to help one another.

For some people, however, being in groups associated with their work may not be healthy, as that sometimes triggers negative emotions or memories or gets the client talking about negative work-related stress rather than helping them unwind. Depending on the person, getting them involved with a recreational group may be better than a work-related group or even a mental health therapy group.

Many SOF members are simply not going to be comfortable in a clinical peer support group. They might be open to an informal gathering of veterans, especially if they're other SOF members. As mentioned, most SOF members don't want to be in therapy in the first place, and they don't want others knowing they're having issues. Also, they tend to be choosey about who they hang out with, and being around "normal" veterans might not make them feel comfortable.

Critical Incident Stress Debriefing

Most therapists will only conduct a critical incident stress debriefing (known in the military as an "after-action review/debriefing" or a "battle reconstruction") if they're embedded with an active-duty unit or working with first responders. However, if the therapist works for the VA or another aligned organization, there may come a time when conducting a CISD may be appropriate.

OSHA (2024) defines the critical incident stress debriefing this way:

> [CISD] is a facilitator-led group process conducted soon after a traumatic event with individuals considered to be under stress from trauma exposure. When structured, the process usually (but not always) consists of seven steps: Introduction; Fact Phase; Thought Phase; Reaction Phase; Symptom Phase; Teaching Phase; and Re-entry Phase. During the group process, participants are encouraged to describe their experience of the incident and its aftermath, followed by a presentation on common stress reactions and

stress management. This early intervention process supports recovery by providing group support and linking employees to further counseling and treatment services if they become necessary.

CISD is usually done routinely for first responders after responding to a critical incident. Essentially, everyone who was involved in responding to the scene will gather together, and a clinician will guide them through the Mitchell model (the seven steps mentioned above). Each participant has an opportunity to speak, where they introduce themselves and explain what they saw and did. This enables everyone to hear the perspectives of others who were involved in the incident.

If there is a missing piece in someone's understanding of a traumatic event, the mind has a unique ability to try and automatically fill in the pieces, and it usually fills the story with wrong information. By having a conversation with others who experienced the same event immediately (within twenty-four to forty-eight hours) after the incident, CISD provides clarity, corrects false assumptions, gives an opportunity for everyone to express and process their thoughts and emotions, and fosters a connection between those who experienced the event. This process often helps reduce the risk of developing stress-related trauma or other mental health issues later on.

One thing to consider when organizing a CISD of military veterans is who is going to be present and what was their relation to the critical event. Former SOF members may be unwilling to participate in a debrief when there will be individuals who were only loosely exposed to the critical incident and may not have even been physically present. I encourage the clinician to limit the circle of participants to those who were physically present and directly affected by the critical incident. A follow up debrief can be scheduled for those individuals who may be affected by the incident but had no on-site relation to it. This is common within the law enforcement CISD operations and has been shown to be beneficial for a majority of the officers. For example, I have held a CISD for dispatchers and on-site officers, then held a separate CISD for the support staff who were exposed to the crime scene but were not present for the incident.

It's important to note that CISD, while widely used, is one part of a comprehensive approach to managing critical incident stress. It is most effective when integrated into a broader mental health support system that includes ongoing support and access to mental health resources. Additionally, the effectiveness of CISD can vary, and it is continually evolving based on new research and practices in the field of trauma and stress management.

PTSD Treatments

Teaching grounding can help people when they have PTSD lapses or flashbacks so they can see, smell, hear, and/or feel the present moment—how their feet are on concrete or carpet in the here and now. You can also teach your client the technique of identifying as many items as they can wherever they are—noticing the furniture, windows, and items on a desk, for example. These tactics can help those with recurring flashbacks to self-identify when they're experiencing flashbacks, to know that they're not real, and to bring them back to the present reality in the bodily senses.

I also talk to clients about secondary trauma and techniques to relieve stress, such as tapping and bilateral stimulation, rectangle breathing, and balling their toes or fists for several seconds, releasing them, balling them again, and rereleasing.

SOF members are very tuned to ongoing world dynamics as part of their job. This constant analysis of world conflicts becomes a habit of nature but can also become an issue when no longer serving. Unfortunately, there is a daily twenty-four-hour overload of news coverage and social media videos of conflict zones from around the globe. This constant access can sometimes be beneficial, but it can also exacerbate ongoing mental health conditions in prior service members.

When this issue comes up in session, I regularly advise the client to limit their exposure and time consuming news and online content to a reasonable level. I try to put it into a time management matrix. I am not advising them to stop altogether, but instead to set a specific topic they will engage with in online media, as well as when and for how long.

As an example, one client often watched interviews of SOF operators recalling Operation Red Wings and the painful loss of fellow brothers. This triggered him, and to cope, he would consume several alcoholic drinks. The client did not regularly consume alcohol but felt it helped him cope when reimagining the events of that particularly tragic operation. This sometimes occurred in the morning before he went to work. To a clinician, the first reaction would be to tell him to stop watching those interviews altogether, but this was a way of staying connected to his SOF brothers, even if it wasn't the healthiest way. Instead, he agreed to engage with this content in a one-hour timeframe in the evenings after work. This reduced the chances of him going to work triggered, depressed, angry, and smelling of alcohol, which, of course, also decreased the risk of losing his job.

Often, the idea of going out to social events, especially to find a romantic partner, can be extremely hard for many combat veterans. As mentioned, veterans often experience fear, anxiety, or anger when dealing with crowds or strangers. I will coach these members on how to get out of their isolation and make social connections without allowing their fear to completely take over. This requires knowing the client and tailoring strategies that fit their interests and lifestyle while not pushing too much on them at once.

Rescripting Nightmares

Rescripting nightmares can help a person gain control over their dreams and reduce the impact those nightmares have on their daily life. One way to do this is to use imagery rescripting, which involves visualizing a different ending to the nightmare and replacing negative images with more positive ones. Imagery rescripting can also be supplemented with other techniques, such as cognitive restructuring and relaxation. Cognitive restructuring involves challenging any negative thoughts or beliefs that may be associated with the nightmare, while relaxation techniques can help to reduce the physical symptoms of nightmares. Additionally, discussing the nightmare with a therapist can help to identify any underlying issues and provide support and guidance.

If the client is waking up during or right after their nightmares, it can be beneficial to have them get out of bed, go to a different room, and do grounding work. Similar to flashbacks, this helps the client learn over time that the threat is no longer real, which decreases the intensity and frequency of nightmares over time.

Post-Traumatic Growth

Not all trauma has to be negative forever. Post-traumatic growth (PTG) is a positive psychological change experienced as a result of adversity and other challenges that a person goes through. As a result, the person rises to a higher level of functioning. PTG is characterized by an increased appreciation for life, relationships, and personal strength, an increased sense of personal control, a more meaningful existence, and spiritual development.

As clients learn to cope with, understand, and learn from traumatic experiences, they can actually become more empowered and have a greater degree of life satisfaction than they did before the traumatic event.

Compassion-Focused Therapy

> I also see that the genuine concern I feel from the Special Forces medics is not because they are medics, men doing their job, but because they are in fact caring individuals. I feel this same care from most all of the men we're working with; some of them are more explicit than others, but even those that are more recalcitrant still have a genuine concern for our well-being. Once you are accepted into their fold they watch over you.
>
> —Richard Strozzi-Heckler (2007, 53–54)

While "Special Forces operator" and "compassion" may not seem to go together, SOF operators are often very compassionate individuals, especially when it comes to their families. But many SOF members may have trouble expressing their compassion, which is why compassion-focused therapy can help them open up, show their compassion in better ways, and be more compassionate toward themselves.

SOF members, being the driven alphas they are, are often harder on themselves than anyone else. It can be good to get them to step back and realize how they're treating themselves versus how they treat others in their life (or how they would want to treat their loved ones).

When a SOF member is emotionally detached, they may be unable to express their love and compassion in ways they would like, or they may be unable to differentiate how they act as a SOF operator and how they act as a spouse or parent. For instance, they may have a military style of parenting where they're barking orders at their kids all the time. In their mind, they think they gave their children all the information they need to know. I do a lot of psychoeducation with folks where I'm teaching them how to break themselves out of that constant stoic, emotionally detached persona and why it's important to connect to their kids in other ways.

As parents, we'll do damn near anything for our kids, yet we won't do the same for ourselves. I've seen grown men go into crisis mode when their kid takes a header on the playground and gets a split lip or something, but that same man will ignore their own pain and suffering and think, "I'll be alright." They're so used to being emotionally detached, pushing through any pain or hardship, that they forget to check under the hood every once in a while. They'll do more for their kids or their spouse or their buddies than they will for themselves. This is where compassion therapy can help them realize that by taking care of their mental health, they're also taking care of those around them.

13. PSYCHOSOMATIC TREATMENT TACTICS

> When I ask [a Green Beret] how he would define a warrior, [his] street fighter face softens into Florentine dignity. "A warrior," he says confidently, "is someone who is always striving for self-mastery, to improve himself and to better serve his goals."
>
> —Richard Strozzi-Heckler (2007, 14)

Special Forces operators often train on "run, shoot, and communicate" drills, where they're sprinting and stopping repeatedly. What they're actually doing is using psychosomatic techniques. For example, they may be sprinting up hills over uneven terrain carrying heavy equipment, then they must immediately stop, get into a firing position, shoot, then get up and sprint again. To do this effectively, they must learn how to instantly focus, hold steady, and slow their breathing and heart rates in order to accurately sight and shoot a target. It's a type of physiological self-control that most SOF members don't realize can be utilized for their personal benefit in other areas of their life.

Additionally, by slowing everything down, they're relaxing and calming their mind in the middle of the storm. When you have SOF members dealing with panic attacks or anger issues and outbursts, you as the therapist can take what they already know and translate it for them to use in the rest of their life, empowering them to adopt healthier behaviors.

I myself learned these techniques as a hostage negotiator when I worked in law enforcement. Many times, I was dealing with someone inebriated and acting chaotically, and I had to be able to slow myself down and be composed in those moments of high stress. Then I started using those same techniques when I had a short temper with my kids.

There's a saying in the military and in martial arts that says, "Slow is smooth, and smooth is fast." That's the foundation of a lot of these methods, such as biofeedback, where SOF members have trained themselves to be able to slow down and focus when everything around them and inside their own bodies is going crazy so they can accomplish the task at hand.

I've successfully used many of these methods with SOF members, and I've eventually taught them how to use them on their own when they're comfortable doing so. SOF clients usually appreciate gaining new tools for their tool belt, so to speak.

Psychosomatic treatment tactics may include biofeedback, body-mind centering (BMC), body-mind psychotherapy (BMP), brainspotting, breathwork, emotional freedom technique (EFT), eye movement desensitization and reprocessing (EMDR), energy psychology (EP), neurofeedback, and somatic experiencing, among others.

Breathing Techniques

When I'm working with first responders suffering from PTSD, one of the calming techniques I give them is rectangle breathing. I have them look at a window or a picture on the wall. Then, I have them "trace" the rectangle with their mind, inhaling for four seconds along the short sides and exhaling for seven seconds on the long sides. This forces the mind to focus, because they have to count the seconds, change from four to seven seconds, and consciously breathe in or out, which helps the brain pivot from the dramatic hamster on the wheel. And as you know, exhaling causes a relaxation response. I especially do this when folks come in and keep repeating the same thing and I can tell their mind needs a break.

This is just one example of breathwork. There are many others that can be employed with your clients.

Eye Movement Techniques

Eye movement desensitization and reprocessing (EMDR) is a form of psychotherapy used to treat trauma and other mental health issues through rapid eye movements that are thought to help access and process traumatic memories, allowing the patient to process the memories in a safe and therapeutic environment. The patient is also encouraged to replace negative beliefs and thoughts with more positive ones. EMDR therapy is a recognized and effective treatment for trauma, PTSD, and anxiety disorders.

Whenever I conduct EMDR, I don't usually use any eye movement. Instead, I use electronic tappers or paddles, and the client will hold one tapper in each hand. The tappers have alternating vibrations. As a clinician, I can adjust the speed as well as the intensity, depending on what we're specifically doing. I like the tapper approach especially when working with law enforcement, because regular EMDR using eye movement techniques is similar to what an officer will do when conducting field sobriety tests, checking the suspect's horizontal gaze and evaluating for criminal activity. A lot of officers didn't like the feeling of traditional EMDR; it made them feel like I was checking them for substance abuse. With the little electronic tappers, they can sit back and close their eyes. They know I'm at least four feet away from them, so they have a safe social distance, which helps them recall a lot more than if they had to concentrate on following my finger or whatever object I'm using for EMDR. That made a big difference.

Similar to emotional freedom technique (EFT), sometimes I have the client tap somewhere on their body. Tapping or paddle vibrations have similar effects on helping the mind and body process traumatic memories while staying in the here and now.

Brainspotting is similar to EMDR and EFT. During brainspotting, the therapist uses relevant eye positions to then help the patient process and release negative memories and emotions in both the body and the mind. According to Brainspotting (2017), "Brainspotting locates points in the client's visual field that help to access unprocessed trauma in the subcortical brain."

With all of these treatments, the therapist determines if certain memories or situations have locked the client's mind in a fight/flight/freeze mode, which is an indicator of PTSD. When that's the case, the therapist uses these psychosomatic treatments to break the repetitive cycle of PTSD.

As mentioned, it's important to gauge your client, not do anything that could be retraumatizing for them for too long, be cautious of their personal space and comfort levels, and make sure they're at a point in therapy where it's healthy for them to try these techniques on their own before giving them too much homework.

Biofeedback

Biofeedback involves using sensors to measure a patient's physiological responses to stress, such as their breathing, brain waves, heart rate, muscle tension/activity, sweat glad activity, or body temperature. The data is then provided to the patient, who can learn to control these responses through relaxation techniques, breathwork, and other mental strategies. While the data must be collected in a medical office, a therapist trained in biofeedback can interpret that information to help the client understand their body's automatic responses and then alter those responses to healthier ones.

Biofeedback has been found to be an effective tool in the treatment of various mental and physical conditions that commonly affect military members, such as post-traumatic stress disorder (PTSD), traumatic brain injury (TBI), chronic pain, anxiety, and depression. It has also been used to improve cognitive functioning and decision-making among military personnel. Research has shown that biofeedback can be a valuable addition to other treatment methods for military members, improving their overall quality of life and increasing their chances of returning to duty or civilian life successfully.

Electroconvulsive Therapy

According to the American Psychiatric Association (2024), electroconvulsive therapy (ECT) is a medical treatment most commonly used when other treatments, including medications and psychotherapy, haven't worked. ECT is also used for people who require a rapid treatment response because of the severity of their condition, such as being at risk for suicide. ECT involves a brief electrical stimulation of the brain while the patient is under anesthesia, administered by a team of trained medical professionals.

Clinical evidence indicates that ECT will produce substantial improvement in approximately 80 percent of patients with uncomplicated but severe major depression. ECT is also used for other severe mental illnesses, such as bipolar disorder and schizophrenia, and is sometimes used in treating individuals with catatonia. ECT's effectiveness in treating severe mental illnesses is recognized by the American Psychiatric Association, the American Medical Association, the National Institute of Mental Health, and similar organizations in Canada, Great Britain, and many other countries (American Psychiatric Association 2024).

However, ECT does not prevent a return of the illness in the future. Consequently, most people treated with ECT need to continue with some type of maintenance treatment such as medication, psychotherapy, and/or ongoing ECT treatments. Some risks with ECT treatment include temporary memory loss and temporary learning difficulties. In most cases, memory problems improve within a couple of months, though some patients may experience permanent gaps in memory (American Psychiatric Association 2024).

Vagus Nerve Stimulation

According to the Mayo Clinic (2024c), vagus nerve stimulation (VNS) was developed as a treatment for seizure disorders like epilepsy but is now also used to treat depression in patients who have not responded to other therapies. The Food and Drug Administration (FDA) has approved a noninvasive vagus nerve stimulation device to treat cluster headaches and migraines. Researchers are studying vagus nerve stimulation as a potential treatment for a variety of other conditions, including bipolar disorder, Alzheimer's disease, rheumatoid arthritis, inflammatory bowel disease, and obesity.

Vagus nerve stimulation can be done in many ways with many devices. Essentially, the devices work by sending electrical pulses to the vagus nerve. (There is one vagus nerve on each side of the human body. The right vagus nerve isn't typically used because stimulation is more likely to affect the function of the heart.) The vagus nerve runs from the lower part of the brain through the neck to the chest and stomach. When the vagus nerve is stimulated, electrical impulses travel to the areas of the brain that lead to seizures and affect mood. Not only can this alter brain activity and treat certain conditions, but for those rehabilitating from a stroke, the stimulation helps create new pathways in the brain as the person performs exercises, thereby helping them regain lost functions (Mayo Clinic 2024b).

Response to vagus nerve stimulation may take months to develop. For this reason, it is not considered a treatment for acute severe depression.

Repetitive Transcranial Magnetic Stimulation

Transcranial magnetic stimulation (TMS) is a procedure that uses rapidly alternating magnetic fields to stimulate nerve cells in specific areas of the brain to improve symptoms of major depression, obsessive-compulsive disorder (OCD), migraines, and smoking cessation when standard treatments haven't worked well. Research continues into other potential uses for TMS, including epilepsy.

Unlike ECT, TMS does not cause a seizure, and the patient remains awake through the noninvasive process. TMS is usually administered four or five times a week for four-to-six weeks. It typically only has mild side effects, including headaches, muscle twitches, and pain at the stimulation site.

Although the biology of why TMS works isn't completely understood, the stimulation seems to ease depression symptoms and improve mood. Methods may change as experts learn more about the most effective ways to perform treatments (Mayo Clinic 2024b).

Aquatic Physical Therapy/Buoyancy-Assisted Psychotherapy (BAPT)

Aquatic physical therapy uses the properties of water to treat cardio-pulmonary, neuromuscular, and musculoskeletal impairments and to promote muscle relaxation and strength. It can also be used to treat certain types of anxiety. The BAPT model has been designed to provide accessible psychotherapy treatment for disabled individuals and others who would otherwise be unable to benefit from traditional methods of therapy. This modality allows those who are physically unable to endure conventional therapeutic settings and methods of treatment to participate and benefit through the utilization of an aquatic buoyancy pain reduction process. BAPT utilizes the effects of buoyancy during active therapy to relieve the gravitational and physical discomforts or sensations that are commonly experienced through traditional seated therapeutic modalities.

It is an accepted fact that pain interrupts and inhibits the cognitive functioning and attention of those suffering from chronic physical conditions. By removing the effects of gravity on an individual through the utilization of buoyancy, the cognitive process is not impacted by the demand of chronic pain on attention. Hydrostatic pressure decreases pain and edema, which, in turn, reduces the interruptive effect of pain signals to cognitive processing.

I developed the BAPT model while completing my master's in counseling psychology, an undertaking that required my complete cognitive attention. Having suffered a major spinal injury a decade prior, I noticed my ability to consistently focus or concentrate on specific cognitive processes was impaired during periods of constant spinal pain. However, while submerged in an aquatic environment, the gravitational pressure on my spine was removed, the pain signal abated, and I was able to consistently focus on complex processes without interruption. After my aquatic experience, I knew BAPT offered many benefits by combining a buoyant environment with psychotherapy for disabled individuals and those with chronic pain who are incapable of enduring conventional therapeutic modalities.

With the BAPT model, the client is submerged to neck or chest depth to allow for the effects of buoyancy on the body. The client is exposed to eye movement desensitization and reprocessing (EMDR) treatment while in a buoyant state with minimal ambient noise.

Sometimes, aquatic therapy that uses hydrostatic pressure can reduce swelling and sensitivity to touch; assist with breathing and strengthen respiratory muscles; decrease muscle spasms; promote relaxation for neurological conditions; decrease pain for those with arthritic joints, healing fractures, and chronic pain conditions; increase range of motion for post-surgical patients and individuals with orthopedic injuries and back pain; and improve muscular strength and cardiovascular conditioning. With the decreased effects of gravity, buoyancy provides relief between joint bones, lessens pain, and facilitates movements that are difficult on land. Buoyancy also reduces the fear of falling and promotes increased circulation, coordination, and balance by providing increased reaction time (California Physical Therapy Association, n.d.).

Hyperbaric Oxygen Therapy

Originally, hyperbaric oxygen chambers were designed to treat divers who got the bends after ascending too quickly from deep waters, though decompression sickness can also occur during high-altitude air travel or any time the air or water pressure changes rapidly. Hyperbaric oxygen therapy now has many other uses. It increases the amount of oxygen the blood can carry, which aids in healing. Our body's tissues need an adequate supply of oxygen to function and even more oxygen to survive when damaged. It has been found that with repeated treatments, the temporary extra-high oxygen levels encourage normal tissue oxygen levels, even after the therapy is completed (Mayo Clinic 2024a).

In addition to decompression sickness, hyperbaric oxygen therapy is sometimes used to treat other medical conditions, such as traumatic brain injury, brain abscesses, burns, severe anemia, carbon monoxide poisoning, sudden deafness, sudden vision loss, crushing injury, infection of the skin or bone that causes tissue death, nonhealing wounds, radiation injuries, and more (Mayo Clinic 2024a).

Facilities that have hyperbaric oxygen chambers are usually along the coasts, near large ports or on naval bases. Civilian medical treatments using hyperbaric chambers can be expensive, though VA programs in Northern California and Oklahoma began referring veterans with chronic PTSD for hyperbaric oxygen therapy at low or no cost in 2017 (US Department of Veterans Affairs 2017). Hopefully, the VA will support more opportunities for veterans in more places soon.

Virtual Reality Therapy

Virtual environment therapy (VET), or virtual reality (VR) therapy, is a fairly new approach to therapy, and it usually evolves around either exposure therapy or talk therapy (Laurence 2024). In virtual exposure therapy, someone can be safely exposed to an environment that causes them stress or anxiety, and the therapist is there (usually via audio) to guide them through the scenario and see how they respond. For virtual talk therapy, an individual or group can attend sessions remotely using avatars so their identity is concealed, making it more comfortable for them to open up and share.

Some VA facilities now have state-of-the-art virtual reality therapy capabilities and are using VR therapy to address conditions such as

PTSD, anxiety disorders, phobias, and other mental health challenges common among veterans. Mostly what the VA is using is exposure therapy. The idea is to teach new coping mechanisms and skills, reduce fears, improve confidence, and help process traumatic memories.

I've heard virtual therapy can have great results, but it's obviously not for everyone. I don't usually recommend exposure therapy, especially for SOF members, but technology is always providing new ways to treat people.

Speech Therapy

For those who have suffered injuries, especially traumatic brain injuries, speech and/or physical therapy may be needed in addition to mental health therapy. Speech therapy can be used for many different speech problems and disorders, from smaller problems like a hoarse voice to bigger problems like a partial loss of speech due to brain damage. Depending on the type of disorder, other medical or psychological treatments may be used as well.

Speech therapy can also help people with speech impediments and other speech disorders communicate better. It can include perception (hearing) and speech (vocal) exercises to improve speech, breathing, and swallowing; help with learning sign language or communication technology; advice for loved ones; and support in implementing these measures in everyday life (NIH National Library of Medicine 2025).

Physical Therapy

Most of us have been (or know someone who has been) to physical therapy when injured or otherwise in need of some physical help. Physical therapy, also known as physiotherapy, generally includes certain exercises, massages, or other treatments to relieve pain, improve range of motion, or strengthen weakened muscles.

These approaches are used for treating acute and chronic symptoms, for preventing future problems, or for rehabilitation after long-term medical problems, such as after surgery.

A SOF member may not like the idea of going to physical therapy and being told how to move by a civilian after they've been in such great shape for years as an elite warrior, on par with professional athletes. However, they may hold less stigma against physical therapy than they would for mental health therapy. So if they're dealing with injuries or other conditions causing physiological problems, physical therapy may be worth mentioning or even researching for your client.

Many of these therapies are not ones that behavioral health specialists might think about to help someone with PTSD, for instance. But a great therapist should keep an open mind and think outside the box, just like a SOF operator does in battle.

14. UNCOMMON TREATMENTS FOR UNCOMMON WARRIORS

These men of the Special Forces have had other options in their lives, other paths, easier paths they could have taken. But they took the hardest path, that narrow causeway that is not for the sunshine patriot. They took the one for the supreme patriot, the one that may require them to lay down their lives for the United States of America. The one that is suitable only for those who want to serve their country so bad, nothing else matters.

—Marcus Luttrell

My main advice to clinicians everywhere, and especially those who want to work with military and SOF veterans, is this: Be open. Be honest. Be flexible. Be proficient in a variety of modalities and techniques. Don't judge. Never stop learning. Never stop improving.

The basic modalities of therapy most of us are taught and practice are not generally that new. And there aren't necessarily a lot to choose from. There are many therapies with different names, but most of them are different ways of conducting talk therapy. And for talk therapy to be effective, you have to get to know each individual client and have cultural competency in where they're coming from. And you have to do it fairly quickly to prove to them that you're worth their time and that healing is possible, and also to know yourself that you can continue with them and what techniques you'll try.

The mental health field is always evolving, as it should. I don't think many of our current models were developed with high levels of trauma and comorbidity in mind. That's why I put an overview of so many different modalities in this book. Special operators do whatever it takes to win the fight. We should do whatever it takes to help them win.

Tough Conversations

Anything that is causing the client anxiety or night terrors or depression or whatever, you have to be aware of those things and be willing to go down that rabbit hole with them, no matter what it is. Not that you need the details or should make them relive their experiences, but you have to know what they're dealing with and be able to handle it.

One example is when I met a guy who was former Army Special Forces, but he didn't want to talk about it, which was strange. Normally, those who have been SOF are proud of their service. Later on, he opened up to me, and I found out why he was reluctant to talk—he was suffering from a severe case of moral injury and organizational betrayal.

His geographical assignment in SOF had been Latin America, where he had worked alongside a particular country's military intelligence and Special Operations Forces. He was an indigenous trainer, so his job was to train their Special Forces on various tactics and techniques. But he was unable to intervene in their missions because they were following their country's rules (or lack thereof). He had no choice but to do his job, which meant watching some horrific stuff.

What he discovered was that, in their fight against the war on drugs, they torture people. If their Special Forces ran across cartel members or people trying to bring down the government, they showed no mercy. But they also extracted information from civilians who had been working with the cartels, like people who had been forced to grow illegal crops, for instance. So, poor farmers, who had been threatened by the cartels and forced to grow illegal crops for them, were then tortured for information by their own country's military. Whatever the cartel would do to somebody to extract information or intimidate them, their own military was doing the same things—torture, dismemberment, outright killings. There was no limit on either side to the level of depravity and barbarianism. As a US counterpart to operations in a foreign country, all this SOF member could do was stand by and watch, and that was his breaking point. It really shook him, and he didn't want anything to do with Army Special Forces or the military after that.

The US Army Special Forces's motto is *De oppresso liber*, which is Latin for "Free the oppressed." Yet what he saw was the opposite of that. It was totally counter to everything he was taught by the US military and our democratic values. Furthermore, he was very religious and so was morally injured by witnessing things that shouldn't exist in a just world.

These tough conversations are what many civilian therapists may shy away from, but it's these experiences that SOF members need our help with the most. As mentioned before, it's important not to focus on the trauma itself, but to focus on how the trauma is affecting the individual so you can help them through it.

Today, that individual runs Christian retreats for kids through his church. By helping him through his trauma, he's now more able to do the good he wants to do and is not held back by his past experiences.

Clinician Self-Care

My advice to any therapist is, before you even decide to work with this population, make sure you have a personal protocol for hard sessions, which you should have anyway. Any person coming into your office might need way more help than you would expect. Take time to put together ideas of what works for you to help you feel calm, grounded, and whole again.

Everyone's different. My own protocol changes based on the situation, but most of the time, it includes some form of being outdoors.

Back when I could run long distances, running or hiking was my therapy. Now when I come home, my wife and our dog, Buddy, are usually all I need to feel better, though I still enjoy being outside in nature and away from people.

Don't wait for the bad session to occur. Have something in place, and "keep it simple, stupid." Make sure it's something you can do by yourself at home, in your car, or even in your office when you're not with clients, so you don't have to rely on a place or person that may not be available.

Animal Therapy

I think animals are probably one of the best mental health tools we have. I've been in rooms full of hard-charging, gritty, tactical law enforcement officers when someone brings in a therapy dog, and it's the most interesting phenomenon I've ever seen. Those hardcore officers suddenly start petting the dog while talking baby talk to it, like, "Oooh, who's a good dog? You are!" Every officer in the room has to pet the dog, and everyone is smiling. I'm like, *Wait a minute, dudes, you're on the SWAT team. You just killed somebody last week!* But a furry animal makes them instantly lose their hardened shell and melt into a bunch of softies. Then as soon as the dog goes away, I see them change back into serious cops.

One US Coast Guard veteran had been dealing with PTSD and suicidal ideation from a decade of search and rescue operations, but after a year together with his service dog, "his doctors told him he had improved so much that they wanted to take him off three anxiety medications" (Sprunt 2024).

A nonrandomized controlled trial of 156 military members and veterans with PTSD concluded that, compared to usual care alone, the addition of a trained psychiatric service dog was associated with lower PTSD symptom severity, lower anxiety, lower depression, and higher psychosocial functioning after only three months of intervention (Leighton et al. 2024).

Animal-assisted therapies (AAT), such as equine psychotherapy, are becoming very popular for military veterans. Animals can be a therapy asset for individuals and for peer support teams. There's a lot of research out there you've probably heard of, but it's interesting to see firsthand how animals can really calm people who are dealing with stress or anxiety.

I mentioned my dog, Buddy, and he's part of my therapy. I could have the worst day in the world, but then I see him get super excited when I come home or take him for a walk, and I forget about whatever happened at work. Usually by the end of a walk with Buddy, I'm feeling good. I'll even talk to him sometimes while we're walking about what I did during the day or how I'm feeling, and he just looks at me like, "I don't know what you're saying, Dad. I'm just happy we're out here taking a walk." And often, that's all I need.

Occupational Therapy & Vocational Counseling

Occupational therapy includes ensuring the client has the appropriate medical care for their condition; is able to manage their condition in their everyday life; and can establish, restore, or adapt the necessary skills for appropriate activities and occupations. The occupational therapist may provide care coordination, case management, physical therapy care, and transition services for the client, as well as consultative services to groups and communities. This includes educating and training the client in self-care, self-management, health management, pain management, home management, community/work integration, school activities, and work performance. The therapist may also provide education and training to others, such as family members and caregivers (RACC 2021).

Similar to occupational therapy, "vocational counseling (sometimes referred to as vocational rehabilitation) is a service for developing skills to find employment . . . It helps individuals find and enter a field that is within their area of interest and scope of their capabilities" (Occupational Assessment Services, Inc. 2024).

For SOF members entering the civilian workforce struggling to find a new career, these services can be extremely useful, especially if they're dealing with an illness, injury, impairment, disability, or other participation restriction. Occupational therapy or vocational counseling can help these individuals manage their health and find activities and employment opportunities.

While similar services may be provided by the area's VA or SOF group (such as the resources mentioned in Appendix I), it's incumbent on you as the therapist to do your homework, know what resources are available in your area, and get your client in touch with the appropriate assistance they need.

I tell my clients, do what you want in life. Do whatever makes you feel good. Too many people overlap someone else's ambitions with their own. So many people are doing amazing things, especially now on social media. It's great to be inspired by them, but they're not you. You have to do what makes you happy, whatever that is.

David Goggins is the only person to date who has completed US Air Force special operations training, Navy SEAL training, and Army Ranger School. Since his military career, he has become an ultramarathon runner, ultradistance cyclist, triathlete, public speaker, and bestselling author. He's famous for his memoirs and for inspiring many other extreme athletes. If you read his books or watch him on social media, you'll know he's an incredibly intense dude. He never does anything half-assed. He's always challenging himself to go further, even though he's a retired SEAL and could slow down. He somehow enjoys that drive and wants to continue challenging himself.

Most SOF veterans don't want to keep waking up at zero dark thirty every day to run twenty miles when they don't have to. They usually still enjoy working out, shooting guns, being outdoors, and swapping war stories with their buddies. But few SOF members keep the same intensity they had during their active-duty service. David Goggins is an outlier in that respect, but that's what works for him and makes him feel good.

I was conducting a training session recently when someone asked me a question that caught me totally off guard. They asked, "What's your spirit animal?" *My spirit animal?* I had no idea what to say. The first thing that came to my mind was a sloth. Even though I tried to go Ranger and Special Forces in the Army and then did a bunch of high-speed jobs in law enforcement, I think being a sloth is the way to go for me. Keep active but move slow, don't be in a hurry all the time, and don't stress about the small shit. That may be the total opposite of David Goggins, but it works for me. And even though I like to take things slow, I still have a lot of things I want to accomplish (like writing this book).

I tell people, you will never be as young as you are today. Right now, in this moment, is the youngest you will be for the rest of your life. That scares some people, but it motivates me to keep accomplishing what I want to do. It's like that quote from George Carlin: "Life should not be a journey to the grave with the intention of arriving safely in a pretty and well-preserved body, but rather to skid in broadside in a cloud of smoke, thoroughly used up, totally worn out, and loudly proclaiming 'Holy shit, what a ride!'" To me, that means doing everything you can while you're still alive and enjoying it as much as you can.

None of us are perfect, so we have to know what we're dealing with. We have to know our good and bad triggers so we can create a new landscape to operate in and address the issues we have. But we also have to live a good life, whatever a good life means to us.

One of the things that hurts me is when I hear about SOF veterans who fall off the cliff and never come back. They might be living in the bushes at the park, or sitting by the freeway off-ramp with a sign that says "Homeless Veteran," or they're alone at home and succumb to their addictions or suicide. That doesn't need to happen, especially to those who served our country in the most demanding units. Everyone deserves a fulfilling life.

That's why it's so pivotal to find ways for these SOF members to find their satisfaction in life. Whether they're missing an arm or a leg, or have a traumatic brain injury, or they've just seen too many people die, we need to get them integrated into society, however they feel comfortable.

I once worked with a former Navy SEAL who told me that all he wanted was to have a job where he was away from people. He ended up working a giant snowplow for a ski resort. He was happier than a pig in poo driving that snowplow up and down the mountain grating snow. He could sit with the heater and radio on and do his job away from people, out in nature on the mountain all day, and that was his therapy. Luckily he was getting military disability, so he didn't need a high-paying job. It was the perfect position for him.

It doesn't matter whether a SOF member wants to be an insane athlete like David Goggins, a serial entrepreneur like Jocko Willink, or hang out driving a snow machine in the mountains, as long as they can find what makes them happy. It may take them a while to make the shift from badass operator to civilian, but they can still have purpose and make a difference.

Mack Alexander

Mack Alexander is an amazing example of someone who was able to overcome his disabilities and find a new purpose in life.

Mack was a breacher for a Navy SEAL team, which as you now know, means he dealt with a lot of explosive blasts up close. Unfortunately for him, soon after he graduated the pipeline and was accepted as part of a SEAL team, he experienced three traumatic brain injuries within a year. One was from a bad HMMWV (Humvee) accident, another was from a big breaching charge blast, and then he was hit in the head during a helicopter landing while overseas. The post-concussive TBI from those compounded injuries led him to have trouble with his vision, balance, and other physical and mental issues, and he was medically retired from the military.

Mack talked about his journey in a *Team Never Quit* podcast interview with fellow retired Navy SEAL Marcus Luttrell:

> It's weird with traumatic brain injury, because you can look at yourself, and you look fine, but there's all kinds of things [wrong with you] that you can't see. What I wish I would've done after that HMMWV accident is take it upon myself to get the necessary help. But being a team guy, it was just: push it under the rug and keep going. I really didn't do a good job taking care of myself . . . I didn't want to leave the guys. You always want to be there. (Alexander 2024)

He also talks about the trauma of losing his SOF career:

> I got my purpose and my paycheck all in one uniform. When I had issues with my cognitive abilities to where I could no longer continue with the boys and could no longer be . . . part of the tip of the spear, my whole life felt kind of worthless. I went to a point where I had isolated myself from everybody who cared about me. I was jacked up on a ton of pills. Like, the list was insane. There was a pill for waking up, a pill for going to sleep, and there were symptoms from one pill, so they stacked another pill on top of that. Dude, I was like a walking chemistry experiment. And I only got worse. (Alexander 2024)

TBI makes it hard to regulate your emotions. That's why with TBI, there may be legitimate causes for mental health issues, such as the loss of career and identity, but then there are emotional issues that don't seem to have a cause. And because of that, Mack says he got to a point where he didn't want to live anymore:

> I didn't see my family as important. I had seen the evil downrange. I had watched these people that need to be killed. And

> I had seen service members give their life. And the first time
> you see a service member who has given his life for freedom,
> with an American flag covering his body coming home . . .
> that American flag means something completely different
> after you experience that. (Alexander 2024)

Unfortunately, soon after Mack got out of the military, COVID-19 hit. All the brain rehabilitation programs the VA was planning to send him to were postponed. And nobody was hiring, so he couldn't find a job. The TBI started causing him to have mini strokes, which affected his speech, and he went through a difficult divorce. All of these issues led to him to live in the back of his truck, essentially a homeless veteran. At the same time, his buddies from his SOF team were no longer in his life. "I had this title that people respected me for," he says, "and when that went away, the inventory of the people in my life also went away." Mack was full of anger, addicted to all of the anti-anxiety and anti-depression pills, started drinking, and hated life.

One day, Mack was shopping at the Salvation Army when he saw an old belt on a rack for one dollar. He was on a waiting list for a service dog, so when he saw the belt, he thought, "Man, that could look like a really good dog collar." Even though Mack had grown up in the city and didn't know anything about leatherworking, he brought the old belt back to his truck, cleaned it with saddle soap, added some hardware, and decided it looked pretty good. He took a picture of it and wondered if he could sell it. He posted the picture on Instagram, and somebody bought it for $45. That's when he realized he could make enough money to stay in Airbnbs and get out of his truck every once in a while, where he continued making belts into dog collars.

Then one of his SOF buddies asked, "Hey, can you make me a belt?" He decided this project would be different. He wanted to honor his brother by making a belt that could handle everything a SOF operator might go through. It had to be durable and high quality but also look the part. He took a picture of the belt before sending it to his friend, and suddenly he had ten orders for belts, which were $100 each—and he knew he had a business.

But it wasn't just the income that helped him to heal. It was the therapy of creating the dog collars and belts themselves. "Leather craft felt good to me," he said. "I'm a breacher . . . but leather craft was quiet. If I made a mistake, I could start over, I didn't have to beat myself up . . . One of my leather belts has seven hundred stitches. At the time I had a single-stitch sewing machine clamped to the Airbnb [kitchen table], so I was sitting there [pushing down the clamp] seven hundred times. But I needed that" (Alexander 2024).

A while later, one of his SOF buddies ended up buying him an automatic sewing machine, which allowed him to scale his business overnight. Eventually, he was able to expand and make sure all his belts were 100 percent sourced and made in America. He now even has vintage World War II automatic screw machines he uses to make the belt buckles. He said in the podcast, "As weird as it sounds, I started a belt company, and I figured out a way to continue serving through that . . . My whole goal is that other people can see that it can be done . . . I'm a small business, but you can be profitable by producing here in the USA."

Mack also explained how his success helped him regain his purpose in life:

> Even though I'm not there . . . getting on the helo [helicopter], there's another guy behind me that's doing that, who's left his family and is putting himself in harm's way. So for me, that was my big shift. I gotta remember [those guys], and I gotta be grateful [for my experiences]. And I have a second chance at life, and I need to make the most of it . . . I carry the names and the faces and the memories of the great heroes . . . [who] paid the ultimate price . . . I reframed it so that I can still serve. I can still be a good example. I can still protect my buddies when they get out, because I can mentor them. (Alexander 2024)

The belt, hardware from a craft store, and online setup initially cost him a total of $41 when he sold his first dog collar. In April 2024, only two and half years later, his company Mack Belts hit $1 million in revenue.

Mack's success gave him a way to make a living. It was also his path to healing.

> The VA gives you your suicide prevention plan. Number one for me was leather craft. There's a therapeutic aspect to it ... I believe in the artistic, creative side for guys like us, who need that quiet between the ears, for [the mind] to shut off, to be working with your hands. (Alexander 2024)

Mack says that for the past five years, he's continually undergone ketamine injections; multiple rounds of stellate ganglion block (SGB) injections; other psychedelic treatments; hyperbaric oxygen therapy; speech, occupational, and vestibular therapy; and cold water immersion. He also continued healing after he became a Christian, prioritized sleep, quit alcohol, followed the keto diet, moved to a quiet environment, and made thousands of leather belts (Alexander 2024).

Mack Alexander's story is a great example of how SOF members can find renewed purpose in their lives and do amazing things. It's our job as clinicians to help them get there.

Final Thoughts

> When you're living in your purest intentions and truth, magical things continuously happen. Through my entire journey, especially regaining my mental and spiritual health and confidence ... I have chipped away at all negative things, and put aside all relationships of any sort that do not fulfill me inside. And that is why I'm living in magic.
>
> —Rudy Reyes (2019)

I hope this book is only the beginning of your journey, and I hope that you continue to research, learn, practice, and (to steal an old phrase from the Army) be the best clinician you can be. Because when SOF members overcome the stigma and barriers to mental health treatment and are brave enough to step into one of our offices and share the problems they're facing, they deserve our best.

Mental illness can oppress the mind and spirit. Be a "warrior healer" and free the oppressed. *De oppresso liber!*

ACKNOWLEDGMENTS

First and foremost, I would like to express my deepest gratitude to **Andrea Kuhlman,** a combat veteran who served as the ghostwriter for this book. Her talent, insight, and dedication were instrumental in bringing this work to life. From our earliest conversations to the final draft, Andrea worked tirelessly to help shape my ideas into a clear, compelling narrative. This book is as much a reflection of her skill and professionalism as it is of the story we set out to tell.

To my wife, **Shannon Ryan**—your unwavering support, patience, and encouragement meant everything to me throughout this process. Thank you for standing beside me through the long hours, the doubts, and the deadlines. Your belief in this book helped carry it—and me—to completion.

I would also like to thank **Jeff Denning**, who not only contributed a thoughtful and powerful foreword but also offered helpful feedback throughout the development of the manuscript. His perspective and encouragement were both valuable and deeply appreciated.

I would like to extend my deepest gratitude to **Dr. Joel Fay** for his supervision, guidance, and enduring friendship throughout this journey. His insight and support were instrumental in shaping both this book and my growth as a clinician.

Thank you to **Thomas LaGrave**, LCSW, for generously sharing both his professional insights and personal journey as a former Navy

SEAL. His contributions brought depth and authenticity to this work, and I'm grateful for his friendship.

In loving memory of **Dr. William Ahern**, Navy SEAL, whose personal and professional insights into the world of special operations left an enduring mark on this book. His wisdom, integrity, and friendship were a gift, and his absence is deeply felt.

Thank you to **Kim Donohue** at the VA for her thoughtful review of the manuscript and for her friendship along the way.

A sincere thank you to **Tim Chen** for generously sharing his expertise, providing thoughtful feedback, and reviewing the manuscript. His insights strengthened the work and helped ensure its clarity and accuracy.

A sincere thank you to **Chaplain Ginger Howl**, whose expertise and compassionate perspective on moral injury added significant depth and clarity to this work. Her contributions helped illuminate some of the most complex and human aspects of the subject, and I am grateful for her willingness to share her time, knowledge, and heart.

I am also grateful to **Dr. Lisa Smith-Rone** for her thoughtful feedback and insight, which helped refine the ideas presented in this book. Her perspective was both encouraging and intellectually grounding.

I would like to thank all the staff members at **Ballast Books**, who have made this process very smooth and have worked with and supported me in every aspect of the book.

I would like to express my deep gratitude to the **First Responder Support Network**, and especially to the **West Coast Post-Trauma Retreat (WCPR)**, for giving me the privilege of working with and counseling some of the most honorable and selfless professionals I have ever encountered. The strength, vulnerability, and commitment of the individuals I've met through this program have left a lasting impact on me and on this work.

Finally, I want to offer my deepest thanks and respect to the men and women of the special operations community. It has been an honor and a privilege to serve this incredible group of warriors. Your strength, sacrifice, and commitment have inspired every page of this book. Thank you for allowing me the opportunity to walk alongside you, to listen, to learn, and to serve in whatever way I can. This book is dedicated to your courage and your stories.

Appendix I:
TERMS & ACRONYMS

The list of terms below is by no means complete or exhaustive, for that would be a book all its own. You do not need to memorize this information. It is simply to help familiarize you with SOF culture. I suggest you read this before finishing Chapter 1 and refer back to it as needed.

Air assault: A tactical assault from the air, usually from a helicopter or specialty aircraft. The US Army's Air Assault School trains soldiers in air assault operations, rotary-wing aircraft (helicopter) sling load operations, and rappelling. Graduates are authorized to wear the Air Assault Badge on their uniform. This is not a SOF-specific course, but many SOF members attend as part of their comprehensive training.

Amphibious assault: A tactical assault from the water, sometimes using a RIB (rubberized inflatable boat).

Airborne: A designation of, or the act of, parachuting from an aircraft. Also the US Army Airborne School. Those who graduate are authorized to wear the Parachutist Badge (also called "Jump Wings" or "Airborne Wings") on their uniforms. This is also not a SOF-specific course, but it is often a requirement for further SOF training.

BUD/S: Basic Underwater Demolition/SEAL training. The initial school to become a Navy SEAL.

CIA: United States Central Intelligence Agency.

CCT: A Combat Controller, an Air Force SOF member trained in establishing airfield landing zones and air traffic control in remote, hostile environments.

Detasheet: A flexible, rubberized explosive.

Delta Force: The nickname for the 1st Special Forces Operational Detachment–Delta (1st SFOD-D), a US Army Special Mission Unit (SMU) under operational control of JSOC (listed below).

Det cord: A detonation/detonating cord attached to explosive charges.

EOD: Explosive ordnance disposal.

Exfil or exfiltrate: To remove a person or team from a hostile area.

Frag: Fragmentary grenade.

Fratricide: An accidental, deadly attack during combat on one's own forces. Also called "friendly fire."

Fast-roping: Sliding down a thick rope (similar to sliding down a fireman's pole), usually from a helicopter. Also called "rappelling."

Green Beret(s): The nickname for the US Army Special Forces. They wear a green beret that distinguishes them from the rest of the Army.

HALO: High altitude, low opening, in reference to a service member who parachutes from an aircraft at higher-than-normal altitudes, usually requiring oxygen, and deploys their parachute at the lowest elevation possible to avoid detection.

HAHO: High altitude, high opening. Similar to above, but with the parachute deployed much earlier than normal. Often used to "float" across forbidden borders undetected.

IED: Improvised explosive device.

JSOC: Joint Special Operations Command.

LZ/DZ: LZ stands for landing zone, a designated place for aircraft to land. DZ stands for drop zone, a designated place for parachutists to land. Both may be hastily set up in hostile territory during combat operations.

MARSOC: United States Marine Corps Forces Special Operations Command.

MOS: Military occupational specialty (and corresponding code) that designates a job in the military, such as infantryman, logistician, computer technician, cook, and so forth.

NVGs: Night vision goggles.

ODA: US Army Special Forces Operational Detachment Alpha.

OPSEC: Operations or operational security.

Pathfinder: The title given to someone who has completed US Army Pathfinder School, which is a two-week course that trains candidates to navigate on foot, conduct helicopter sling load operations, establish and operate helicopter landing zones, provide air traffic control and navigational assistance to rotary-wing and fixed-wing aircraft, and establish and operate parachute drop zones (DZs), among other skills. Graduates are authorized to wear the Pathfinder Badge on their uniform. This course is not exclusively for SOF members but may be an additional SOF training requirement.

Pipeline: The various schools, certifications, and training a member of the US Armed Forces must go through in order to serve in a special operations combat unit.

PJ: Pararescue, an Air Force SOF trained in combat medicine and search and rescue.

PT: Physical fitness. Also the time and/or place where physical fitness training is held (In context: "When is PT?").

Q Course: The qualification course to become a Green Beret (Army Special Forces).

Raiders: The name of US Marine Corps Special Operations Forces.

Ranger: Someone who has graduated US Army Ranger School and wears the Ranger Tab on their uniform, especially when serving in a Ranger unit.

RIB: Rubberized inflatable boat.

RPG: Rocket-propelled grenade.

SAC, SOG, and PAG: The Special Activities Center (SAC) is a division of the CIA responsible for covert and paramilitary operations, comprising the Special Operations Group (SOG) and the Political Action Group (PAG).

SEAL: The Navy's most elite Special Operations Forces. SEAL stands for sea, air, and land.

SERE: Survival, Evasion, Resistance, and Escape is a military school that teaches candidates how to survive and evade capture in enemy territory in a variety of terrain, as well as how to resist torture and other enemy tactics. SERE School is recommended or at times required for service members at high risk of capture, such as pilots, and is required by US Army Special Forces candidates.

SFUWO: Special Forces Underwater Operations, the Army's special operations use of dive equipment to infiltrate beach landing sites and other underwater enemy targets undetected.

Shaped charge: An explosive charge shaped to focus the effect of the explosive energy to penetrate armored vehicles.

Shock tube: A nonelectric explosive initiator in the form of a small and hollow plastic tube used to initiate an explosive by means of a shock wave.

SOAR: 160th Special Operations Aviation Regiment (US Army), a major support unit for SOCOM and JSOC.

SOF: Special Operations Forces.

SOP: Standard operating procedure.

SOWT: Special operations weather technicians, part of the Air Force SOF.

SQT: SEAL Qualification Training, the next phase after BUD/S.

SWCC: The US Navy's special warfare combatant-craft crewmen.

TACP: The US Air Force's tactical air control party, the communications specialist who helps coordinate air fire support.

TOW missile: An anti-tank missile. TOW stands for tube-launched, optically tracked, wire-guided/wireless.

USAF: United States Air Force.

USAFSOC/AFSOC: United States Air Force Special Operations Command.

USASOC: United States Army Special Operations Command.

USMC: United States Marine Corps.

USN: United States Navy.

USNSWC/WARCOM/NSW: United States Naval Special Warfare Command.

USSOCOM/SOCOM: United States Special Operations Command, the command that oversees and coordinates joint training exercises and operations all over the world for all the special operations contingents in the US Armed Forces.

Appendix II:

RESOURCES FOR SOF MEMBERS & THEIR FAMILIES

A good therapist will be knowledgeable about various mental health resources in their area regionally, as well as medical, financial, legal, and housing resources. They will also be knowledgeable about groups, events, and specialists that may help people suffering from issues that cannot be solved in therapy alone.

Below is a list of the organizations and resources available specifically to those who served in the special operations community, as well as their families. Many Special Operations Forces veterans may have heard of some of these organizations, while other resources are fairly new.

Military and Family Life Consultants (MFLC)

MFLCs are licensed mental health professionals who work closely with active-duty military families to address various personal and psychological challenges. Their services are tailored to the military environment, ensuring a deep understanding of the military culture and the specific pressures faced by military families. They provide support through flexible, informal consultations and can meet families in a variety of convenient and comfortable settings, such as schools, homes, and military bases. MFLCs offer nonmedical counseling for issues such as stress, anxiety, depression, grief, and marital problems. Their approach is solution-focused, aiming to provide immediate, situational support rather than long-term therapy.

MFLCs also provide workshops and presentations on topics relevant to military life, including stress management, conflict resolution, and effective communication within families. In times of acute stress or crisis, MFLCs can provide immediate support and intervention to stabilize families and connect them with additional resources if longer-term or medical intervention is needed.

One of the cornerstones of the MFLC program is confidentiality. No records of the consultations are kept, providing families and service members the freedom to discuss sensitive issues without concerns about impacts on the service member's career.

Active-duty service members and their families can reach out to their chain of command for MFLC specialists and services.

Preservation of the Force and Family (POTFF)

The POTFF program is a comprehensive initiative designed specifically for US Special Operations Forces to address the unique pressures and challenges faced by both SOF personnel and their families. Therefore, it goes above and beyond the MFLC program that is available across the regular military. POTFF aims to enhance the well-being, resilience, and readiness of SOF members across all domains: physical, psychological, social, and spiritual.

POTFF ensures that specialists such as strength and conditioning coaches, physical therapists, psychologists, and chaplains are embedded within SOF units to provide immediate, contextually relevant support. These specialists hold regular workshops and seminars for SOF personnel and their families to educate them on resilience techniques, stress management, and healthy lifestyle choices.

Similar to MFLC, POTFF programs are available on base to active-duty SOF operators and their families.

USSOCOM Warrior Care Program (Care Coalition)

The US Special Operations Command Warrior Care Program (Care Coalition) provides wounded, ill, or injured SOF service members and their families assistance and advocacy after life-changing events. Through specialized medical treatment, the Care Coalition helps SOF members navigate recovery, rehabilitation, and reintegration as quickly as possible. Whether the SOF member is returning to operational status, moving into a different field, or transitioning into veteran status, the Care Coalition assists SOF members with continued medical care, benefits, and career opportunities.

This resource may be available for those no longer on active duty, depending on the SOF member's veteran status. Hopefully, any SOF veteran in need of the Care Coalition has already been connected with them, but there may be various reasons why a SOF veteran or family member didn't get in touch with the right resources during their transition.

Website: www.socom.mil/care-coalition

The Special Forces Association

The Special Forces Association is a 501(c)(19) nonprofit veteran service organization with over 9,700 active members and eighty-five chapters located throughout the United States and eight countries around the world. One of the primary missions is to promote and support the general welfare of the Special Forces community, which is accomplished through three funds: the Emergency Relief Fund, which provides immediate financial assistance to eligible members, their spouses, children, and grandchildren in times of natural and unexpected disasters; the Scholarship Fund, an annual education assistance program providing education scholarships based on merit to children and grandchildren of SFA members; and the Patriot Fund. Established in 2007, the Patriot Fund provides support and assistance to the JFK Special Warfare Center and School, the Special Forces Command, and seven

Special Forces groups and their families primarily through family readiness groups and the US Special Operations Command Warrior Care Coalition.

Website: www.specialforcesassociation.org
Phone: (910) 485-5433
4990 Doc Bennett Rd, Fayetteville, NC 28306

Operation Healing Forces

Operation Healing Forces is a 501(c)(3) nonprofit corporation dedicated to America's Special Operations Forces who have served at the tip of the spear in our nation's battle to defeat violent extremists around the world. Their work focuses on helping to restore the relationships wounded by the call of duty faced by special operators and their families.

Website: www.operationhealingforces.org

Special Operations Warrior Foundation

The Special Operations Warrior Foundation is an American 501(c)(3) nonprofit organization founded in 1980 to provide college scholarships and educational counseling to the surviving children of American special operations personnel killed in the line of duty.

Website: https://specialops.org

The Green Beret Foundation

The Green Beret Foundation serves the Army's Special Forces, our nation's most elite soldiers. The foundation believes that Green Berets are our nation's greatest assets. Every day, the Green Beret Foundation honors its commitment to Green Berets past and present, as well as their families, by connecting them with the right resources to prosper and thrive.

Website: https://greenberetfoundation.org

Special Operators Transition Foundation

The Special Operators Transition Foundation, formally Your Grateful Nation, is a 501(c)(3) nonprofit corporation dedicated to supporting special operations veterans and their families during and after their transition from the military to civilian life. The foundation is funded through private and corporate gifts, contributions, and grants. Services they provide may vary by case but will include employment transition services, paid internships, cooperative education, and family stabilization support.

Website: https://www.sotf.org

Special Forces Shield Maidens

The Special Forces Shield Maidens is a 501(c)(3) nonprofit is comprised of women representing the 1st, 3rd, 5th, 7th, 10th, 19th, and 20th Special Forces Groups, all other unique Green Beret assignments, and veteran and retired SF. Its members are wives, sisters, mothers, daughters, and Gold Stars. The Special Forces Shield Maidens was established to operate independently within the Green Beret community, developing its own programs, missives, and guidelines.

Website: www.specialforcesshieldmaidens.org

Military Special Operations Family Collaborative

MSOF is a nonprofit public health initiative for the special operations community. It enables the success of SOF warriors and families through collaborative health and well-being research and programs.

Website: https://msofc.org

All Secure Foundation

All Secure is a small foundation focused on special operations soldiers and veterans. It has been able to impact thousands of lives through one-on-one coaching and couples programs.

Website: www.allsecurefoundation.org

Navy SEAL Foundation

The Navy SEAL Foundation (NSF) provides critical support for the warriors, veterans, and families of Naval Special Warfare.

Website: www.navysealfoundation.org

Marine Raider Foundation

The Marine Raider Foundation is a 501(c)(3) nonprofit organization that provides benevolent support to active-duty and medically retired MARSOC Raiders and their families, as well as to the families of Raiders who have lost their lives in service to our nation.

Website: https://marineraiderfoundation.org

Pararescue Foundation

The Pararescue Foundation is a 501(c)(3) nonprofit organization dedicated to exclusively support US Air Force Pararescue and Combat Rescue Officer service members, veterans, and their families.

Website: www.pararescuefoundation.org

Special Operations Wounded Warriors

Special Operations Wounded Warriors provides unique outdoor experiences and targeted therapeutic treatments to the deserving men and women of US Special Operations Forces that have sustained wounds in battle and/or in significant service to our country.

Website: https://sowwcharity.com

SOF Support

The primary focus of SOF Support is keeping our active warriors in the fight. SOF Support provides special operators and their families with specialized, confidential, and fully paid mental health services.

Website: https://sofsupport.org

TARA Mind

While open to anyone, TARA Mind's founder, Marcus Capone, is a former Navy SEAL who struggled when his special ops career ended. He credits psychedelic-assisted therapy for saving his life. TARA Mind is a public benefit corporation on a mission to combat the mental health crisis in America by expanding safe and equitable access to psychedelic-assisted therapy through a vetted network of providers and in partnership with employers and payors, so that people who are struggling with their mental health can get the help they need in a way that is financially feasible.

Website: https://taramind.com

Veterans Exploring Treatment Solutions (VETS)

VETS's mission is to end the veteran suicide epidemic by providing resources, research, and advocacy for US military veterans seeking psychedelic-assisted therapies for traumatic brain injury (TBI), post-traumatic stress disorder (PTSD), addiction, and other health conditions. Marcus Capone (of TARA Mind) is the founder.

Website: https://vetsolutions.org

Warriors Heart

Warriors Heart treats active military, first responders, veterans, and other frontline workers in every walk of life by offering treatment for chemical dependency, alcohol abuse, and co-occurring psychological disorders relating to PTSD or the psychological effects of MTBI (mild traumatic brain injury). They have two inpatient rehabilitation centers, one in Texas and one in Virginia. They also offer a detox center, a sober living facility, and an intensive outpatient treatment program.

Website: https://www.warriorsheart.com
Phone: (888) 598-4241

Intrepid Fallen Heroes Fund

The Intrepid Fallen Heroes Fund (IFHF) is a great resource for those suffering from TBI as well as PTSD. IFHF maintains a series of twelve major treatment centers at military bases nationwide wherein advanced care is provided for traumatic brain injury, post-traumatic stress, and other severe injuries suffered by American military personnel. IFHF now provides ongoing support for these centers to assist with additional needs important to patient care.

Website: https://www.fallenheroesfund.org/intrepid-spirit

Additionally, the NICO Corporation is a separate company that conducts minimally invasive neurosurgical care for those suffering from TBI, which many veterans are referred to when seeking help if there is a NICO facility nearby that works with the regional VA.

Appendix III

RESOURCES FOR CLINICIANS

If you are new to serving military members, veterans, and their families (and even if you aren't), I highly recommend the resources below. They provide invaluable information and expand on many of the topics covered in this book.

Books

- *On Killing: The Psychological Cost of Learning to Kill in War and Society* by Dave Grossman
- *In Search of the Warrior Spirit: Teaching Awareness Disciplines to the Green Berets* by Richard Strozzi-Heckler
- *Better Broken: The Hidden Advantage of a Challenging Life* by Sean J. Rogers
- *Warrior SOS: Military Veterans' Stories of Faith, Emotional Survival and Living with PTSD* by Jeffrey Denning
- *Operator Syndrome* by Chris Frueh, PhD
- *Counseling Cops: What Clinicians Need to Know* by Ellen Kirschman, Mark Kamena, and Joel Fay
- *Emotional Survival for Law Enforcement: A Guide for Officers and Their Families* by Kevin M. Gilmartin, PhD

- *EMDR with First Responders: Models, Scripted Protocols, and Summary Sheets for Mental Health Interventions* edited by Marilyn Luber, PhD
- *War and Moral Injury: A Reader* edited by Robert Emmet Meagher and Douglas A. Pryer
- *Soul Repair: Recovering from Moral Injury After War* by Gabriella Lettini and Rita Nakashima Brock
- *Moral Injury Among Returning Veterans: From Thank You for Your Service to a Liberative Solidarity* by Joshua Morris
- *The Warrior Elite: The Forging of Seal Class 228* by Dick Couch

SOF & Mental Health Podcasts

- *SOFcast* (www.socom.mil)
- *The Shawn Ryan Show*
- *Mike Drop* (Mike Ritland)
- *GBRS Group* (DJ Shipley)
- *The Team House* (Jack Murphy and Dave Parke)
- *FNG Academy* (Sean "Buck" Rogers)
- *Team Never Quit* (Marcus Luttrell)
- *Mike Force Podcast* (Mike Glover)
- *Cleared Hot* (Andy Stumpf)
- *American Heroes Network* (Gary Ray)
- *Veterans Helping Veterans* (Pat Farrell)
- *American Veteran: Unforgettable Stories* (PBS)

REFERENCES

Alexander, B. 2013. "Marcus Luttrell: Dealing with 'Lone Survivor' wounds." *USA TODAY.* https://www.usa-today.com/story/life/movies/2013/12/22/marcus-luttrell-lone-survivor-melanie/4009687/.

Alexander, M. 2024. *Team Never Quit*, hosted by Marcus Luttrell. "Mack Alexander: How A Veteran Turned $41 Into A Million Dollar American Made Belt Business." April 11. Podcast. https://www.youtube.com/watch?v=zFBFSn3bAnU.

American Addiction Centers. 2024. "Drug Use among Those with Complex Post-Traumatic Stress Disorder." https://americanaddictioncenters.org/trauma-stressor-related-disorders/complex-post-traumatic-stress.

American Psychiatric Association. 2024. "What is Electroconvulsive Therapy (ECT)?" https://www.psychiatry.org/patients-families/ect.

Brainspotting. 2017. "What is Brainspotting?" https://brainspotting.com/about-brainspotting/what-is-brainspotting/.

Britzky, H. 2022. "100 women have now graduated US Army Ranger School." *Task & Purpose*, March 11. https://taskandpurpose.com/news/100-women-army-ranger-school/.

Bullock, A., and Skomorovsky, A. 2017. "The impact of deployment on children from Canadian military families." *Armed Forces & Society*, 43(4), 654–673.

California Physical Therapy Association. n.d. "Aquatic Physical Therapy." Accessed on July 18, 2024. https://med.stanford.edu/content/dam/sm/pain/documents/AquaticTherapyKeyMessages.pdf.

Cherian, K. N., Keynan, J. N., Anker, L. et al. 2024. "Magnesium–ibogaine therapy in veterans with traumatic brain injuries." *Nature Medicine*, 30, 373–381. https://doi.org/10.1038/s41591-023-02705-w.

Cleveland Clinic. 2024. "Traumatic Brain Injury." https://my.clevelandclinic.org/health/diseases/8874-traumatic-brain-injury.

Cooke, T. J. and Speirs, K. 2005. "Migration and employment among the civilian spouses of military personnel." *Social Science Quarterly*, 86(2), 343–355. https://doi.org/10.1111/j.0038-4941.2005.00306.x.

Cooper, A. D., Warner, S. G., Rivera A. C., et al. 2020. "Mental health, physical health, and health-related behaviors of U.S. Army Special Forces." *PLOS One*, 15(6), e0233560. https://doi.org/10.1371/journal.pone.0233560.

DAV. 2024. "What Are the Symptoms of PTSD?" https://www.dav.org/get-help-now/veteran-topics-resources/post-traumatic-stress-disorder-ptsd/.

Dittrich, K. A., Lutfiyya, N. M., Kucharyski, C. J., et al. 2015. "A population-based cross-sectional study comparing depression and health services deficits between rural and nonrural U.S. Military veterans." *Military Medicine*, 180(4), 428–435. https://doi.org/10.7205/MILMED-D-14-00101.

El Camino Health. 2023. "Understanding Brain Injuries: Concussion, TBI, and CTE." https://www.elcaminohealth.org/stay-healthy/blog/understanding-brain-injuries.

Farmer, C. M. and Tanielian, T. 2019. *Ensuring Access to Timely, High-Quality Health Care for Veterans*. RAND Corporation. https://www.rand.org/pubs/testimonies/CT508.html.

Fleming, L., and Nelson, K. 2022. "As Evidence For Treatment Potential Grows, So Has Psychedelic Legality." *Verywell Mind*, updated November 18. https://www.verywellmind.com/where-are-psychedelics-legal-for-therapeutic-use-6827701.

Garner, J. D. 2018. "Identity Development and Loss in Military Transitions from Special Operations Forces to Civilian Life: An Exploratory Conceptualization for Treating Our Nation's Elite Warriors." PhD diss., University of Chicago. ProQuest (13419439).

General Discharge. 2023. "Recon Training & Assessment Program (RTAP): The First Gut Check of the Recon Marine Pipeline." https://gendischarge.com/blogs/news/recon-training-assessment-program.

Gribble, R., Goodwin, L., and Fear, N. T. 2019. "Mental health outcomes and alcohol consumption among UK military spouses/partners: A comparison with women in the general population." *European Journal of Psychotraumatology*, 10(1), 1654781. https://doi.org/10.1080/20008198.2019.1654781.

Grinspoon, P. 2024. "Ketamine for treatment-resistant depression: When and where is it safe?" *Harvard Health Publishing*. Harvard Medical School, February 15. https://www.health.harvard.edu/blog/ketamine-for-treatment-resistant-depression-when-and-where-is-it-safe-202208092797.

Grossman, D. 2009. *On Killing: The Psychological Cost of Learning to Kill in War and Society* (3rd ed.). Back Bay Books/Little Brown and Company, Hachette Book Group.

Grossman, D. n.d. "On Sheep, Wolves, and Sheepdogs." MWK-Works.com. https://www.mwkworks.com/onsheepwolvesand-sheepdogs.html.

Hanwella, R., and de Silva, V. 2012. "Mental health of Special Forces personnel deployed in battle." *Social Psychiatry and Psychiatric Epidemiology*, 47(8), 1343–1351.

Hanwella, R., Jayasekera, N., and de Silva, V. 2014. "Mental health status of Sri Lanka Navy personnel three years after end of combat operations: A follow up study." *PLOS One*, 9(9), e108–e113. https://doi.org/10.1371/journal.pone.0108113.

Hisle-Gorman, E. H., Susi, A., and Gorman, G. H. 2019. "The impact of military parents' injuries on the health and well-being of their children." *Health Affairs*, 38(8), 1358–1365. https://doi.org/10.1377/hlthaff.2019.00276.

Kirschman, E., Kamena, M., and Fay, J. 2014. *Counseling Cops: What Clinicians Need to Know*. The Guilford Press.

Klein, C. 2023. "How Green Berets Became the US Army's Elite Special Forces." *History*. https://www.history.com/news/green-berets-armys-special-forces.

Laco, K. 2023. "'Psychedelics saved our lives': Ex-Navy SEALs including the Lone Survivor credit drugs for helping them readjust to normal life: 'I was reborn' and my marriage was 'saved' Rep. Morgan Luttrell said after seeking treatment upon returning from brutal combat." *Daily Mail*, June 19. https://www.dailymail.co.uk/news/article-12204431/Psychedelics-saved-lives-Ex-Navy-SEALs-credit-drugs-helping-readjust-normal-life.

html#:~:text=A%20GOP%20lawmaker%2C%20and%20 ex,broadly%20accessed%20by%20service%20members.

Laurence, E. 2024. "Virtual Reality Therapy: Everything You Need To Know." *Forbes.* https://www.forbes.com/health/mind/ virtual-reality-therapy/.

Leighton, S. C., Rodriguez, K. E., Jensen, C. L., et al. 2024. "Service Dogs for Veterans and Military Members With Posttraumatic Stress Disorder." *JAMA Network Open.* doi:10.1001/ jamanetworkopen.2024.14686.

Luttrell, M., host. 2024. *Team Never Quit.* "Mack Alexander: How A Veteran Turned $41 Into A Million Dollar American Made Belt Business." April 10. Podcast. https://www.youtube.com/ watch?v=zFBFSn3bAnU.

Lyon, G., host. 2023. *The Dr. Gabrielle Lyon Show.* "The Warrior Mindset: How to Overcome Challenges and Achieve Success | Rudy Reyes." December 7. Podcast. https://www.youtube. com/watch?v=EgZeIPTfTjI.

Mailey, E. L., Mershon, C., Joyce, J., et al. 2018. "'Everything else comes first': A mixed-methods analysis of barriers to health behaviors among military spouses." *BMC Public Health*, 18(1), 1013. https:// doi.org/10.1186/s12889-018-5938-z.

Marine Forces Special Operations Command. 2024. "Career Paths." *Marine Raiders.* https://www.marsoc.com/career-paths/.

Mayo Clinic. 2024a. "Hyperbaric oxygen therapy." Mayo Foundation for Medical Education and Research (MFMER). https://www. mayoclinic.org/tests-procedures/hyperbaric-oxygen-therapy/ about/pac-20394380.

Mayo Clinic. 2024b. "Transcranial magnetic stimulation." Mayo Foundation for Medical Education and Research (MFMER).

https://www.mayoclinic.org/tests-procedures/transcranial-magnetic-stimulation/about/pac-20384625.

Mayo Clinic. 2024c. "Vagus nerve stimulation." Mayo Foundation for Medical Education and Research (MFMER). https://www.mayoclinic.org/tests-procedures/vagus-nerve-stimulation/about/pac-20384565.

McElhinny, G. 2021. "Veterans and Social Isolation." *NVHS National Veterans Homeless Support*. https://nvhs.org/veterans-and-social-isolation/.

Mental Health Match. 2024. "A Glossary of Therapy Approaches & Modalities." https://mentalhealthmatch.com/articles/therapy/glossary-therapy-approaches-modalities.

Meyer, E. G., Writer, B. W., and Brim, W. 2016. "The Importance of Military Cultural Competence." Curr Psychiatry Rep, 18(26). https://doi.org/10.1007/s11920-016-0662-9.

Mizokami, K. 2021. "Confused by All the U.S. Special Forces? Here's a Guide." *The National Interest*, August 21. https://nationalinterest.org/blog/reboot/confused-all-us-special-forces-here's-guide-192216.

Morin, R. 2011. *The Difficult Transition from Military to Civilian Life*. Pew Research Center. https://www.pewresearch.org/social-trends/2011/12/08/the-difficult-transition-from-military-to-civilian-life/.

Mosel, S. 2024. "Post-Traumatic Stress Disorder (PTSD) and Alcohol Addiction." American Addiction Centers. https://alcohol.org/co-occurring-disorder/ptsd/.

National Center for PTSD. 2022. "PTSD and Problems with Alcohol Use." U.S. Department of Veterans Affairs. https://www.ptsd.va.gov/understand/related/problem_alcohol_use.asp.

Navy Recruiting Command. 2024. "Special Operations Careers." *America's Navy.* https://www.sealswcc.com/navy-seal-swcc-training-main.html.

Navy SEALs. 2025a. "Navy SEAL History." https://navyseals.com/nsw/navy-seal-history/.

Navy SEALs. 2025b. "Hell Week." https://navyseals.com/nsw/hell-week-0/.

NIH National Library of Medicine. 2025. "In brief: What is speech therapy?" IQWiG (Institute for Quality and Efficiency in Health Care). Last updated January 24. https://www.ncbi.nlm.nih.gov/books/NBK561506/.

Noller, G. E., Frampton, C. M., and Yazar-Klosinski, B. 2017. "Ibogaine treatment outcomes for opioid dependence from a twelve-month follow-up observational study." *The American Journal of Drug and Alcohol Abuse*, 44(1). https://doi.10.1080/00952990.2017.1310218.

Occupational Assessment Services, Inc. 2024. "What Is Vocational Counseling?" https://www.oasinc.org/what-is-vocational-counseling.

Official United States Air Force website. 2024. "Air Force Special Operations Command History and Heritage." https://www.afsoc.af.mil/About-Us/AFSOC-Heritage/.

OSHA (Occupational Safety and Health Administration). 2024. "Critical Incident Stress Guide." US Department of Labor. https://www.osha.gov/emergency-preparedness/guides/critical-incident-stress.

Perez, Z. 2024. "VA-sponsored psychedelics studies get green light in FY24 budget." *Military Times*, March 14. https://www.militarytimes.com/news/your-military/2024/03/14/va-sponsored-psychedelics-studies-get-green-light-in-fy24-budget/.

Prez, S., interviewer. 2024. *VladTV.* "Ex-Sniper Nicholas Irving on War Stories, Who Snipers Aim For, Body Parts to Target." March 15. Podcast. https://www.youtube.com/watch?v=zlxDpR1bEyU.

RACC (Representative Assembly Coordinating Council). 2021. "Definition of Occupational Therapy Practice for the AOTA Model Practice Act." *Occupational Therapy Scope of Practice.* https://www.aota.org/-/media/corporate/files/advocacy/state/resources/practiceact/ot-definition-for-aota-model-practice-act.pdf.

RAND Corporation. 2023. "Veterans' Barriers to Care." https://www.rand.org/health-care/projects/navigating-mental-health-care-for-veterans/barriers-to-care.html.

Reyes, R. 2019. *fightTIPS*, hosted by Shane Fazen and Marcus Kowal. Season 1, episode 10, "Recon Marine Rudy Reyes on Going Dark." December 16. Podcast. https://www.buzzsprout.com/361331/episodes/2291036-recon-marine-rudy-reyes-on-going-dark.https://www.youtube.com/watch?v=fi137eSRGb0.

Richer, I., Frank, C., and Guérin, E. 2022. "Understanding Special Operations Forces Spouses Challenges and Resilience: A Mixed-Method Study." *Military Behavioral Health*, 10(2), 100–111. Routledge Taylor & Francis Group. https://doi.org/10.1080/21635781.2022.2067921.

Richman, M. 2017. "Study yields insight on sexual disorder and its effects on Vets." US Department of Veterans Affairs, June 7. https://www.research.va.gov/currents/0617-study_yields_insight_on_sexual_disorder.cfm.

Ritland, M., host. 2023. *Mike Drop*. Episode 156, "Recon Marine Fox Special Forces Host Rudy Reyes Part One." October 1. Podcast. https://www.youtube.com/watch?v=8a9j8Ge2DqM.

Rogers, S. J. 2024. *Better Broken: The Hidden Advantage of a Challenging Life*. BenBella Books, Inc.

Ryan, S., host. 2023. *The Shawn Ryan Show*. Episode 80, "John Lovell - How a 75th Ranger Built One of the Biggest Tactical Training Networks, Part 3." October 25. Podcast. https://shawnryanshow.com/blogs/the-shawn-ryan-show/srs-80-john-lovell-part-3.

Seck, H. H. 2024. "Few women are trying for elite special operations roles, new data shows." *Military Times*, March 8. https://www.militarytimes.com/news/your-military/2024/03/08/few-women-are-trying-for-elite-special-operations-roles-new-data-shows/.

Shea, M. T., Stout, R. L., Reddy, M. K., et al. 2021. "Treatment of anger problems in previously deployed post-911 veterans: A randomized controlled trial." Depression and Anxiety, 39(4), 274–285. https://onlinelibrary.wiley.com/doi/10.1002/da.23230.

Shneidman, E. S. 1998. The Suicidal Mind. Oxford University Press.

Skipper, L. D., Forsten, R. D., Kim, E. H., et al. 2014. "Relationship of combat experiences and alcohol misuse among U.S. Special Operations Soldiers." *Military Medicine*, 179(3), 301–308. Oxford Academic. https://doi.org/10.7205/MILMED-D-13-00400.

Skovlund, J. 2024. "How to ace the Marine Basic Recon Course." *Task & Purpose*, April 2. https://taskandpurpose.com/military-life/marine-basic-recon-course/.

Smith, P. H., Potenza, M. N., Mazure, C. M. et al. 2014. "Compulsive sexual behavior among male military veterans: Prevalence and associated clinical factors." *Journal of Behavioral Addictions*, 3(4), 214–222. https://doi.org/10.1556/jba.3.2014.4.2.

SOF For Life. 2021. *2021 SOF for Life Survey Results 2020-2021*. Global SOF Foundation. https://sofforlife.org/wp-content/uploads/2021/08/SOF-for-Life-Survey-Results-2020-2021-FINAL.pdf.

Sprunt, B. 2024. "Service dogs are helping veterans with PTSD. A new bill would help expand access." NPR, September 22. https://www.npr.org/2024/09/20/nx-s1-5116573/lawmakers-push-for-funding-to-help-groups-train-service-dogs-for-vets-with-ptsd.

Stringer, H. 2024. "The emergence of psychedelics as medicine." *American Psychological Association*, 55(4), 50. https://www.apa.org/monitor/2024/06/psychedelics-as-medicine.

Strozzi-Heckler, R. 2007. *In Search of the Warrior Spirit: Teaching Awareness Disciplines to the Green Berets* (4th ed.). North Atlantic Books. Kindle Edition.

Sullivan, J. R. 2018. "The Ex-Navy SEAL Who Inspired 'Lone Survivor' on His Recovery Routine." *Men's Journal*, January 26. https://www.mensjournal.com/health-fitness/the-ex-navy-seal-who-inspired-lone-survivor-on-learning-to-recover.

Turban, J. L., Potenza, M. N., Hoff, R. A. et al. 2017. "Psychiatric disorders, suicidal ideation, and sexually transmitted infections among post-deployment veterans who utilize digital social media for sexual partner seeking." *Addictive Behaviors*, 66, 96–100. https://doi.org/10.1016/j.addbeh.2016.11.015.

US Army. 2024a. "U.S. Army Rangers: Heritage & History." https://www.army.mil/ranger/heritage.html.

US Army. 2024b. "U.S. Army Rangers: The 75th Ranger Regiment." https://www.army.mil/ranger/.

United States Army Special Operations Command. 2021. *Breaking Barriers: Women in Army Special Operations*. https://www.soc.mil/wia/women-in-arsof-report-2023.pdf.

Ursano, R. J., Bell, C., Eth, S. et al. 2004. "Practice guideline for the treatment of patients with acute stress disorder and posttraumatic stress disorder." American Psychiatric Association. https://psychiatryonline.org/pb/assets/raw/sitewide/practice_guidelines/guidelines/acutestressdisorderptsd-1410199309090.pdf.

US Air Force. 2024. "Special Warfare." https://www.airforce.com/careers/special-warfare-and-combat-support/special-warfare.

US Department of Veterans Affairs. 2017. "VA to Provide Hyperbaric Oxygen Therapy to Some Veterans with Chronic PTSD." *VA News*. https://news.va.gov/press-room/va-to-provide-hyperbaric-oxygen-therapy-to-some-veterans-with-chronic-ptsd/.

US Department of Veterans Affairs. 2023. *2023 National Veteran Suicide Prevention Annual Report*, 5–8. https://www.mentalhealth.va.gov/docs/data-sheets/2023/2023-National-Veteran-Suicide-Prevention-Annual-Report-FINAL-508.pdf#.

US Department of Veterans Affairs. 2024a. "Anger & Irritability." *Make The Connection*. https://www.maketheconnection.net/symptoms/anger-irritability/.

US Department of Veterans Affairs. 2024b. "Coping with Survivor Guilt." *Make The Connection*. https://www.maketheconnection.net/read-stories/survivors-guilt/.

US Department of Veterans Affairs. 2024c. "Depression." *Make The Connection*. https://www.maketheconnection.net/conditions/depression/.

USSOCOM. 2022a. "About Us." United States Special Operations Command. https://www.socom.mil/about.

USSOCOM, host. 2022b. *SOFcast*. Season 5, episode 3, "1SG Jason Belford – A Ranger's journey to the brink of suicide and back." Podcast. https://www.socom.mil/SOFcast/Pages/default.aspx.

Veterans Help Group. 2024. "PTSD Triggers." *Disabled Vets*. https://www.disabledvets.com/claim-types/mental-health/ptsd/triggers/.

Wikimedia Foundation. 2025. "Joint Special Operations Command." Last modified May 3, at 17:19 UTC. https://en.wikipedia.org/wiki/Joint_Special_Operations_Command.

Williams, S. 2024. *Wayfaring Stranger Podcast*. "Life After Special Forces: Challenges of a Green Beret's Retirement." July 26. Podcast. https://www.youtube.com/watch?v=1DmLsl1iSxE&t=108s.

Williams, S. C. P. 2024. "Psychoactive drug ibogaine effectively treats traumatic brain injury in special ops military vets." *Stanford Medicine*. https://med.stanford.edu/news/all-news/2024/01/ibogaine-ptsd.html.

Willink, J. 2020. *Discipline Equals Freedom: Field Manual MK1-MOD1* (Expanded ed.). St. Martin's Press.

Your Next Mission. 2024. "New episode alert! Emerging Therapies for Veterans with PTSD." LinkedIn. https://www.linkedin.com/posts/your-next-mission_suicideprevention-veterans-ptsd-activity-7244356944080052225-Bvde.

Zabalo, J. n.d. "What is a Marine Force Recon & What It Takes." *USAMM Armed Forces Super Store*. https://www.usamm.com/blogs/news/marine-force-recon-guide.